FIRESTARTERS

IGNITE THE FAITH WITHIN YOU

GARY SNOWZELL

[1] Lewis, C. S. The Lion the Witch and the Wardrobe. ZonderKidz, 2005.

[2] Stallone, Sylvester. Rocky IV. MGM/UA Entertainment Company, 1985.

CONTENTS

This book is dedicated to Heather.
Without you the story never would have been written.

'The most unremarkable spark can set a fire ablaze.'

INTRODUCTION

Therefore, since we are receiving a kingdom that cannot be shaken, let us be thankful, and so worship God acceptably with reverence and awe, for our 'God is a consuming fire.'

- Hebrews 12: 28-29 NIV

The rain was falling and our boots were covered in thick Herefordshire mud. We huddled under a tree on the edge of an old rampart of an iron age hill fort. Josh passed me a cup of tea from his flask and a piece of Victoria sponge that he'd packed in his rucksack as he asked me questions about my memories of a miracle that God had done almost 20 years ago. This was the first interview that we did for the book, father and son retracing the steps of our family walks and recounting the story that God has written through our lives.

Heather and I began a church in 1988 with six other brave souls, starting in our home with a belief that we could change our town of Leominster (pronounced locally as 'Lem-stuh'). We wanted to make a difference and all we had was the belief that God had called us to be Firestarters. This journey took us through so many valleys and mountain tops. It's twists and turns are more than we could have ever imagined and as you read the stories you may question did that really happen, well it did. We wanted to chronicle the journey, to inspire others who have the yearning within them to make their life count, to become Firestarters. We represent the ordinary believer, the nameless volunteer who carries Jonathan's armour, who dares to believe their spark of faith ignites hope in the unbelieving, whose actions redeem a nation, it's for those daring dreamers who have something in them, who refuse to compromise and believe 'impossible is nothing' for God. So we have reflected on the journey, we have recounted the stories and shared the lessons without dressing up the rawness and reality of what we experienced so this may inspire, prepare and encourage the potential within anyone anywhere to create a breakout and become a Firestarter.

We have five sons and Josh, my eldest, was about to move to the USA with his family when their paperwork fell through and they were temporarily unable to move. In this season of waiting for paperwork to be resolved, the long-awaited dream of writing our story came to life. Josh arranged to interview me and capture the most important moments of our journey and write them into this book.

This story follows Heather and I as we navigate through our own insecurities, our own journey of challenge and how we became Firestarters in the small town we lived, but the story of our church didn't stop there; it grew past our wildest expectations into a global church planting movement. We share the incredible stories of those heroes who have helped continue to write this story all over the world.

We have also written into the narrative some of the most important and relevant lessons and teachings along the way with some questions to help you apply these truths in your own life. *So as you read this book, it swings back and forth from the narrative of our story and then to teaching to equip you.*

This is not in a completely chronological narrative, so sometimes we move up and down the timeline too. Some names have been changed in the more sensitive stories.

We called this book, 'Firestarters' because we have realised that all it takes is a spark of faith to set a forest on fire; a common, ordinary, unremarkable, tiny spark and when God breathes life upon it - there's a breakout. For too long the mission of the church has been left to the 'qualified' and the special few, we've abdicated our calling and potential by being sheep when He called us to be Lions. I've come to realise we will only truly impact our world when the common, ordinary person realises that they can make a difference, they can start a fire, and that the Holy Spirit is ready and waiting if only we realise we are qualified.

It is also a call to the potential that is unlived within every believer and to the many church leaders who have accepted their lot, their disappointment, and how their story ends. To cause a revolution within their souls and to challenge them to consider once again that 'perhaps' they were born for more than ordinary.

We have devoted our lives to taking the light of Jesus into the world, and want to see others burn with that same wildfire too, so that more and more may come to Him.

AN ARMY ARISES

'*The kingdom of heaven is like a merchant looking for fine pearls. When he found one of great value, he went away and sold everything he had and bought it.*'

Matthew 13: 45-46 NIV

In May 2014 I walked on to the stage of our Saturday night Cave gathering, my heart beating out of my chest and adrenaline coursing through my veins. I had been building to this moment for months. Praying into it, fasting, planning, discussing and strategising. Now the time had finally come.

The whole room was filled with excitement and anticipation. Filled with Fire. We run the Cave as an in-house conference, though the word 'conference' doesn't do justice to the passionate, fever-pitch, prophetic gathering of our church members from around the world.

We had our frontline pastors there, flown in from all over, surrounded by our church members, all eagerly listening and leaning in. All buzzing with excitement and faith as the Cave 2014 weekend was coming to its climax. There were less than 300 people in the converted warehouse.

We had started in 1988 with just eight people in our small living room in an insignificant, often overlooked town. This Cave gathering was beyond our wildest dreams. A group of people of all ages and all backgrounds, ready for more: with us heart and soul. Truly believing our God is who He says He is and that the Church can change the world.

Through the course of the Cave weekend, we'd unveiled plans to plant 10 churches over the next four years, including going to five new nations. The vision was called 10|04, and it was audacious at best, ridiculous at worst. We didn't have the money, the resources or the leaders to accomplish this crazy vision. We had unveiled our plans to our church through the day, and had built to a crescendo for our evening event.

I spoke with our whole church about the parable of the pearl (Matthew 13:45-46), that once we find the pearl, everything else loses its value in comparison. We should do everything we can to go after the pearl, which represents the kingdom of God.

Would we as a people do whatever it takes for that pearl? With great reverence, I led our church to the outworking of this in our own lives by making an invitation to our whole church to be a part of the vision.

Now, if you're a leader, you'll know that you can come up with as much vision as you want, but if you don't have the people who are willing to follow you and to execute it, it won't make much of a difference. I heard it said 'A leader without any followers is simply a man, taking a walk'.

We needed people to move to these cities across the world. To make huge sacrifices of their jobs, their homes, their families, their future security, and take the plunge in giving everything for the Kingdom. To dare to move across the world to take the gospel of Jesus and share the life giving hope of church community, and all with no guarantees of 'success'. We needed pastors, kids leaders and evangelists, people who thrived on building relationships.

It was a huge ask. We didn't have all the answers, and people would have to make their own way, standing on their own legs financially. We didn't have the resources to support them. We didn't even have anything to pay towards the pastors for these new church plants.

During the three years leading up to this, we had been planting churches, learning, exploring, succeeding, failing and evaluating. We understood more of what it would take for people to do this. I was brutally honest with people about the challenges that lay ahead for the people that were to answer this call. I didn't want even one of our people to go into this commitment thinking that it would be easier than it would be. They had to make the choice with the full knowledge of the challenge and stretch that was to come.

When I finished laying out the vision and the realities of meeting that vision, it was time to allow people to answer the call. The weight and the tension in the room was palpable. The anointing that came, the significance of the call, was falling on our church in a truly powerful and unforgettable way.

My wife, Heather and I had thought that perhaps 40 people would respond to help us plant these 10 churches. As I made the call, people began to leave their rows. Couples holding hands, tears streaming down their faces. We had 14 year-olds responding who worked out that by the end of the vision timeline they would be old enough to 'go'. Whole families responding together. All bowing on their knees at the front of our church.

More and more came. We started having to put away chairs just so people had space to respond. In the end, more than half the room, about 160 people, had responded to the call to plant these churches over the next four years.

It was absolutely staggering. Heather and I were filled with emotion as we saw these incredible people's willingness to answer the call. Could this really be happening? After all the battles that we had been through in the last 25 years? These brave saints were Lionhearts.

This book is a story of some very ordinary people doing some extraordinary things because they believed in an all powerful God. I dedicate this book to them and to every person who has chosen to sell everything to get the pearl.

'When I saw the lion, I saw that he was a fighter and warrior.'

2

———————

THE ROAR OF THE LION

If you want to be as bold as to go change the world, you have to know who you are. To truly know who you are, you have to know who Jesus is. We have the Lion of Judah emblazoned on the front of our church buildings throughout the world, celebrating this iconic imagery from the book of Revelation. There is something of the majesty and might of the Lion of Judah that inspires and communicates Christ.

When you're on safari, what you really want to see are the lions. I have been lucky enough to go on safari in Africa, and have seen some amazing animals that fill you with awe when you see them in the wild. Elephants, giraffes, zebra - each extraordinary in their own way.

But when the lions came, it was different. We were blessed to be able to see them at the end of our safari day, and we marvelled as we saw these magnificent beasts in their natural habitat. Our guide quickly radioed to the network of other guides in the area to let them know we had stumbled upon the pride. Jeeps started arriving in every direction, cameras in hands as dusk was falling. Everyone was desperate to see the lion.

Lambs are a different story. Living in rural Herefordshire, I have seen many sheep, and I have never seen that response to a lamb. Never seen people flocking to a lamb in the wild. They're cute, but they don't command respect and awe.

There are many churches, denominations and Christians that have identified Christ as the lamb. They fell in love with a soft saviour that they could cuddle in their arms. But this is a misunderstanding that has stolen away from the church the true nature of Christ.

Jesus' identity is the lion, his role was the lamb.

> 'I saw a scroll in the right hand of the One Seated on the Throne. It was written on both sides, fastened with seven seals. I also saw a powerful Angel, calling out in a voice like thunder, 'Is there anyone who can open the scroll, who can break its seals?' There was no one—no one in Heaven, no one on earth, no one from the underworld—able to break open the scroll and read it. I wept and wept and wept that no one was found able to open the scroll, able to read it. One of the Elders said, 'Don't weep. Look—the **Lion from Tribe Judah**, the Root of David's Tree, has **conquered**. He can open the scroll, can **rip through** the seven seals.' So I looked, and there, surrounded by Throne, Animals, and Elders, was a Lamb, slaughtered but standing tall...' Revelation 5:1-6 MSG

I love the imagery of Christ as a lion. I love the precious sacrifice that has redeemed the world, represented by the lamb.

As the powerful angel calls out to see if there are any that are worthy to break the seals and open the scrolls the writer, John, sobs, fearing there is no one. That is where the Lion of Judah enters the scene and rips open the seals with powerful imagery that shows us the authority of Christ. But then the scriptures describe him as a slain lamb, depicting the sacrifice that was paid on the cross and entitles Christ to be the one worthy to open the scroll.

This image of a lamb is actually much more common in the Christian understanding of Jesus than the lion. For some reason Jesus has appeared holding a lamb, with a chiffon robe, blonde hair and blue eyes, looking serene, meek and mild.

Maybe religion deemed the lion too offensive, too aggressive, too powerful. Perhaps the soft and friendly face of a lamb felt more appropriate, more relevant for the masses than the snarling teeth of the lion.

The juxtaposition of the lion and the lamb is a funny contrast. John gets told about a lion, and then sees a lamb. They represent completely opposite qualities. When you think of a lamb you think of weakness, vulnerability and harmlessness, but when you think of a lion, you think of strength, courage and danger. Christ took on the role of the lamb to become our sacrifice, yet there are many Christians that have spent their whole life only seeing him in this role. The character of Christ has often been misunderstood and at times lost, and this has cost the church.

You don't have to study the life of Christ long to see his character was that of a lion: his boldness, the respect he commanded and the authority he walked in. This is so important because we will model our own character on who we understand Christ to be.

As a child in Sunday school, I saw Christ as the lamb, meek, mild and gentle. There are elements of this that are true, but it does not present you with the full reality of Christ. You can get away with knowing a lamb-like Christ when you're young, but as you become an adult, it will not captivate you in the way the Lion of Judah will.

When I was 10, I got a glimpse of the lion. I looked into his eyes, and it changed my whole life. When you meet the lion, that's what will happen to you too. In the fire of his eyes your soul will find life, purpose and calling.

I sometimes wonder what would have become of my life if I had never got a revelation of Christ the lion. Maybe I would have become one of those Christians whose wife goes to church alone on Sundays. Who believes but 'doesn't need the church'. Pray when I need something, give him as little as possible. Who gives their life for a lamb anyway?

But the lion demands nothing less than all of your life. When I saw the lion, I saw that he was a fighter and a warrior. He went into battle for me! On understanding this, my heart surged to fight for Him.

Lambs go to slaughter rather than to battle. Perhaps this is why so many churches are empty of men. They got sold the lie of a lamb-like Christ whom they could never relate to and walked away. The Lion inspires loyalty to the call.

There has been feminisation of Christ by the enemy to deceive his followers and stop them from truly knowing him. But Christ was the ultimate man. The most inspiring figure of all mankind, born into a stable in relative poverty, and going on to impact every nation in the world for thousands of years to come and for an eternity beyond our understanding.

The lion of Judah is raising up a roar for willing sons and daughters to come and give Him everything.

C.S. Lewis famously represented Christ as the character of Aslan the lion in the Chronicles of Narnia:

> *'Aslan is a lion - the Lion, the great Lion.' 'Ooh' said Susan. 'I'd thought he was a man. Is he-quite safe? I shall feel rather nervous about meeting a lion'...'Safe?' said Mr Beaver ...'Who said anything about safe? 'Course he isn't safe. But he's good. He's the King, I tell you.'* [1]

When you follow the lion, it is exhilarating, inspiring and even dangerous. But that's the life he has called us to: not the comfort blanket Christianity that so many settle for.

In the Second World War at the battle of the Bulge, there was a commander who was warning his men of the difficult battle ahead and instructed them to build fox holes, dug out pits to shelter in against enemy fire, to prepare for the attack of the enemy. One of his privates responded, 'Why don't we attack the enemy and get them to be the ones who build the fox holes?'

If you go on the attack in your life, you summon inspiration, bravery, courage and self-belief from within you, rather than hiding in your fox-hole waiting for the enemy to attack. I know many Christians who have been in the battle and get overcome by their circumstances, so they stop taking ground and hide away in a fox hole. If you're in a fox hole right now, you need to find a way to get out of it.

We are taught to pray to God as our Father in the Lord's prayer, meaning we are his children. Christ was the son that we take our example from: he embodies the fullness of the family DNA that we have within us. If Christ was a lion, then it makes us lions and lionesses.

Maybe you're an artist who hasn't painted anything in a while. Maybe you're an entrepreneur who never started a business. Maybe you're a musician who is so afraid of rejection, you never took the risk to share your gift and it's slowly dying within you. Perhaps your dream has been discouraged or delayed.

You need to embrace lion-like thinking and learn to roar again. Lambs are afraid of the big bad wolf, Lions fear nothing. Lions triumph, defend their territory and understand their dominion.

> *'Then God said, 'Let us make mankind in our image, in our likeness, so that they may rule over the fish in the sea and the birds in the sky, over the livestock and all the wild animals, and over all the creatures that move along the ground."*
>
> Genesis 2:26 NIV

Man was made to rule, not to be owned. God is calling us as Christians to that first call that we ever had: to rule over our lives and not be ruled by our circumstances. Lions roam their land with confidence.

When I run in a field with a lamb, they flee at the sight of me, even when I pose no threat. It's instinctive for them to be afraid. If I was in a field of lions, I'd be running the other way!

We are under God's authority but given dominion over the earth. Under God but over despair. Under God but over poverty. Under God but over discouragement.

Lamb-like thinking easily infiltrates your mind. Cynical thinking, self-absorption, fearful mindsets, indecision. Lambs can only think of themselves, Lions think about the whole family unit. Lions inspire others and lead their families. Lamb-like thinking responds to circumstances as a victim. Lambs are Incapable of triumph: they are slaves to the past, consumed by historical mistakes, decisions and disappointments.

The lion of Judah wants to set you free from these things. Our society is trying to eradicate lion-like thinking with its participation trophy mentality. Where the winner doesn't get a specific trophy, instead everyone gets an award. Yet we find Paul telling us in 1 Cor 9: 24 'To run in such a way as to win the prize'. To fight, to overcome, to be victorious!

I pray this stirs you to remember who you were called to be. To get your swagger back. Get your roar back, or discover it for the first time. I can't tell you how many people I know who didn't think there was a roar inside of them. They discovered it only when they looked into the eyes of the lion.

When adversity comes, and it will come, you have to embrace it. You need to discover the boldness, the confidence and aggression that the lion of Judah gives. A determination from passion in our spirits that fights for the purposes of God and heaven's call.

Jesus was not a lamb: it was only his role. If we get confused by seeing Christ as the lamb we will bear the likeness of what we choose to see. Become the lion you were born to be.

I'm on a mission to establish Christ as the lion in the hearts and minds of every believer. To live my life with the passion and the tenacity of a lion and to raise up lions and lionesses in this generation, those with the hearts and minds of Christ.

As you read the story of Heather and I and our church, you will see that we are continually faced with the question: do we back down in fear and leap away like lambs, or do we make a stand and believe with all our hearts that the Lion of Judah lives within us, he has called us to be bold and courageous?

There are times where I didn't get it right and where the enemy almost caused us to cave in. To back down and become lamb-like. But the lionheart within us has always endured in the end. As you read this story, I pray that the roar of the lion will get louder and louder within you as you turn every page and follow him with the faith and boldness that he is calling you to.

———

THE ROAR OF THE LION QUESTIONS TO CONSIDER:

- Reflecting on your own church background, were you encouraged to view Christ as lamb-like or lion-like?
- How has that perspective shaped your relationship with Him now?
- We are invited to lock eyes with Jesus Christ, Lion of Judah. How would doing so affect your prayer life? Your daily confidence? Your faith?

3

DARE TO BELIEVE

I didn't look like a firestarter. I was ten years old, crying my eyes out in a cupboard, and trying to make sense of what had just happened to me. My life had been shaken to its core, and it had all started with me pulling the shortest straw.

I grew up attending church in the Salvation Army and was attending as a 10-year-old at the Corp in Hereford. My dad was the bandmaster, and so of course, I was in the band as a default and played the second cornet (which is basically a trumpet).

Sundays were busy days. We had young people's meetings in the morning, then the morning service with the adults. After that we would often do a march in town, playing our salvation songs to the public and finish by heading back to our church building for the evening services.

As well as being busy, Sundays were often boring. I love the Salvation Army and what they did and still do around the world to impact people, but in the 70's, for a ten-year-old, it wasn't a favorite place to be.

One Sunday, me and four of my buddies concocted a little bit of fun. We knew what was coming at the end of the speaker's message. At gospel services, they would give an appeal. We had never seen anyone actually respond to it. Wouldn't it be funny, we thought, if, when he gives the appeal tonight, that one of us goes forward and responds?

We all agreed that this was going to make the rest of our evening a lot more entertaining. But who would take the hit, who would go forward to give the rest of us the laughs? We decided to draw straws, which is biblical at least, and out of the five of us, I drew the short straw. I had been chosen to go 'give my life' at the mercy seat.

The mercy seat was a red cushioned place to kneel, where you could come and receive your salvation. It was a public declaration at the front of the church, where everyone could see you putting your trust in Jesus. No 'raise your hand while everyone keeps their eyes closed', no privacy at all.

I couldn't believe I had to go through with it. But as I wasn't one to avoid a dare, I readied myself as the moment came at the end of the message. We were sat in a horseshoe shape on the stage just behind the speaker, looking down at the mercy seat on the floor. The speaker made his appeal to see if anyone wanted to come to kneel.

My friend gave me a nudge. I nervously put my Cornet down and shuffled my way down to the mercy seat, to the delight of the speaker. As I knelt, putting my hands together, trying to give the impression to the congregation that this ten-year-old was taking this all very seriously, I looked up at my friends who were struggling to contain their laughter.

But then something happened to me that would change my life forever. I felt a hand rest upon my shoulder. And I heard a voice, so clear and so close. 'Gary, I want your life.' I looked around. There was no one there. I knew instantly that I had truly heard God.

And then, what no ten-year-old boy wants to happen in public, happened. I began to cry. I knew that I had been touched by God Himself. I fled the room, leaving through a side door to go to the band room. The tears really started to flow now. Could this really be happening to me?

I didn't know how to stop crying, and I didn't want my friends or my parents seeing me like this. In the band room there was a cupboard to keep all the empty cases of the instruments. I climbed into it before anyone could follow me or find me and sat in the dark for almost an hour, crying and crying. They weren't sad tears, but I was overcome with emotion, knowing that God was not only real, but He knew me, and He was calling me to follow Him with everything that I had. That's a lot to take in for a ten-year-old boy.

I waited in that dark cupboard until the building had emptied so I wouldn't have to face any questions from anyone about what had happened.

Finally, my parents came to pick me up. I got in the car and I felt distinctly different: it was as though God was sitting right next to me. I knew in the depths of me that He was truly real. That He was a father to me, that He loved me.

In that dark band cupboard, I had also been made aware of my sin, the wrong things that I had done, and had asked for forgiveness. I had an innocent simple awareness that my life was to be lived for God. This was no longer just my father's religion; this was a new found faith all of my own.

My ambition had always been to be a soldier: to join the army, escape my four sisters, escape having to practice the cornet and live a life of adventure. But this encounter with God changed the desires of my heart. I had heard God tell me that He 'wanted my life'.

The only person that I'd ever known that had given their whole life to Jesus was a missionary, someone living in a foreign land without electricity and other basic amenities. I always take God at his word and when God said 'I want your life' I looked for a way to give it to him. I grew up as a teenager telling everyone I was going to be a missionary, which most people found funny. It was the only way I could imagine living a life completely devoted to God, to give up my current life and live in relative poverty in a third world country. So that was the life for me.

It would take me many years to discover that it's not about where you are, or the means that you live with, but the willingness you have to give Him every part of your life.

I didn't end up going to be a traditional missionary, but my life was going to be wrapped up in mission in ways that I never would have understood as a ten-year-old boy.

HE MUST SUFFER FOR MY NAME

In Acts 9, we read of Saul being struck off his horse by the presence of Jesus. He had been on his way to Damascus after getting specific permission from his religious elders to stamp out this new sect, these followers of 'the way', those that had seemingly lost their minds and were believing in a resurrected carpenter from Nazareth. But Jesus altered his destiny by appearing to him and knocking him from his horse.

I walked down to that mercy seat and was not intending to give my life to Jesus. I was kneeling in the name of mockery, to give my friends a good laugh and to hold up my end of a dare.

But Jesus was calling me, he chose me. But his words were not, 'Your life is mine' but, 'I want your life'. It was my choice. What was I going to do in response to this invitation?

Even from that young age, I knew that if the Holy Spirit is calling me to do something, then I will always make the choice to fully embrace his will over my own preference. No matter the cost, no matter the stakes. There is nothing worth having that is greater than his will.

After Saul has been struck from his horse and made blind, he was in such a shock that he couldn't eat or drink anything for three days. I feel quite blessed that I only cried in front of my friends and shut myself away in a band cupboard for an hour.

Jesus spoke to Ananias, one of the believers in a city near to Saul, and told him to go and give him back his sight, and fill him with the Holy Spirit.

Jesus told Ananias of Paul:

> 'This man is my chosen instrument to proclaim my name to the Gentiles and their kings and to the people of Israel.'
>
> Acts 9:15 NIV

Saul had this immense privilege and calling to impact the nations. But it is quickly followed by:

> 'I will show him how much he must suffer for my name.'

Acts 9:16 NIV

That's not one of those Bible verses that makes it to the front of our fridge or that we get tattooed on our arm. It is a reality to the Christian call that sometimes we like to think was for another age. Jesus said to his disciples at the last supper:

'If they persecuted me, they will also persecute you.'

John 15:20 NIV

How does this fit with our modern christianity, which is often a convenient, consumer-driven version of the faith-filled persecuted courageous church we find in Acts?

I pray that your spirit would be electrified by the call of Christ. Many people have had that voice come and invite them to give everything. Some give themselves to that call for a time and then turn away. Whatever the dream, the vision that God has placed within you, may it be stirred and awoken.

In our story, something was about to be awoken in me, a love for my team mate, my partner that would help me answer the call that God had for us both.

DARE TO BELIEVE QUESTIONS TO CONSIDER:

- Jesus invites us to give our whole lives. How are you currently responding to that invitation?
- Reflecting on your journey of faith up to this point, can you identify times when you have suffered for Christ?
- Are there any areas you are withholding from God? Parts of your life that you are unwilling to give him control of?

4

A DATE IN THE VALLEY OF DRY BONES

I knew that I was not going to be able to start fires alone. I was 17 when I met Heather. My Dad was involved in running a young people's choir and drama group to tour around Herefordshire churches. If you grew up with your parents involved in something like this, you'll know that the first name on the team sheet is your own; you get signed up to anything and everything.

But I was starting to be my own man. So I showed my Dad I was gonna do what I wanted to do. Instead of signing up to the choir, I joined the drama group. What a rebel.

This did prove to be a great choice. A girl named Heather was also in the drama: she was a beautiful blonde with an amazing smile and she caught my attention immediately. She had a joy and fun that was so attractive. As quickly as I noticed her, however, I also wrote off any chances of her being interested in me. She was older than me and out of my league. And then the moment came when we had to use our creative prowess to act like the valley of the dry bones in Ezekiel 37.

As we both lay in a bone-like state on the floor, our eyes met. As I looked at her, and she looked at me, I suddenly fancied my chances. The next part of our drama had the bones coming to life, and we were up on our feet, shaking our bodies about representing the bones coming together through the breath of God. Can't beat a bit of 80's drama.

It was the last night of the production, and after it was all over and everyone was heading home to contemplate what they had just witnessed, I seized my moment to ask her out on a date. This would be my last chance. She said yes!

We got on as friends immediately, laughing together and enjoying getting to know one another. We went on all kinds of adventures together that summer, going walking and fishing because I thought it was romantic. We were falling in love, and I just knew that she was the one for me.

So just before I headed off to bible college in the south of England, I put on my best skinny leather tie, drainpipe jeans and trilby, then took her up to Woolhope Common on a summer evening, when the moon was full and shining. With my heart going, I got to the big moment and asked her a life-changing question for both of us. 'Do you fancy being a missionary's wife?'

Heather had a certain perception of what a missionary looked like, and it wasn't me. It took her a moment to realise I was referring to myself.

This moment was perhaps not navigated with the most wisdom or clarity, but the heart behind my proposal was to ensure something: That Heather was going to be willing to go wherever God called us to in the world. To perhaps live without means and possessions as we counted the cost of a life on mission. I wanted her to know that if she was going to marry me, that it would be a life driven by God's agenda and not ours.

I may have been young, but I did understand the power of agreement even then.

'Do two people walk hand in hand if they aren't going to the same place?'

Amos 3:3 MSG

If we were to set out on this epic adventure of life being married together, then we had to both be in agreement that we would follow the direction of the Holy Spirit and that we wanted the same things. As much as I loved Heather already, I couldn't compromise on the call of my life.

Heather, understanding what I was implying, gave me an emphatic yes. She was willing, to not only be my wife but to answer the call of God, united and together.

'Seek first his kingdom and his righteousness'

Matt 6:33 NIV

If the church could only discover this priority, this urgency of the kingdom, we would be an unstoppable force for change in our world. But many Christians segment their faith into only part of their life as they pursue their career, their holidays, their finances, and their relationships.

What a community of Christ we could see if they were to position his kingdom front and centre. It is what we are all called and created to do. That the kingdom would be the sun that our whole lives orbit around. There is nothing greater, nothing more important than this eternal building work that we are called to undertake.

There can only be one master. A lot of us are comfortable with God as a friend, a comforter, a saviour even. But how about the sovereignty and lordship of God in our lives? Because we all serve a master. If we are not intentional to choose God, then our flesh will choose something else: money or fame or satisfaction. But whenever you serve that master, you are inevitably choosing something that is other than God.

As Heather and I started out in our marriage, there was so much we didn't know. But we had resolved that Jesus would be our master, and we would be submitted to his calling and direction for our lives, no matter the cost.

Before anyone starts a fire they have to first prepare what they are going to burn. What will my resources be, what will sustain the fire. What will it cost me?

'No one else can carry what you are called to carry.'

5

PICK UP YOUR CROSS

'Whoever wants to be my disciple must deny themselves and take up their cross daily and follow me. For whoever wants to save their life will lose it, but whoever loses their life for me will save it.

Luke 9:23-34 NIV

We cannot profess to be a true disciple unless we take up our own cross. Remember when Jesus spoke this, the cross had no representation of what we now know it to be. We think of the cross and we think of Jesus, his forgiveness, his redemption, his power to overcome.

When Jesus spoke these words to the crowd, they would have been very familiar with the cross in a very different way. They marked their roads and towns, and they meant death. Final and painful.

Carrying your cross is about embracing personal death. Jesus was asking for those that will embrace the pain of death to themselves and surrender their lives completely, so that they can be genuine disciples. These verses show us that you can be a believer but not a disciple. Jesus called us to go to all the world and make disciples (Matt 28:19), not believers. Jesus is not just expanding his fan-base but establishing a Kingdom where he is unquestionably the Lord and King. He is looking for people who will truly lay their lives down for the call.

We display our love and devotion to Him by dying to ourselves daily: dying to those selfish desires and agendas.

When Jesus talks to the crowd in Luke 9, there are a lot of people following him. He speaks about discipleship. In any gathering there is always a 'crowd' group and a 'disciples' group. As church leaders we want to see the crowd grow bigger: but not for its own sake. We know that the larger the crowd, the more disciples will emerge.

God brought this scripture to life for me very vividly a few years ago. I saw the image of the cross that was for me, that I was called to carry. Jesus had his name written above his cross, and mine has my name on too. Even when I was ten years old, He gave me this cross to carry. No one else can do it; this is mine and mine alone to carry. You have got a cross with your name on that you were called to carry. So has every believer.

The journey we go on is long and tiring. Over the years of carrying, there were many times when I wanted to lay down the cross that I had been given and be free from its burden. I was tempted to look back at the life that I had left, and think, 'This is too heavy for me. The cost is too much.' But to me, it seemed that the cross had something like a radio frequency that seemed to ring out and remind me to not look back but to look ahead. That if I would only keep going and persevere, eyes focused on Him, I would answer His call on my life.

Carrying a cross through your day is challenging enough in the day-to-day movement of life, but when you come up against an obstacle and have to clamber over it or find a way through, that cross can become even heavier.

The pressure of facing bankruptcy.

The miscarriage of a baby.

When people criticised us.

When those close to us betrayed us.

When we faced health problems with our children.

When it looked as though our son would go to prison.

The cross was heavy. It was awkward to carry. I had to often get underneath it and lift it once more. Keep moving forward, unrelenting and undeterred.

What I discovered is that my cross was not something to resent. It has been given to me by Jesus and so is not a curse but something to cherish. My flesh makes me feel entitled, but the cross kills that. Your life is not safe when you pick up your cross; your finances are not safe when you pick up your cross. But we are called to this life. No one else can carry what you are called to carry. I have my cross, and I'll fight you for it.

So many that were once called to follow Jesus have abandoned their cross. They left them in the pursuit of an easier call, at a difficult time, or because of disappointment. Self-sacrifice and putting the kingdom first became too much, so instead they laid it down to pursue their own way instead of His.

My cross carries more names than just my own. There are the names of every person that has been saved through my obedience to Jesus and my choice to follow Him, building his church. That's why this cross is glorious!

It represents not only my personal death but the life that I am called to in the redemption of others. That's why it is so important that we own our cross and that if we have abandoned it, we go pick it up again and embrace the call that we have, death to self, for our redemption and for others.

Heather and I have always been motivated by others, but to reach those that were beyond us, I would have to first overcome my fears.

PICK UP YOUR CROSS QUESTIONS TO CONSIDER:

- Are you currently living as a believer or a disciple? How can you tell the difference?
- The crosses that we are called to carry are heavy. Have you ever been tempted to put yours down and walk away? What stopped you?
- Whose names are written on your cross? And who are you believing will be added in the coming days?

6

DISCOVERING THE SPIRITUAL WORLD

I grew up in the Herefordshire countryside until the age of 11 in a little village called Burghill. My parents would both be out when I got home from school, and I had to let myself in and be at home alone. In winter it got dark as early as 4pm.

There was a psychiatric hospital just down the road, where my uncle was a patient. There had been some patients that had managed to escape and my parents told me, 'If your Uncle, or anyone else comes knocking on the door, DO NOT let them in.' This was terrifying.

Every night I would build myself a barricade in the front room with sofa cushions, arming myself with a kitchen knife, not sure what I'd do with it but being prepared as a good Cub Scout. When I heard my parents parking in our drive I would quickly disassemble my barricade and put back the kitchen knife before they got in. I did this most nights, and this is when fear, particularly fear of the dark, really got hold of me.

Years later I was in Bible College, a married man, but still carrying the same fears. During that time we lived next to the woods in our cottage. I was determined to conceal my fear of the dark, but I kept my shotgun next to the bed.

Heather never knew that it was loaded. I'd managed to keep this fear from her, as I was too embarrassed to confess it. I wanted her to feel protected by me and to respect me. The boy that used to be terrified and wielded a knife behind the sofa cushions had got a significant upgrade, (although I did keep a knife there too for good measure). I may have been a married man on the outside, but the little boy who was full of fear was on the inside, still calling the shots.

I couldn't bear the thought of Heather thinking I was a coward and thought I needed to keep up my manly appearance, so I used to go out shooting at night. But what I was actually doing was walking towards the main road, avoiding the woods.. Lots of cars were going past with their headlights, which I found comforting. I would crouch next to the road in a hedge, holding the shotgun until I felt enough time had passed and that Heather would think I may have gone to hunt.

But one night there was a power cut as we were going to bed. The fuse board that reset the system was at the other end of the house. I froze, I was close to a panic attack. Fear flooded my heart and Heather knew immediately that something was wrong. I had no choice but to tell her everything, that I had grown up with this overwhelming fear and I struggled every day to try to hide it.

'So, is that why you've got a gun next to the bed, and you put a lock on the bedroom door?!' I knew that it was a spiritual fear, and she told me that I needed prayer. It wasn't normal behaviour to be living with such fear that controlled me. Hard to argue with that.

The next time we went back to visit my parents in Herefordshire, we opened up about it, and my dad identified it as a spirit of fear. They prayed over me and took me through a methodical prayer, where I renounced my fear. I didn't really feel any different in the moment. There were no fireworks going off as they prayed for me.

When I got home I went out shooting as I normally did. This time I felt the courage to venture into the woods: I wanted to put the prayer to the test and see if I was truly free. As I walked, I startled a bird and it made me jump, but I wasn't afraid. Nothing. No fear as I walked through the dark trees. The fear that had plagued me since being a child had finally gone. The power of the prayer and the declarations I made in the name of Jesus had brought me the freedom that I so desperately desired!

Walking in my new found freedom, I went on to study God's word, theology, ministry and concepts of church leadership over the following years. After completing three years of Bible College, you might have thought I was prepared and equipped to minister and lead. But as you'll see that was far from true.

'It was a miracle. A real bonafide jaw-dropper.'

7

THROWN INTO THE DEEP END

We knew that one day we would start a fire of our own, but it was important to us to mature and grow in experience. In 1985 Heather and I had the opportunity to volunteer as missionaries with Christ For All Nations, led by the great evangelist Reinhard Bonnke. They were holding huge rallies across the African continent and seeing thousands of people being saved, set free and healed.

It was too good an opportunity to miss and felt like a great fit in relation to the calling I had as a boy. As we got on our plane we had no idea how much this trip was about to impact us. It was to be a deep immersion in the realities of spiritual forces.

'For our struggle is not against flesh and blood, but against the rulers, against the authorities, against the powers of this dark world and against the spiritual forces of evil in the heavenly realms.'
Ephesians 6:12 NIV

A huge proportion of Christians never understand what this really means, leaving the spiritual world as a mystery. Until our trip to Africa, we were definitely in that group. But our eyes were about to be opened.

When we arrived in Zimbabwe, the country was still fraught with tension, having not long ago come to the end of a white minority rule. We were young and naive and had no experience of Africa. As we came through the security at the airport Heather was detained and given an intensive search and questioning.

They began to question me too: where we would be staying? I had no idea. I had just been told that a 'Jane' was picking us up. What's her second name? Didn't know that either. Where is she taking you? Not sure.

The soldiers, with their automatic weapons, were getting more agitated. They allowed me to go through to find our contact Jane and prove our story, but they were going to detain Heather until I could assure them that we were genuine.

I went through to the arrivals in the airport frantically looking for Jane. Having never met her, I had no idea what she looked like. After an extensive search, it seemed she had not arrived. This was before the days of mobile phones or emails; I had no way to contact Jane or anyone else and nowhere to go.

Time passed, and I grew anxious wondering what on earth we were going to do and hoping Heather was okay. She had followed me to the missionary lifestyle, but we'd only arrived a few hours and she had already been left behind with a group of Zimbabwe police, armed to the teeth!

I was praying my socks off and declaring by the name of Jesus that the mysterious Jane would turn up. Then I heard a voice over the airport tannoy: 'Gary Snozil, please come to reception, there is someone to see you.'

Sure enough, it was Jane, 'So sorry, I got delayed in the traffic...' We went to get Heather, who although a bit intimidated and anxious had been fine with the armed guards. We were relieved to exit the airport and get on the road and start to see a bit of Zimbabwe. Before we knew it, there were sirens going behind us. 'They've changed their minds and are coming after us!'

No, it was President Mugabe and his entourage of vehicles: jeeps armed with fixed machine guns driving right behind our car. Jane drove into a ditch and told us to keep still, we saw Mugabe and his motorcade fly past us at 50MPH, which they did to make him a harder target for gunfire. Jane told us that if we hadn't pulled into the ditch we would have been shot off the road. It was turning into quite the day.

Later that week we drove up to Zambia, and it was wild. The colours, the smells and the sights were like being in a different world. It was a culture shock, but we absolutely loved it. We saw wild animals, like cheetahs, hyenas, and elephants casually crossing the road.

There were lorries lining the road too, covered in bullet holes. We asked our driver what had happened. He said they had been attacked by local people who wanted to try and loot them. Heather and I looked at each other, wondering what we had got ourselves into. We were uncertain what lay ahead but sure that this was a real adventure.

The first gathering in Zambia had about 25,000 people attending. People travelled from all over to attend these gatherings, walking miles and miles from the surrounding villages. We had never seen anything like it: the arena, the stage, the set up and the huge number of people gathered to hear what this man had to say about Jesus Christ.

It was a cauldron of expectation. We were given the choice to sit wherever we liked. Volunteers usually sat down at the front, but we wanted to be right in the thick of it so we sat in the middle of the local people. Heather got a lot of attention, particularly because seeing blonde hair was so unusual in Zambia, so people were reaching across from different directions to try and touch it.

Reinhard preached very powerfully, sharing about the love and acceptance of our saviour. He made an appeal for people to respond to God and the uptake was staggering. There were huge crowds of people moving forward for prayer, some being carried by loved ones as they sought healing.

This was our cue as volunteers. We were to head out behind the stage where these people had gathered. It was carnage with people everywhere: laid out, receiving prayer, waiting for prayer and calling out. It was hot and loud and completely overwhelming for this ill-equipped English couple.

People were shaking on the floor and screams sounded around us. I had read about Jesus delivering demons in the gospels and the disciples following suit in Acts.

But there had been no mention of it in Bible College. During those three years of preparation, there was almost a disdain towards any denomination that would believe in or allow such wildness. I had never imagined I would see people in our day and age being set free of demonic spirits. Having no under-standing of my authority in Christ, I felt nervous, unsure of what to do next, and intimidated.

One of the first guys I was asked to pray for was about 20 years old. He was flat on his back, and there were eight local church volunteers praying for him already. Thankfully they knew what they were doing as I was way out of my depth. I began to pray for him with the others and he was writhing around. The group praying held the man so that he didn't injure himself or anyone else.

But as I helped and prayed for him, I knew that something supernatural was happening. He was trying to lift my bodyweight from the floor with just his one arm. I didn't even want to look. I had my eyes shut tight, and all I could think to do was to pray in tongues.

I eventually opened my eyes and looked at his face. As I did so, he opened his eyes, looked straight back at me and to my surprise, spoke in English, which very few people did in the middle of this rural area.

He said:

'What are you doing here? You have no power.'

I felt he was right. He continued 'This is my home. I'm not leaving'. I shut my eyes again, praying even harder. This was a demonic intimidation. This man had come forward responding to prayer; he wanted help, but as we prayed there was great resistance in his spirit.

As we continued to pray, I was observing what else was going on around us. I could see others praying but with a different outcome. People were seeing breakthroughs in a matter of minutes as their groups prayed whereas we had been praying for over 15 minutes.

Our team was getting exhausted, looking at one another and saying something was wrong.

'The powers of our prayers should be working, we have all authority in Jesus, to set this man free from the darkness that is oppressing him.'

One of the things that were common in that area was involvement with witch-doctors. They went to them for a blessing or curse or ritual, and this 'blessing' was often represented by a bracelet around their wrist. This physical bond that we could see embodied a spiritual bond of darkness that we could not see.

The prayer team would cut the bracelets off as they were praying. As they coupled this with rebuking the evil spirits and praying for freedom in the name of Jesus, the individual would find unparalleled freedom.

The bracelet had been cut off our guy a long time ago. It had made no difference, he was still being ravaged by this spirit. I wondered if it was to do with me being there, not having a clue what I was doing.

But the Holy Spirit led someone to say, 'Pull up his t-shirt.' When they did there was something tied around his torso. It was a handmade charm from the witch doctors. This represented a major curse showing he had been involved at a higher level.

They cut it off. Immediately we prayed again and he was delivered. He came round, now speaking in his right mind and visibly changed! We could see that he had been completely set free. There was a relief now that his soul was at peace.

We were there for the following two weeks. I was observing, learning, asking questions and trying not to get too freaked out. I felt so unqualified. I came away with more questions than I had before we had travelled. But God was working. I was being humbled.

Attending bible college can create an arrogance in students that makes them presume that they know all the answers. Some form all their conclusions before even beginning ministry. I'd picked up an element of that too.

As I came face to face with this context of spiritual darkness, where the light was shining so brightly, my conclusions got blown to smithereens. One of the greatest fruits of this trip was not becoming fully equipped to handle the spiritual world but committing myself to have a teachable spirit.

With the cutting of the bands, my logic couldn't relate to how this made sense. How could this physical bond relate to spiritual freedom? But the Holy

Spirit was promising to teach me, to help me understand and to see beyond the physical. This would turn out to be just the foundation stage of my education.

As well as deliverance, we had our first experience of healing at these huge meetings. There would be huge piles of crutches on the stage, where people who had come with ailments, were walking away without them, throwing away their crutches as a celebration of their healing.

There was an unconfessed cynicism in my heart, as a lot of these ailments were things you couldn't really see. Someone hopping along, then the next moment, they could walk. Nothing that was going to have your jaw dropping to the ground. A lot of you may know what I mean. We can see someone say they are healed or feel better, but for some of us there is a voice in the back of our minds that questions its validity.

My doubts wanted a jaw-dropper. The second week that we were there I saw an opportunity for this to happen. As volunteers we were there from the start of the event, welcoming everyone. A father and son arrived early so they could sit near the front. The father was pushing his son in a homemade wheelbarrow. As he passed me, I could see the boy, who was about nine, had lame withered legs. It was clear he had never walked. As this father pushed him past in the rough rickety old barrow, my heart broke for the little boy.

I prayed for him, saying to God:

'If you heal this little boy, and I see him walk, I'll never doubt you again.'

I sat close by to them both, eager to see what would unfold. At the end of the event the appeal was given for anyone who wanted to receive healing. The father seized his moment, pushing his little boy down to the front.

A team of volunteers were on hand to pray for those who had responded. They worked their way down the lines of hundreds of people, eventually coming to the small boy in the wheelbarrow. They tapped him on the head with their hands, saying: 'Be healed, in Jesus name.' That was it. They moved on, tapped the next one, and the next one.

Nothing seemed to happen for the little boy that I had been watching so closely. After a while his father picked up the wheelbarrow, pushing his son home. The next day came around, and the rally with it. The father had returned early again with his barrow and his boy. When the appeal came for healing people began to respond.

The father pushed his son through the masses of people. Arriving at the front, positioning him for prayer once more. The volunteers prayed with a tap on the boy's head once again. Just as before there was no change. The father wheeled him away another night.

He returned again the next day for a third time. The father, not discouraged or dismayed but determined with his precious boy. As the event came to an end the appeal was given, I watched the pair head towards the front, praying in my spirit, asking that this would be the night.

Once again the volunteers prayed for all those who had responded, people all over the group were standing up, throwing their crutches on the stage, it was an amazing sight. But the best part was watching what happened next.

The little boy, after being quickly prayed for with another tap, sat himself up in the wheelbarrow, holding on to his legs, as if he could feel the change. He swung his legs over the side, jumping up onto his feet! Full of joy, full of laughter, he sprang into the air, again and again with this new found, God-given strength! The joy to be able to walk, and to leap, was magnificent to the little boy that had never before experienced it.

It was a miracle. A real bonafide jaw-dropper. It was evident that he had never walked before; he began to learn to balance, walking like a young foal getting to its feet for the first time after being born. But very quickly he became more assured and more confident.

He was now running and jumping through the crowd. His father picked up the wheelbarrow which had been his son's transport all this time, pushing it behind his son as he followed the miracle running out before him.

The father's faith, prayers and determination had been rewarded. I have never seen someone smile as widely as the father did that day. I can only imagine how heaven responded.

Just before we left Africa, we decided to see some of the sights and to go have some fun. We travelled back down to Zimbabwe to stay with Jane and her husband John. John took us out horse riding through the African bush, exploring the wild country. As sundown approached, we headed back to the farmhouse, but Heather's horse got spooked, it bolted, throwing her to the ground violently, landing her on her back. It was clear immediately that Heather was in a lot of pain. After the initial shock, she told us through tears that she couldn't move her legs. She began to panic, thinking that this would impact our ability to have children. John quickly rode away to get help.

As dusk descended upon us, we became more nervous being in the middle of nowhere, hearing all kinds of noises and movements coming from animals in the surrounding vegetation.

After what felt like a lifetime, John was back, this time with a cigarette in his mouth. He had given up smoking, but Heather's accident had caused him a significant relapse. He was chain smoking now.

We lifted her into the back seat of the car, making a bumpy and painful journey back over the rough terrain. John drove back to his farmhouse that we were staying at, as we were two hours from the closest hospital. Heather was still in a lot of pain, but Jane strongly discouraged us to go there because of the risk associated with the hospital. It was so distressing seeing Heather like this. I didn't know if she had broken her back, and then she passed out.

The pressure increased on making a decision on what to do, I was praying once again for my wife, asking God to come through in a miraculous way. She eventually came round, so we decided to see how she was in the morning. The next day I took her to a little clinic instead of the hospital.

To our great relief, she was able to begin to move her legs again. God had answered our prayers. The clinic gave her a pair of crutches, allowing us to head back to England. We were loaded up with African paintings, furniture, ornaments and souvenirs.We would remember our trip forever.

Our trip to Africa had a huge impact on our lives. We had witnessed the spiritual in ways that our rural English upbringings had never exposed us to. We came home feeling more alert to the presence of the spiritual in our everyday lives, more aware of the goodness of God personally and over the church.

But it's also fair to say that we felt spiritually disturbed on our return. It was as though things that had been dormant in our lives were now activated. We both had an underlying sense that our trip had also exposed us to some things that we carried back to the UK with us. We could not identify exactly what it was, but we did have this uncomfortable sense that something wasn't quite right, or out of place..

Only a few months after we had got back from Africa, Heather became pregnant, putting to rest our fears that her accident would have impacted her ability to bear children. Nine months later our first son Josh arrived and we were so grateful to become parents.

Heather struggled to heal and recover from giving birth, she spent weeks, which became months, unwell, some days spending all day in bed. She started to become low in her spirit too. This was so unusual for Heather who is always laughing.

We sought the help of doctors, but they couldn't do anything to help her recovery other than give her painkillers. After praying into it with my parents, the Holy Spirit revealed to us there was more to this than ill health. There was a spiritual dynamic to the trouble in our household.

My parents began to pray around the house, declaring the favour and peace of Jesus in each room. They prayed in our bedroom, where they stopped, 'There is something dark in this room.' They encouraged us to search the room to see if there was anything in there from last year's trip to Africa.

It was a tiny room so there were not many places to search. I went over to the wardrobe and pulled everything out of it; towels, bedsheets, spare pillows. Right at the back, tucked away in the corner was a small, wooden, hollowed out pot with a handle on it. It came back to me: we had been given this by a local man as a free gift when we went horse riding, the day that Heather had the accident that had temporarily paralysed her.

He had urged us to take it with a smile on his face, wanting nothing in return. It had ended up travelling all the way back to England with us and ended up hidden at the back of our wardrobe. We took it outside to burn it.

As quickly as the fire went out, health was returning to Heather's body. Within just a week she was back to herself. This little wooden mixing pot that we were given was most likely from a witch doctor, who would have practiced incantations and curses and used the pot to mix his remedies. As the witch doctor had seen us coming that day, he presented us not with a gift but with a curse.

Now I know this sounds pretty crazy. If you are still reading, then well done. But let's just give a little biblical context here.

> 'God did extraordinary miracles through the hands of Paul, so that even handkerchiefs and aprons that had touched him were taken to the sick, and the diseases and evil spirits left them.'
>
> Acts 19:11-12 NIV

If it is possible for blessings to be carried via something physical, don't you think that the things of evil will try to imitate the things of God? For a curse to be carried on something physical? I can only tell you our direct experience. When we destroyed these things, we prayed, and then saw the immense breakthrough we had been asking for.

In the years following we've picked up many things from our trips around the world. We love collecting things to remind us of the people we've met and the amazing things God has done, but we're always conscious of the potential connection to negative spiritual things if you're not careful.

Church leaders are often so cautious of these explosive elements of ministry that they neglect to speak or teach on them. Our churches need to be aware and equipped to deal with the supernatural as a part of our faith.

As well as being aware of the supernatural power of darkness, we need to be embracing of the supernatural power of God. That was about to come into our lives and spark our fire into life.

8

CHURCH PLANTING IN LEOMINSTER

We were part of my Dad's church in Hereford in 1987 when an American group came to minister to us. They were a part of the awakening to the 'five-fold ministry' outlined in Ephesians 4 that was happening across the church at that time. This was primarily focussed on the offices of the apostle and the prophet, and it was about to change our lives hugely.

We were there with our baby Josh, Heather not wanting to miss out. One of the Americans visiting our town to minister that night was Clem Ferris. He was a smartly dressed, serious chap and seemed to be Mr. All-American. The full suit and formal shoes seemed an old-school combination on the young man, certainly compared to our informality.

The team were prophesying into the lives of people across the room and spoke with an amazing boldness and authority. The things they were saying made you think someone must have given them inside information.

We were sitting right at the back of the room, listening intently, with our heads down. We didn't want to make eye contact with these people, in case they saw into your soul. Clem, who was in training at the time, walked straight up to us. We were blown away as he began to speak some things into our life: things there was no way he could have known.

He began to describe things that related to Heather's childhood and passions that were in her heart. He then said to me: 'You're trying to hide, but God sees you.' It was spot on for me at the time. I didn't like the limelight or having anyone's attention on me at all.

He went on to speak about us planting a church. Those words lit a fire in our spirits. The conviction we had for mission was about to take shape right on our doorstep.

We were a part of the Hereford church, but we were living in neighbouring Leominster. We had moved there originally because we couldn't afford house prices in the city of Hereford. We had been leading a small group of others who lived in the town, and up until this time we had been serving in my dad's church, doing what we could with the things that fell into our hands. But as the prophet spoke out something new, a fire began to burn within us, a new vision for our town.

One of the profound things for us was that we knew God saw us. As he pulled us out in front of the whole room, it was a huge affirmation but also an encouragement that He was with us on this journey and knew us by name. These are things that we already knew in our minds, but these truths take on new power when they become alive in our hearts. Up to this point, we didn't believe in ourselves, but this prophetic encounter birthed courage and conviction in our souls.

From that point on, we had a vision: we were going to plant a church in the market town of Leominster. It had a population of about 10,000 and was an insular place known for antique shops and a quiet lifestyle. But we saw that God was calling us to reach the people of this rural town.

My dad was a pioneer. He had planted the church we were going to and had shared plans to start other churches in the surrounding area. It just made sense. Of course we would start a church in Leominster.

After praying into it, Heather and I approached my dad and shared our plan. We suggested that we take our Leominster group and turn it into a new church. He said that the whole Eldership team would need to hear our thoughts.

A week later I went to the church offices and there were a group of desks lined up. My dad and the elders sat looking on, with a chair placed on the other side for me. This was more formal than I had anticipated. I thought we were going to have a chat about it over a cup of tea.

They questioned me for about an hour. It was a proper grilling. They wanted to know how we were going to make it work. I was just 22 at the time, and they hadn't seen me do much at the church since coming back from Bible College.

A week later they came back to us with their prayerful response. They told Heather and I to pray into it for the next year and see if we still felt the same in twelve months. I knew that this was to test us, to see how serious we were.

I went back and told Heather and we were both pretty deflated. We had been raring to go, ready to get started and see what God had on the other side of this decision. But now we would have to wait for a whole year with this burning inside us.

So we prayed for that next year, carrying the vision close and handing it to Jesus again and again. Instead of dwindling, the fire burned even stronger within us. We came back after those twelve months and told them that we were ready to go and were fully convinced that God had called us to do this.

They gave us their blessing and we started doing pre-launch meetings in our home. We set a launch date for New Life Community Church: May 22nd 1988. We had just moved house, and our second son, Luke, had been born 13 days before. We rented a community centre in Leominster and had a turnout of 40 people, with a number of the church in Hereford travelling over to support us for that first Sunday.

We were buzzing, full of life, energy and excitement in expectation of what God would do! We had two items that were given to us to launch our new church: an overhead projector, (which you can Google if you need to), and a tambourine.

Today we plant our churches with thousands of pounds to invest in equipment, so it is extraordinary now to look back and see how small the beginning was. The rent for the community centre was paid out of an overdraft: we went into the negative to get the church started. None of our group had any money and most of us had debt. We kept the church going out of an overdraft for the first few years.

The next week we had a group of 10 people show up, including ourselves. We had no musicians. And I couldn't really avoid preaching and being the centre of attention anymore. It was a juxtaposition of having a passion to answer my calling and to do this for the kingdom; at the same time as it being my worst nightmare.

———

As I began to preach, I spent so many hours preparing messages. I filled the waste paper basket with page after page of content that just didn't seem good enough. It took years before I had any confidence that what I was saying was half decent.

We felt alone. We were only 13 miles away from our mother church, but it was enough to feel disconnected and isolated. I was learning how to lead a church. It was a slow and painful process. I couldn't help thinking that no one thought we would last very long and that maybe once we had failed and learned our lessons, we would end up retreating back to the safety of our church in Hereford.

The community centre we were meeting in would be rented for parties on Saturday nights. We would come in on Sunday morning and the place would be a mess: beer glasses everywhere, rubbish all over the floor, cigarette butts to pick up, the stench of smoke to air out and sticky spillages to clean up. The first thing to do each time was to try and get the place usable again.

In the winter, the owners wouldn't put the heating on; we weren't paying enough for that apparently. Our young group that we started off with included three babies, so by the time I got up to speak the mothers had left the room to nurse their children. They were pretty dire days.

Through this time, there was so much pressure on me. God was deconstructing me and teaching me about who I was called to be in Him. Have you ever seen that survival film where the desperate individual needs a fire and uses a bow drill until his hands get red raw, then he throws the thing in anger? That was a bit like trying to get our first fire started.

I was the only speaker in the tiny church and would spend my Saturday afternoons, evenings and Sunday mornings preparing my message. Then I would wrestle out a midweek message too. Alongside working a full time job, preparing and carrying the preaching was intensive and immersive.

We started reaching out to some really broken young people. They had messed up lives and were full of complex issues but were responding to the care and love of our little church community.

We saw some of them get baptised and it was a huge encouragement to us all. Then one week a visiting speaker came along so I could have a moment's relief from the speaking rota. He rebuked these young people for coming in and out of the room while he was speaking. After that we didn't really see much of them. Our first fruits had been scared off, felt judged and it was a discouragement to our fledgling congregation.

We had a family come and join us that were travelling from another town. It was great to see another family getting involved and even making the effort to get in a car to be a part of what God was doing.

The husband was about 10 years older than me and had been involved in ministry, leading youth work in his past church. He had also attended bible college, and he had all the confidence I didn't have.

He would make notes through my message; I could see him as I was speaking, scribbling away. His note-taking wasn't because my preaching was so inspirational and he wanted to learn. Quite the opposite. After the service, I was presented with a list of criticisms and questions he wanted to address with me
.

I look at our church, where it is now, and this guy wouldn't bother me. But when someone like that was one of a dozen people in the room and I was as young and unsure of myself as I was, it was a huge battle to have him sitting in front of me each week.

He didn't believe in tithing and would enjoy debating the issue frequently with me. He felt he had a prophetic gift and would often get up to share a word for the church, although it seemed to me that it was most relevant to himself. He would get up and start speaking in tongues in front of the church, then do interpretation too.

He had massive issues with authority and with leadership. God used this to strengthen a steel in me, to get me to confront, to be direct and to challenge. I had to get over not just my fear of speaking; I had to take it a step further and stand up for what I just preached.

I went to his house and told him that he couldn't come freely up to the front and prophesy over others any longer. I challenged him about his character not matching up with his gifting. I gave him a challenge of withholding from his gifting and working on his character for six months.

I found out that he had been dismissed from a previous role for inappropriate behaviour some years previously. He told me later on that he was planning on getting a new job, but it meant it would take him away from his family. I advised him against it and that he should focus on his marriage. He ignored me and went for the job regardless.

Unfortunately that decision led to significant hardship and challenge for his family and weighed heavily on our fledgling church as we worked to sort through the mess that came from it.

Facing up to this man had been an intense and stretching challenge for me. God often grows our character not just through affirmation but through challenge and resistance.

9

TAKING A SHORT CUT

We tried everything we could think of to make an impact on our town. We would go door to door, Jehovah's Witness style, sharing our faith and offering to pray with people. We were so desperate to see people come to know Jesus.

I had two men who were leading with me at the time, and we would meet early in the mornings to run and pray several times a week so that we could see Leominster have a breakthrough of the gospel.

Heather had befriended a woman that had connected to my dad's church in Hereford. She was in a relationship with a guy called Bill. Bill was a notorious criminal with a big reputation in the town: he had been in prison for kicking a man close to death. Drugs, drink, violence and a sense of humour was a pretty good summary of Bill.

God said 'Reach him,' so I struck up a friendship through us spending time with him and Sarah. I went to the local pub with him. It was called the Queens Head, and Bill tried to talk us into not coming as it was too rough and full of criminals and rascals.

For us nowhere was off limits for the hope that we carried within us. Determined to be a light in the darkness, we entered this old pub, which was a crumby dive, to see what God would do. Bill would do the sign of the cross when we saw him. He thought it was hilarious that we wanted to spend time with him, but there was a weird respect forming.

As time went on and we kept visiting the pub, his whole group of friends would do the sign of the cross. It was a big joke but also a sign of respect. If anyone swore in front of us, Bill would give them a harsh rebuke and remind them to behave themselves around the church people. We had a lot of conversations with him and I built a friendship with him, but he never came to church.

Prayer. Friendship. Outreach. Time. Investment. Patience. Repeat. If only there was a quicker way to get this fire burning.

I had been told that we would not have a breakthrough in our town unless we were promoting unity across churches and building relationships with other pastors in the area. So, I was regularly attending a joint church leaders meeting. One week, one of the pastors approached me. He knew we were looking for some momentum in our small church and had an idea to help.

He had a friend who did healing and evangelism, travelling around and ministering into different places. He said 'Why don't we see if he will come to you guys in Leominster, we could do some healing meetings there?'

Seeing people healed and get saved through a minister who had confidence and experience felt like a no brainer. 'That sounds great, but where would we do it?' I responded. He suggested we get a big tent, like a circus tent, and put it in the middle of the town in a public park with permission from the local council.

We were offered help from another church and leader, and for the first time, we had a plan of how we could impact more people in the town and really get some momentum. It felt foolproof. We were willing to do WHATEVER it takes to see people reached, so our group of around 30 took on this event.

We made arrangements and planned details, not deterred by our lack of experience. We advertised by giving out leaflets and arranging to go into the local school to talk about the event. We got the permission we needed, found a tent to hire and prayed into the event, expectant that this was going to catalyse our church and give us the impact that we so desired. We assembled the tent then we had a 24-hour guard duty, never leaving it unmanned in case it was vandalised or misused.

The first night came around and we were so excited to see what God would do. The pastor from Hereford had brought some of his church and had brought the speaker too. He had written a number of books and was probably my first experience of a so-called Christian celebrity.

I saw that he had arrived and as the hosting pastor, went to greet him and introduce myself. As I approached him, he put his hand up, indicating he didn't want to speak to me. This made me a bit worried about who we had brought in, but I chose to believe the best and that he just needed some time to prepare himself.

When the start time came, the place was packed. We had a lot of Christians who had travelled quite a distance because they knew of the speaker, but we had a number of local people too. We had advertised the night as a place to come and get healing. As he shared, he spoke about the gospel and said: 'I know that a lot of you have come for healing tonight, but before I do that, I want to ask if you want to accept Jesus as your saviour.' It felt manipulative. If you want the healing you heard about, come to Jesus first.

On the second night, we had advertised a youth event for the school children after the main healing meeting. We had communicated this to our guest speaker and we were so excited to see the young people beginning to turn up to our big circus tent in anticipation of our youth event. If you have ever built church, you'll know that getting people to show up is most of the battle.

The time to start our youth event came round. All the young people were gathered outside, and kept popping their heads in to see what was going on. Our guest speaker went on for another hour. We tried to keep them waiting, telling them that he would probably be finished soon. But as they kept getting glimpses of people being prayed for they thought it looked crazy. A few key young people decided they had enough and left, and the group followed along with them. We were absolutely gutted.

———

Despite that disappointment, over the two nights we had 106 decisions for Jesus! This was revival. Three times the number of our weekly gatherings had just got saved. We were so grateful and full of joy that we had seen this happen. We got information cards for all the people that had made a decision with their names and addresses.

A week later, Heather and I got some other volunteers and split the decision cards between us and went about following up each and every person. We wanted to connect and build a relationship so that we could see them become a part of a church community and receive some discipleship.

Door after door we would knock, and people would answer with a bewildered look on their face, wondering what we were after.

'Hello, you came along to our church's healing meeting and made a decision to follow Jesus? We would love to invite you along to church this Sunday, where you can learn more about who Jesus is...'

The usual responses were:

'I'm not interested'

'No thanks'

'Leave me alone'

'I wanted prayer for healing, but I'm not interested in your church. Don't call here again'

The banging of a closed door in our faces became a familiar sound.

It was a devastating and discouraging exercise. It was so tough on our team; we had put so much hope, prayer and work into this, and it was bitterly disappointing. We had seen little fruit from our efforts so far.

Just before the tent meetings we had one of our most authentic and tangible fruits of our new church plant. A man who had come in as an atheist found Jesus. His life had been dramatically turned around. The tent outreach was one of the first times he had ever got involved in a church event. After being involved in running the event itself and then in door knocking, I had to scrape him off the floor. He was so discouraged, questioning everything. 'Is this really what it's about? It's really knocked my faith.' He was about to give up.

48

Not only did we not see people coming in as we had dreamed or make the impact we had prayed for, but it also dealt a gut punch to the people we did have, the people who had followed me into battle and backed the vision. I had to get people back on their feet and get fresh faith again.

We did have an old couple who came along after the tent outreach though. They seemed to have a Christian background and were in their seventies. We were glad to see someone come in after all our efforts. However, towards the end of our worship time that morning, the wife was in some distress. Everyone stopped and set about helping her, realising that she must be having some kind of seizure. We called an ambulance and they took her and her husband away.

Heather went to visit her at her home, and she was okay, but we never saw them again. The one couple that we had seen come in from this healing outreach had come to church once and left in an ambulance. If we didn't laugh, we would have cried.

Next we had a message from the council telling us that they had a number of complaints from the local community about the noise we had created. We had also gone longer than we should have thanks to the guest speaker.. Because of this we would never be allowed to hire council land again. We were banned! It was another blow.

Then we had another letter. Someone had attended the healing outreach on one of the nights and had tripped on the chain link fence that was around the perimeter of our tent. It was a council fence, but the lady who tripped was saying that it was our responsibility because we had not lit the area sufficiently. She said she would be suing us for damages. And she was a Christian!

I wrote back to her, and told her she could sue us if she wanted, but we didn't have anything. None of us owned any property, the church didn't own assets or have any finances, so it would be a fruitless endeavour. I never heard from her again.

It had been tempting to think that we had found a golden goose.

It turned out to be more of a trojan horse.

We thought that this would be a way to jumpstart this church planting process and see an instant influx of growth. 'If we just go and knock door to door..', 'If we just get in this gifted speaker...' 'If we go in and invite them from the schools...' All this had royally failed. It appeared to be a gift, but it almost destroyed us.

———————

I knew from this point onwards that the only way to build this church was to consistently work at it. There was no easy route round the back. I would be looking for God to move and looking to Him alone.

I also decided that I would never put the church in the hands of other leaders that I have little or no relationship with. That approach was a roulette, and this one had almost finished us off. We were going to have to work hard and pray harder.

I learned to rely on God and not rely on others and to trust the leadership that was within me. There is a constant pressure as a leader to know the vision and direction. When someone approached me and came up with a plan, it was a welcome lifting of weight. I had embraced it and seized the opportunity for someone else to bring vision.

This would be a valuable lesson in the future: to know that I had to accept the mantle of my own leadership and not try and pass it off to others.

> And don't allow yourselves to be weary or disheartened in planting good seeds, for the season of reaping the wonderful harvest you've planted is coming!
>
> Galatians 6:9 TPT

'David found strength in the Lord his God.'

1 0

SELF-LEADERSHIP - LESSONS FROM DISAPPOINTMENT

The early days of church planting were brutal, but throughout my years of ministry God has used disappointments such as the tent outreach to teach me how to overcome discouragement. There have been a lot of disappointments along the way, but the tools I have found to overcome it are well-displayed in the story of David at Ziklag.

You can read the story in 1 Samuel 30. David and his band of warriors are living in Ziklag, which is Philistine territory. They return from a war campaign and find that enemies have burnt it down and taken the women and children.

These are devastating circumstances. They cry and wail so deeply that they can cry no more. The men look for someone to blame and want to stone David to death.

Then the scripture tells us that when all hope seems drained away and David is about to meet his end, that: 'David found strength in the Lord'. This is a small phrase, but the entire destiny of David and his legacy depends on this moment. Instead of wallowing in self-pity or going on the offensive against his disloyal men, David opts for a different approach. A turning of the heart to the Lord.

This is a game-changer. The ability to not become consumed or overwhelmed when you are receiving fierce, personal criticism is extremely important in any form of life, and especially in ministry. David strengthens himself in the Lord and then gets up from his mourning to make a plan.

There are some key thoughts from this story that have helped me, that I would like to equip you with too.

PEOPLE WILL DISAPPOINT YOU.

The men threatening to kill David were not just ordinary soldiers. These men had been with David a long time, fighting many battles alongside him. David had originally taken them in when they were broken and purposeless, flocking to him for leadership in Adullam's Cave (1 Sam 22: 1-5). Everything they had now gained was because of their association with David. Even that didn't stop them from wanting to kill him when they felt let down by his leadership.

Given David's position, we could understand him being hurt, defensive and angry. But he doesn't hold his men's emotions against them. He leads them out of those feelings instead. People will disappoint you: they will fail you and even betray your trust, even after you have devoted yourself to pouring into their lives. But how you deal with that disappointment is the key.

If you have unrealistic expectations, your heart can become bitter towards that person and to others in the future too. If you don't manage your expectations, you can spend a lifetime managing your discouragement. People will let you down; you have to accept that. We're involved in the redemption business though. That means that it never has to be final. But you can only move on from it if you are willing to lead out of it, instead of waiting for them to do so.

Just like David's men, those that are closest to us can hurt us the most. We must put our trust in others but not be naive to think that those people will never fail.

If the growth and strength of your faith depends on others performing, you'll end up in trouble. It's easy to lead when things are going well. Part of maturity is experiencing rejection. Maturity looks like experiencing rejection and drawing confidence through it.

I know that sounds like a paradox, but that's how you start getting rid of the fear of man: being free of what others think of you. You can't test that when everyone agrees with you, only when you face opposition and disapproval. Don't allow a tough heart to develop to protect you. Instead have tough skin.

You alone are responsible for the condition of your heart. You can't control others or determine how they treat you. Put your focus on what is in your control. If you don't deal with your heart, the enemy will use it to remove you from the race. Your heart can be the biggest obstacle or the biggest blessing.

YOUR RELATIONSHIP WITH JESUS IS YOUR NUMBER ONE STRENGTH.

You can have the greatest church culture to work in and you can have brilliant people around you, but if you try to sustain yourself on any other strength apart from the one that comes from God, you will be on shaky ground. David strengthened himself in the Lord and that is what sustained him when all else was failing.

Reading leadership books is great, going to conferences might be helpful, listening to a podcast might be inspiring, but you must be sustained first and foremost through your daily relationship with God. David on his most difficult day accessed the source and it changed everything.

The source is unhindered: God never turns off the river of his presence. It is our willingness to connect to it and choose Him over our feelings that determines our connection to him. I don't believe that anyone should ever have to suffer from 'burnout'. If we are consistently connecting to Him through prayer, worship and his word, we will be sustained no matter what we face.

PASSION AND VISION ARE CONTAGIOUS

David found strength in the Lord his God. That's all the detail that the Bible provides us with at this pivotal moment. But in my experience, here's what that might have consisted of:

Reflecting on God's heart for him, not the hearts of the angry men.

Remembering God's promises, not his desperate circumstances.

Rooting confidence in God's unfailing faithfulness, not the fickle nature of the men he was leading.

Surrendering his human feelings and fears and picking up the boldness that God has provided for him.

After David's strengthening, he and the priest begin to enquire of the Lord the next steps they should take, and a plan is made. As soon as he does this, there is no more talk of stoning.

When David begins to cast vision, there is no more anger, no more threats. Vision runs like an infection through the camp, hope revives and unity recovers. Vision unifies people. The best way to bring unity is to cast a compelling, clear vision.

One of the most awesome things I have seen in our church is our people's willingness and response to vision. It has allowed us to do all that we have done through these years. It's a well known concept that leaders should be temperature setters and it's true: David sets the temperature for the whole group by focusing on his response rather than reacting to their feelings.

Set the temperature. Choose to believe that God is doing something mighty rather than letting your hope seep away. Take ownership. Employ your voice. Division drains vision, but unity causes momentum.

BE CONFIDENT IN GOD'S DOT-TO-DOT.

After strengthening himself in the Lord and surviving a plot to be killed, David rouses his men and leads them out to find the enemy. The Lord promises that they will find them but doesn't indicate which way to go. So David and his men, in faith, go on the pursuit.

In 1 Sam 30:11 they find a starving Egyptian in a field. They feed and revive him and he turns out to be a slave who was abandoned by the raiding party because he was ill. He leads them to the attackers and David and the men recover their wives and children and take all the plunder that the enemy have accumulated. God did not reveal a location, but he did direct their footsteps to a half-dead Egyptian slave.

Self-leadership is a lot about the faith that we have in God's dot-to-dot. Just like a child's dot-to-dot picture, we don't get to see the overall image until we keep going from one dot to the other, joining them together in order to create the finished picture.

Some of the miracles I have seen have been amazing, but they have rarely been simple. It has been trusting God from one dot, to the next, to the next, all the while leading others on that same process, and reassuring them that God is responsible for the picture and he cannot fail.

BE GRACIOUS TO THOSE WHO FAIL

David returns with his men, women and children and all the plunder. But 200 of the 600 men had been too exhausted to make the whole journey (1 Sam 30:10) so they stayed behind and rested in a valley.

When the 400 that had been successful saw those that had not made the journey, they declared that they did not deserve to have any of the spoils of the plunder. Their families would be returned to them, but they could not have anything else. There is a big part of me that agrees with this. By all means, take your family back, but why should you receive the reward when it was others who risked their necks?

David's response was very different.

> David replied, 'No, my brothers, you must not do that with what the Lord has given us. He has protected us and delivered into our hands the raiding party that came against us. Who will listen to what you say? The share of the man who stayed with the supplies is to be the same as that of him who went down to the battle. All will share alike.'
>
> 1 Sam 30: 23-24 NIV

Sometimes we can decide that we are finished with someone. They let us down too many times, they betrayed our trust, they weren't there when we needed them. Our hearts can become bitter against them.

Self-leadership requires us to protect our hearts against this. We cannot lead effectively by harbouring our disappointment. We have to lead with grace, forgiveness and humility, keeping a short account with others. Anything else will be a burden that will cause the integrity of our leadership to rust and decay.

We so quickly forget all the chances we were given, all the times that we failed. If we're not on our guard we can fall into entitlement and judge others by a vastly different scale to the one used for us.

You have to laugh at the men suggesting that the 200 that were too exhausted to keep up the pursuit didn't deserve any plunder. All of them had been talking of killing David earlier that very same day! Isn't that a picture of man's arrogance?

Self-leadership requires us to remember where we came from and to keep ourselves grounded. It is a privilege and an honour to lead. You will see others come in and receive the blessing that you fought for. That's a part of the deal. Is that not what Christ did for us 1000 times over?

SELF LEADERSHIP QUESTIONS TO CONSIDER:

- Are there any relationships in your life where you have unrealistic expectations of others? How can you adjust those?
- How are you cultivating your relationship with Jesus right now?
- Where can you set a temperature of faith and share vision with others?
- God rarely shows us the whole picture but rather invites us to follow one step at a time. What is the next step of obedience in front of you today?
- Forgiveness, grace and understanding help keep our hearts soft. Is there anything you need to do to remove pride and judgement from your heart and to protect it for God's purposes?

' Therefore put on the full armor of God, so that when the day of evil comes, you may be able to stand your ground, and after you have done everything, to stand.' **Eph 6:13**

11

SPIRITUAL WAR

After being baptised, Jesus set out on his 40-day fast in the desert. It was there that he had his conversations with Satan, right at the beginning of his ministry. Perhaps this is where the enemy thought that Jesus might be most vulnerable to temptation.

We were certainly at our most vulnerable when we started the church. We were low on confidence, lacking experience and still intimidated by the thought of dark spiritual activity.

As well as learning new lessons, we were also getting an upgrade in ones that we had begun already. Going to Africa had exposed us to a spiritual world far beyond our understanding. We were now seeing similar, intense demonic attacks in the lives we came in contact with through the work of New Life Community Church. These are just a few encounters that we experienced in the first years of planting our church.

A police woman who was not a Christian started to attend the church. She was tough-skinned; she would often deal calmly with bodies at crime scenes. But she called us by phone one evening in a hysterical state. She lived alone in the countryside and had gone to bed that evening, only to be disturbed by knocking at the door: constant banging, banging and banging. She had been so terrified that she hid in her bed, anticipating a break-in.

Eventually it stopped. Nothing and no one seemed to be there in the old stone cottage. She had a dog, but since she had moved in, it would never go upstairs because it was afraid. Now she never wanted to go up there either. She asked me to go to her house and pray.

I took one of the other leaders from the church and we found her curled up in a chair, clinging to a Gideon's Bible and holding it up as some kind of deterrent. She said this was the only comfort she could find. The dog was howling and obviously distressed.

We went upstairs and began to pray for God's peace in each room. We also prayed the name of Jesus over the home. When we had finished praying, the dog immediately went upstairs for the first time and she followed it.

'It's gone, isn't it?' she said with relief. We confirmed that there is nothing that can withstand the name of Jesus.

She found out later that the people next door had been carrying out occult rituals. They had no idea that we had been around to pray, but knew something had happened. They approached our friend and were indignant. 'What have you done? What's happened to our poltergeist? He's gone!' They were angry and upset, but the home, the woman and the dog were free.

Another experience we had was with two ladies called Nina and Pat who started coming along to our church. They had recently moved to Leominster. Nina had been very involved in practicing witchcraft. Pat had too, but to a lesser extent. They had come from a witches coven in another part of England.

They had been involved in some dark satanic, sexual and sacrificial rituals, things too dark to write about on these pages. Their dabbling in high levels of Satanism had scared them thoroughly and they had literally run away. After a while, they met someone from our church who invited them along.

Nina became very distressed when she had walked into our church meeting room for a time of prayer. She was afraid and clinging to the sides of the room. 'There's blood everywhere!' She shrieked. 'I can't be in here. It's covered in blood!' The room was as clean as a whistle. I looked back and forth. I knew that she had been involved in witchcraft, and it dawned on me that what she was seeing was the blood of Jesus. I tried to comfort her, 'It's okay, this is where we worship. This is the blood of Jesus and it will heal and save you.'

They gave their lives to Jesus and repented from the terrible things they had been involved in. We prayed with them, cutting off and banishing every past influence and spirit. Soon after that, Nina and Pat got in touch to say things had been kicking off in their home. There were noises and things were moving around. Quite understandably, it was scaring the life out of them. So they asked us to pray.

I went around with another leader as we did things in pairs as the Bible shows us in Luke 10:1, and we prayed around the house. This was not an old country house, like the one before, it was a modern build on a housing estate. We took communion together and started praying over the house, coming against anything that was lingering there and speaking the peace of Jesus into every room.

It was all fine, and we worked our way through each room until we came to the last bedroom. It was foggy in there. We turned the light on and off and we could see there was a strange opaqueness to the room. We did a double take and checked we were both seeing the same thing. Yes. So we prayed our routine prayers with renewed vigour, taking authority and declaring peace in the name of Jesus.

The room slowly cleared. We wanted to do the whole house, so we went up into the attic. My prayer partner gave me a leg up, I popped open the attic door and pulled myself up. There was no light in the attic, but there was light coming through the eaves below. I managed to get up fully into the dark and dusty space and began to pray my usual prayer.

While I was praying, to my surprise I saw something running at the other end of the attic. It was about three foot tall and looked like an imp-like dark creature. I couldn't believe my eyes. I was actually seeing a demon. I called quickly to my partner: 'Get up here and join me now!' As he scrambled up, I was already praying against the little beast.

As the pair of us were praying in the name of Jesus, it was running back and forth with nowhere to go, running faster and faster and faster. And then all of a sudden it vanished. We knew that the house was clear. Nina and Pat reported back to us in the coming weeks that there were no more noises and their home was now peaceful.

All of this allowed us to see into the spiritual world that was at work among those we were reaching in our community. These stories have been the exception, but still opened our eyes to what the enemy is really doing when we pray and to the influence his demonic activity has through sin in the lives of people.

These experiences aren't the norm for most people but were lessons that would prove to be invaluable as we put together our ministry teaching that many people have benefited from, gaining freedom from the dark aspects of their pasts. For many people freedom looks different to these extreme situations, but as believers in Jesus, we all have the opportunity for the fullness of freedom that he gives.

12

FREE AND FREE INDEED

Many of the things we face in life have a spiritual connection or context. Even though our world is obsessed with the spiritual in films, media and entertainment, we overlook the reality of it in our own lives. We often can't see it because we're so deep in the cycles of feelings, relationships and the busyness of life. The early experiences we had and years of pastoring have taught us that if we don't deal with the supernatural things, we will always be living a partial version of God's fullness.

We also learned that it wasn't just spiritual. Much of how we are doing comes down to our mentality, the habits of what we say or don't say, our actions, discipline and even the people we do life with. True freedom is a combination of the spiritual and physical. So we developed ministry teaching to bring these aspects together in something that really helps people get free and stay free.

WE ARE SPIRITUAL BEINGS

The Bible teaches us to love God with our heart, mind, soul and strength. Therefore it teaches us that whilst we are one person, we have these compartmentalised elements that all work together.

The spiritual element is the most real part of who we are. The fact that we're going to live out eternity with God in Heaven shows us that this spiritual dynamic of our lives will outlast the rest. God's word is full of examples where there was more going on than just the physical dynamic. As Christians, we have to engage with the spiritual world; it's an essential part of our faith. As we open up to the reality that there may be spiritual dynamics to why we are who we are, we need to understand who God is in this. We also need to understand how the enemy works.

God is sovereign, the enemy is subject. Whilst the enemy has time-limited power, he doesn't have eternal authority. If you're walking with Jesus, you're on the winning side. God is the creator, the devil is created. The unseen battle of good and evil is not between two equal parties. The Bible says that God will destroy the enemy with a breath, it will not even be a wrestle. This should give us confidence. It's not easy resisting the enemy, but it is possible.

The devil is a master of getting us to ignore him or obsess over him and in either extreme he wins. We need to strike the balance between the two. Genesis 3 describes the devil as crafty, clever even.

The popularised idea that the devil appears with flames coming out his nose and horns on his head is far from the way he works in most situations. In Genesis 3:1 the devil comes and asks a question that instigates doubt (the first tactic) 'Did God really say?'. Have you ever heard that kind of question in your life? 'Are you really saved?' 'Did you really marry the right person?' 'Did God really move in that moment?'.

The devil is too cunning to appear in front of you. He will instead, in the most normal moments of your life, start asking questions that sow doubt. Doubt is like a virus. It attacks the immune system of trust and relationship.

The devil wants to erode your idea of who God is. He tried it with Jesus in Luke 4: 'If you are the son of God...'. It was a tactic aimed at inciting doubt. It tested Jesus' identity and relationship with God the father.

Back in Genesis 3, we see Eve replying with a religious quote of God's command rather than a relational revelation. Just think about it. There she is in the most amazing place of all human history, a place of provision, perfection and closeness to God. She could have replied with 'What does it even matter? Look at all this God has given us and is to us'. Just like Eve, we are so susceptible to look at what we don't have rather than what we do have. It's in those moments that we're vulnerable to the questions that the enemy raises.

Once the enemy has sown doubt, he starts to water it with deception, his second tactic. 'You surely won't die.' That's the first lie, but maybe not the most important. 'For God knows that when you eat…' The enemy makes out that God is withholding something. With his third tactic the devil distorts Eve's perception of the heart and nature of God. This is his ultimate lie.

Look at Luke 4 again: 'Cast yourself down because if God loves you He'll catch you'. It's a deception and a distortion, trying to test Jesus' trust of the heart and character of God. It's a similar tactic. But Jesus does not make the same mistake as Eve. He focuses on who God is and uses the truth of Scripture to resist the temptation. We are vulnerable to this doubt, deception and distortion more than we realise. When we stop that process with the truth of the word of God, like Jesus does in Luke 4, it starts to change the way we see things.

Let's go back to Genesis 3, it says: 'When Eve saw the fruit was good…'

Do you really think that day was the first time Eve had ever seen the fruit on the tree? Her perspective had changed because of the dialogue with the enemy. When we give in to the enemy's tactics we feel entitled to the praise, power or pleasure we would have walked past and ignored any other day of the week.

At this point, the enemy turns into a tempter and our own flesh thinks up every reason we should do what we know we shouldn't. As soon as we give in, the devil changes his tune. Out comes the accuser. 'How dare you do it again?' 'God won't forgive you for this!' 'Yet again you've done it; you will never change.'

Next we need to learn to identify these patterns in our own lives. One ministry tool that we use is called fruit and root. The fruit in your life; attitudes, actions, addictions etc, don't just appear. They have roots. For example, if you've experienced a significant rejection in your life, a moment of someone leaving you or letting you down, it can become a root issue. The root grows into a plant system within who you are, shaping your life.

Rejection attacks your sense of value. As a result most people either reject the world around them as a subconscious form of self-defence so that no one can reject them again or run around 'people-pleasing', subconsciously hoping to fill the gap or deal with the pain created.

The fruit in our lives often looks very different to the roots. Most of us spend time pruning but not truly uprooting the issues. These patterns are psychological, emotional, and experiential but also spiritual. The lies we believe in these moments of vulnerability are often sown by the enemy, and they become strongholds in our thinking. Identifying them can be painful, but it's the beginning of freedom.

A CHOICE TO CHANGE

Many of us are more comfortable with the enemy we know than the unknown sacrifice of change. Someone once said: 'Before you heal someone, ask them if they're willing to give up what makes them sick'.

If you have an issue with pornogrphy, it will almost always have a spiritual start, a root and pattern you can identify. But if you're not willing to go without your smart phone for a season, you can pray until you're blue in the face and still find yourself giving in to temptation. If you want to win the battle to take hold of your freedom, you will have to change.

UNDERSTANDING AUTHORITY

As we begin to understand and identify issues and make changes in our lives, we then need to take authority. Jesus said it is finished. It's over. He has all authority (Matthew 28:18) and we can pray in his name and see chains broken and the strongholds of the enemy disempowered in our lives.

Some of the stories we've shared of our early experiences are pretty full on. More often than not, the process of ministry is more simple. In fact, it can be misleading to think that a more supernatural or 'spiritual' moment is more authentic. What is authentic is change: people living and being different.

We have to have the confidence to deal with supernatural moments and even a desire to see God move supernaturally. However, we also have to make sure we don't get caught up or distracted. Many people can be fearful of 'something spooky' happening, so we developed a simple and clear ministry format. Like any format, it is a framework which should shift around what God is doing in particular moments.

These are not rigid rules to follow, but biblical principles that work and we believe are in the right order.

MINISTRY FORMAT

Repentance

The first step to freedom is getting right with God. Jesus has done it all on the cross, but there is power in confession and repentance before God. This is where it all begins. Whether it's you on your own or helping someone else, start by confessing out loud the actions, motivations, and thoughts that aren't right, and ask for forgiveness.

It is often powerful to repent of false agreements we've made with concepts of who we are or who God is. For example, 'I repent of taking on board the idea that I'm worthless,' or 'I repent for believing you never loved me'. Repentance means to turn away from and apologise for something and make it right, through Christ.

Forgiveness

We can never underestimate the power of forgiveness. In 2 Cor 2:11, the Bible teaches us that holding unforgiveness in our hearts actually gives the enemy an advantage over us. Some people want the hyper-spiritual experience, but aren't willing to forgive. Without forgiveness, we can go through a religious practice that does not actually make a real difference in our lives. So we make forgiveness a core part of the ministry process.

Forgiveness has layers to it. We encourage people to begin by forgiving the key people and moments that have marked their lives. It's not a check-list of absolutely everything but moving through the moments that became roots and digging them up again.

We also encourage people to forgive themselves, which can be challenging. These moments are so moving and often the most powerful as the weight of shame falls off. If you're ministering to someone, this is often the moment that God's healing floods in. As people let go of debts they hold to others, it's incredible how God sweeps in to heal.

. . .

69

Communion

Once we feel we've covered the right things in the above, this is a powerful moment to take communion. Communion is an act of remembrance and a defiant declaration that we are defined by what Jesus did on the cross. Never underestimate its power. We've seen the Holy Spirit move particularly profoundly in this time.

Declaration and Breakthrough

As a statement of faith, we encourage people in this next section to speak out and declare their freedom and identity in Christ. This is the moment where we address the enemy and command him to leave our lives and renounce any strongholds he once had.

These moments can take many different expressions: from very vocal and demonstrative, right through to very calm, gentle and almost uneventful. Ministry should always be done with the person's best interests at heart. Treat everyone as unique individuals rather than assuming it's a one-size fits all approach. Be mindful and wise about where and when you do it and always with the individual's agreement and understanding.

Refilling and Healing

By this stage you will have seen God already move significantly. To finish, ask the Holy Spirit to come and fill the person or yourself. Be ready for Him to move powerfully and be open to bringing prophetic encouragement or direction.

Ministry is not just about 'dealing with the enemy', it is really about becoming more of the person Jesus died for us to become. As you end these moments, it's amazing to see people leaving lighter, freer and more whole.

'The challenge was on, the Holy Spirit was inviting us to trust him wholeheartedly.'

13

THE BROOK HALL MIRACLE

Spiritual warfare does not always look like personal deliverance; it can look like fighting for a home.

Heather and I had a growing family with four boys, all under the age of 10. It was quite a house-full. We had faith for a bigger house and we found ourselves looking at a small plot, which was a piece of someone's garden that backed onto a car park. It was covered in nettles and had been neglected, but it had lots of potential.

The land came with planning permission for a four bed house and would be the perfect base for our next chapter with our wild boys. We had always dreamt of designing something that specifically fit our family. We picked up the details of the plot and went and had a look at it, but it was on the market for £30,000. The highest we could raise for the land was £21,500. So with a heavy heart, I picked up the details and threw them in the bin. It looked like another dream that needed to be delayed.

Heather has a reputation for loving anyone and everyone and making them smile with the joy and vibrancy she has for life. My sons will tell you she was always the last one to leave the school gates as she would be chatting away to another mum, encouraging someone, or speaking words of life into a person's dark moment. Not that the boys always had grace and understanding for this loving heart of Heather's, they wanted to get home and watch Teenage Mutant Ninja Turtles.

She could take a small task of popping into town to run an errand that should take fifteen minutes and turn it into a half day activity as she chatted to everyone she met.

This particular quality, which has caused me so many delays over the years, every now and then delivers an absolute gift. Not long after I threw away the details for the plot of land, Heather happened to get talking to an architect in town, and he told her about what he had been recently working on. A nettle covered garden that looks on to a car park. She couldn't believe it, telling him: 'Oh, we went to see that, really loved it! But we couldn't afford it. We could only muster £21,000.' And the architect responded with a tip off from heaven. 'I happen to know, if you submit the offer of £21,000, they'll take it.'

Submit it we did, and take it they did. God made a way for us to build our own house, against the odds, and we named it 'The House of Promise.'

After eight years of hiring and moving around different venues in our little market town, the church had a core of 40-50 people, and we were beginning to see some good things; young families joining and occasionally people being saved. God began to prompt us to start looking for a more permanent home, a building all of our own.

Leominster is a small place, so there were limited options. God directed us to a building that had been on the market for a while, it was an old Brethren Church building that had been a base for an incredibly powerful community revival in the early 1900s.

People had been raised up and sent to impact the world from this old church building. But the congregation had ceased to grow and were left with a small group of elderly people who had grown up in the church and now met in one small corner of the building. The rest of it was full of relics and reminders of their glorious previous era.

Sadly, the building was deteriorating and falling apart as it was being neglected and used less and less as each decade passed. Now it was used mostly for funerals as their elderly members died out one by one. It had been on the property market for a while at the price of £150,000, but no one was interested in it. It was then reduced to £120,00 to try and ignite some interest.

I looked through the printed details from the estate agent. What a building, what history, what potential! But we couldn't afford that kind of price, so once again I found myself picking up the papers and throwing them in the bin. A dream to be delayed.

The Holy Spirit had other plans. The House of Promise, as well as having a car park at the back of it, had a pavement and road running right in front of this church building. Not very long after throwing those papers in the bin for Brook Hall, I stepped out of the house at precisely the same moment as Edward, one of the church elders there, was walking past.

Edward was in his seventies. He was a kind and gentle soul and looked pleased to see me. He started asking me questions about our church and how things were going. I told him we had been looking around for a building. 'Well, why not come and buy ours!' He spoke as if it were obvious. I told him that we could not afford it. Edward urged me: 'Gary, just come and take a look at it.' I couldn't deny I was curious to see it, so I arranged to go and pay Brook Hall a visit for the first time.

The smell of death, damp and decay was overpowering as I walked through the doors. The amount of work needed to make it usable again was daunting. It was in a fantastic location though and had the space for us to house our young church family comfortably for the coming years.

After praying into it with my leadership team, we knew that God was calling us to purchase the building. But as God spoke, He disturbed me by telling me specifically how much to offer for Brook Hall. £60,000. Half of what it was on the market for.

You expect to knock a little off the asking price, but to offer 50% felt arrogant and even offensive. But God was directing me to submit an offer on behalf of our church to these elderly, traditional trustees and offer them half of what they were asking. It felt disrespectful, like a slap in the face. But I had always committed myself to be obedient to the direction of God's voice, no matter what it cost, so I wrote a letter and put in a formal offer.

To the elders of Brook Hall,

After prayerful consideration we have decided to submit the offer of £60,000 for the purchase of Brook Hall. It is non-negotiable. The reason being, that this is what God has told us to offer, and not a penny more. So please consider this carefully. It's down to you to decide whether you accept this is from God or not.

Yours respectfully,

New Life Community Church.

Then we prayed. I had contact from Edward and he told me they had received the letter, but it had not been received well. Some of them were outraged. They were dumbfounded that this young, charismatic lot would have the cheek to put in such an offer. They would be having an initial meeting to discuss it and had invited me along as they had some questions. I didn't know if they really wanted to get me there to tear some chunks out of me.

It's one thing being obedient to God by submitting a letter but a whole other challenge to go and see the people that you have been so seemingly cheeky too. But I walked in, full of conviction that God had directed me to submit that figure, and ready to answer any question they threw my way.

The twelve grey-haired elders looked at me solemnly as I walked in. Edward welcomed me and looked a bit nervous. They had their solicitor there, in his pinstripe suit, bowler hat and pocket watch. The solicitor was the mouthpiece for the men, and after our introductions he began to question me, 'What do you and your church intend to do with this building?'

I went into my best sales pitch of how we would use it to reach children, young people and to truly impact the community for Jesus. Maybe this was the moment where they would see that what we were doing was all about the Kingdom. They sat there silently, non responsive, looking at me and giving nothing away. I wondered if they had understood me at all. Apart from Edward of course, who was nodding and smiling with subtle encouragement.

The solicitor proceeded to tell me that the group had discussed between them that we should not expect any charity from them at all. The fact that we were all Christians would not entitle us to discount in any way. They had, after all, only just reduced the asking price by £30,000.

He took it a step further and said that if they had a group of Muslims wanting to turn it into a Mosque, and they offered a better price than us, then they would go with the Muslims. Ouch. Things didn't look good. But you should know never to make conclusions off the way things look when God has given you a promise to hold on to.

They would be meeting again, without me present, to take a vote. It would have to be a unanimous agreement for them to accept the offer.

———

So what were we to do? What we had learnt that we must always do when we are given a promise from God that we know is ours but not yet in our hands. We prayed. With fervour, with passion, with declaration and fasting, that God would convict their hearts to give us the building at the £60,000 we were offering.

Edward, who was a good man, believed in us. He backed us and went to advocate on our behalf that they should really consider this offer. So the group met again, talked it through and came to a unanimous decision.

When Edward called me and asked if we could meet, his voice was shaking over the phone. I knew something must have happened, but whether for or against us, I was not sure. He asked me to meet him at the building.

When I arrived, Edward met me at the door and he looked visibly shaken. He told me that something extraordinary happened in the meeting.

'Everyone was opposed to you. Opposed to the whole idea of it. Moaning, complaining. It seemed inevitable that your bid to buy Brook Hall would never get all the votes that it needed.'

I waited for the 'but' with bated breath. 'But.. something came up from our past, a division between two of the Elder's wives.'

He told me that someone had been brave enough to mention the elephant in the room, a story of bitterness and unforgiveness that had soured their church community for the last four decades because of an argument between these two women. The whole group had refused to deal with it, to bring any reconciliation or healing, and this unresolved hurt had destroyed their community like a terminal disease.

It had never been spoken of until that night. God had used our outrageous offer to address something that had gone unchecked for forty years. The question was asked: 'Who are we to stand in the way if this is God's purpose and we can't even sort our own house out?'

As Edward recounted this moment to me, he could no longer hold back the tears and began to cry. He said, 'I'm handing this place over to you right now. Please pray for me, on behalf of us all, pray for forgiveness that we never dealt with this years and years ago.'

In that damp, dark building, I lay hands on this broken old saint and prayed for God's healing, upon my friend Edward and upon them as a group, that it was never too late to put things right.

We finished praying and Edward told me, with a smile on his face, and still with tears in his eyes, that they would accept our offer of £60,000 to purchase Brook Hall.

———

We had around three months for the purchase to go through from the point of our offer being accepted. There were rumours starting to circulate around our small town, (Leominster always did love a good rumour), that we did not actually have the money.

The rumours were true.

God had told us to offer the £60,000, and it was an amazing miracle that it had been accepted. But we were a congregation of fledgling families and young people, and had no more than £1000 to our name. No commercial bank was interested whatsoever in giving us the money we needed to complete the sale. Our young, low-earning, relatively new congregation was not an appealing prospect to the mortgage lenders.

After several months, the solicitors had done all of the legal work and told us that they were ready for us to send the money over. I told them in faith that it would be coming through the bank.

God began to investigate my heart. 'Are you doubting me?' 'Do you really trust me?'. We had been working so hard to build a good reputation in our town and there was a part of me that was nervous that this reputation was about to collapse all around us, that we would become a laughing stock. We had been continuing to pray and believe fervently that God was going to deliver every penny that we needed. But honestly, the pressure was growing, and things were becoming more intense as each week passed by and we still had no way of paying for our miracle building.

One option that we were pursuing was a charity bank specifically for churches that may lend us the money. Our main prayer point became that the charity bank would give us the approval we needed.

The Holy Spirit had upped the stakes. He told us to end the lease for our current building, an Old Methodist chapel that was just a few streets away from Brook Hall.

God said to me: 'Is that building your security? Or am I your security?' Well, then. The challenge was on, the Holy Spirit was inviting us to trust him wholeheartedly.

So we gave notice on our building and told them we had no further need of it. Our whole church was praying together, and we all knew that it was the last week for the money to arrive from the charity bank. With one Sunday to go in our current church building, we received the news that even the charity bank had deemed that we were not fit for a mortgage. Our application had been rejected.

Now things were really going to the wire, and with our only sensible and logical route having been royally burned to the ground, it was time to pray for a miracle. Isn't that just how God works best? He often deliberately increases the pressure, closing the options so that you can know that there is no way this could have happened without Him.

The final Sunday approached and that week, through the post, I had a letter from a solicitor telling us that a client of theirs had decided to give us £60,000 as a loan. I'd never heard of this solicitor, they were from another town. My first thought was that it must be a hoax. Someone knew of our plight and was winding us up!

I pulled out the Yellow pages and looked up the solicitors. It was a real business and belief started to flow through me. The letter said that I needed to give them a call. When I spoke to the solicitor, they already had the money waiting and asked us which bank we wanted it sent to. The only condition to the loan was that their client was to remain anonymous.

Those were terms I could live with. I put the phone down and oh, the relief! The celebration! The joy! To have the backing from God, so undeniably, so clearly, was a huge boost to Heather and I. That Sunday we met at our old building, and marched with our children through the streets, with banners and tambourines (don't judge, it was the 90's), and hearts full of gratitude, beaming with smiles, laughing at the goodness of God to us and we went to claim our land that God had promised us.

Like our spiritual ancestors, the Israelites, who had walked so boldly into Jericho when its walls had come tumbling down, we walked with assurance, knowing that God's favour and affirmation was upon us.

When you see God move so tangibly and you're on such a high, you can be tempted to wonder if this is the peak of his provision, but this miracle of trusting in Him would only be the foundation of what he was about to do.

I often reflect how much more God would do in us and for us if we were just willing to trust in Him more than ourselves. Take away the safety net, burn plan B, get out of the boat onto the water and dare to believe.

' *God wants to stir up the dreams and mischief that he has placed inside of you.*'

14

WILD DOG FAITH

There was a faith and a mischief in me to go after the Brook Hall Miracle. I got up to different kinds of mischief when I was younger. I was a tree climber, I would go exploring for animals, and I would play with knives. I would also fall out of the tree too, I would get lost, and I would accidentally cut myself.

Our world has become so sanitized that it wants to discourage children from adventure and exploration. When my boys grew up, we used to play games called the endurance tests. They would usually be just in their pants and would have to do all kinds of tests to see how long they could endure it. We would get the pet rat and put him on their bare tummy, seeing how long they could take it for. Or they would put their heads under a freezing cold waterfall for as long as possible when we were out on a walk.

What if they caught a cold? What if they got hurt? What if they cried when they lost a round to their brother? A civilised nature comes upon humanity to try to make sure no one gets hurt and no one feels left out. It tames us and cuts off our curiosity and adventure. We were born wild, but many of us have become domesticated. This is true for our faith too.

Many of us came into faith with great ideas and imagination of what we could do to change the world and to be used for God's kingdom. Many of those dreams have been dormant through the years as a result of life getting in the way. God wants to stir up the dreams and the mischief that he placed inside of you, awakening the adventurer to come alive and believe for the impossible once more.

This reminds me of Jonathan in 1 Sam 14. He was a prince, next in line to the throne after his father Saul, the first king of Israel. If there is anyone who should be dignified, respectable and sensible, it should be the prince.

Not Jonathan though. There is a wildness to him. The Philistine army had invaded and encamped themselves in Israel and King Saul was sitting morosely under the pomegranate tree, deliberating on what to do next, his surrounding army immobilised by his indecision. Jonathan began concocting a wild, audacious, faith-filled plan to take the fight to the enemy.

> 'One day Jonathan, son of Saul, said to his young armor-bearer, 'Come, let's go over to the Philistine outpost on the other side.' But he did not tell his father.'
>
> 1 Sam 14:1 NIV

I believe he didn't tell his father because he knew that his father would disapprove. His 'wisdom' would say that Jonathan's idea was foolish and impossible. We can be so reasonable, so full of 'common sense' and our own wisdom that we fail to be audacious with our faith and think of the impossible.

Jonathan was not interested in trying to appease his father but in exercising his faith. If only more of us could be free of the opinions of others and free of people pleasing and focus our hearts, thoughts and actions on pleasing God and moving boldly in faith. There are many of us that are not taking the risks of faith because we are not free of people yet.

> 'Jonathan said to his young armor-bearer, 'Come, let's go over to the outpost of those uncircumcised men. Perhaps the Lord will act on our behalf. Nothing can hinder the Lord from saving, whether by many or by few.'
>
> 1 Sam 14:6 NIV

The Philistine army was at an advantageous position at the top of a cliff. Between Jonathan and his young armour bearer they had just one sword: two men taking on a whole army with one weapon. This crazy plan gets even better though; the name of one of the cliffs that they were to climb to get to the Philistines was called 'Sineh,' meaning thorns. It would be a sharp and difficult climb, and when you got to the top, there would be an army waiting to kill you, as Jonathan's plan was to show himself to them.

Sometimes we are praying for God to move the mountain when God is wanting us to climb up its jagged rock face instead. You might get cut, be sore or uncomfortable, but God is calling you to apply your faith unswervingly to take possession of what He has called you to do.

I can't tell you how many times people have told Heather and I that we are believing 'too big,' that we are taking our faith to a bit of an extreme level. 'You need to be a bit more realistic.' When was faith ever realistic? When people start speaking doubt over me, it is provocative: it causes me to be more determined to believe for impossible things. There is a fight in me that rises up. A fight to believe. And there was a fight in Jonathan and the armour bearer that day to act audaciously in line with the faith they had in who God was.

Saul was sitting enveloped in his deliberation under the pomegranate tree. He had no movement and no vision. We all have a pomegranate tree, a place whose shade and reflection seem more attractive than the confrontation of the task in front of us. Discouragement and past experience can come and keep us under the pomegranate tree. But if you choose to unleash the wild faith within you, you can ascend the cliff with a fight and tenacity to overcome and to believe. We have to learn to tap our wild nature and calling within.

We once had this cat called Babby who was not your average cat. If you stroked her, she would hiss at you. She would disappear for days at a time. She would bring me gifts of all kinds of dead animals that she had hunted. She would open up these poor victims, their entrails hanging out, sometimes just their heads remaining, then leave them on the doorstep as a love offering for me.

The cat next door was indulging in cans of tuna, scooped out generously by her owner. The cat next door was fat and lazy. Not Babby, she was a feral cat. Feral means 'to be in a wild state, especially after captivity or domestication'.

Babby would not be domesticated, though we did try. More of us need to be like Babby, breaking free from our docile domestication and finding the wildness of our feral faith.

The reason that we are wild is that we knew what it was to be captive. Now that we have found our faith, we should exercise it wildly. But many of us got set free from captivity and found ourselves wandering back inside to live indoors and see what food had been dished up for us, snuggled up in a nice warm cosy bed. It's time to wake up and live wild once more!

Take the poodle for example. It's probably the most iconically pampered dog of all time. The ridiculous haircuts, bows, sparkly collars, some even being pushed in a pram by their owners, have made this breed of dog a bit of a joke.

Did you know that the origin of the poodle, the history of its breed, is a hunting dog? The poodle's heritage is brave, intelligent and determined. They could even be used for hunting bears. This bear-hunting, madly brave dog has become a laughing stock.

There are too many dressed-up poodles in Christianity that need to remember they were born to be hunting dogs and to go up against the bears. It's not the size of the dog in the fight but the size of the fight in the dog that counts!

No dog is born tame; they have a wild nature, but it is trained out of them. It is the same for the Christian. There is a natural wildness to our faith, but it can be tamed and trained out of us. This is done to lower our expectations, to 'keep our feet on the ground', and to be more reasonable.

Coming back to our 'wild dogs' Jonathan and his armour bearer, there is a key moment in the story where Jonathan says: 'Perhaps the Lord will act on our behalf'. No guarantees. No assurances. But a hope, a faith, a wild possibility. And with that hope they acted. So many Christians are immobilised by the desire for a guarantee, but a wild-dog faith within is all about saying 'perhaps' and then moving on that belief.

Jonathan and his armour bearer ascend the cliff, defeating 20 Philistines, and then God sends a panic that ripples through the whole Philistine army that causes them to run. King Saul and his army can see the Philistine army retreating and begin to pursue them.

There is a great victory for Israel, started by two men with one sword, then finished by a small army in a weak position.

It all began with someone who held to faith in God more than his own circumstances, someone who refused to be tamed by his circumstances and his peers, and held onto the hope that if he were to move, that perhaps God would bring about a great victory.

WILD DOGS QUESTIONS TO CONSIDER:

- Are there any areas of your life where you are praying for God to move the mountain, and He is asking you to climb the rock face?
- Where might you need to have a wilder, less-tamed faith?
- Jonathan and his armour-bearer provoked faith in each other. How can you put yourself in an environment or community where that boldness of faith is encouraged, not flattened?

15

BUSINESS AND THE BRINK OF BANKRUPTCY

Our next chapter was going to require that faith to lead us at our rock bottom.

When I became a pastor it did not come with a wage packet: there was no job offer, no benefits, no pension. Becoming a pastor was the answer to a call from heaven, not a job opportunity. It would be eight years before I would receive any financial contribution from the church towards our living costs.

So when I started the church, I also needed to work full time to support Heather and our two sons. I had been working for my dad, first at his factory and later for his business selling garden buildings at a garden centre. I had never had a heart for business; it never had been a dream. Working was a means to an end. My life was about building the kingdom, and if I had to support myself to do that, then it was just a part of the call.

One day my dad came to me and told me that they were going to be moving to Northern Ireland. I was completely taken by surprise. They were selling their home and selling everything they had: including the businesses. As a result I found myself facing redundancy. It was a blow. With a young family, we were only just getting by. How were we going to cope now?

That was when it came to me: I had been doing this for my dad, but maybe I could do it for myself. I spoke to him, shared my idea and bought the office from him to keep the business going. I had to borrow some money from the bank and it was an exciting beginning to my own venture.

Our main business came on Saturdays at the garden centre, so I had to work a lot of weekends, which was not ideal when I was doing church on Sunday too. It was hard work, and I couldn't earn enough to provide for our family.

I went about thinking of what else I could do to earn some money. I had been passionate about animals my whole life, and so naturally I thought: 'That's it, 'I'll start a pet shop.' I could run the business out of the same buildings, making the most of the space I had and hopefully improving the cash flow too. My pet shop was called 'Dr. Doolittle's' and we sold exotic animals; tarantulas, snakes, lizards, crabs, tropical fish and monkeys. I even had a fruit bat called Kevin!

I fulfilled a lifetime ambition of having all the pets I had ever dreamed of. I also had the idea to use my white vehicle to promote the business by getting it covered in black stripes in a zebra style with my business name on. I'd see people staring at me while I was driving, and wonder out loud asking what their problem was. Heather would say, 'We're driving around in a zebra car Gary...'

I was all in. We were going to make it work. We started with a small number of animals, and then every time we made some sales, we would sow the money back into the business by buying more. We accumulated so many exotic creatures, but we ended up losing animal stock to illnesses. If it was a particularly cold night, I would come into the store to find that we had lost 500 fish. That was money, and fish, down the toilet.

We kept having break-ins too, criminals looking for cash. But when they had broken in, they opened the doors to the snakes, so customers were soon to be arriving and I was looking around the pet shop trying to find where the snakes had hidden. They would hide in such small spaces, and when they are out of their environments, they become a lot more volatile. Once four snakes escaped at once.

I also had an African grey parrot called Benji. He sat on a perch rather than in a cage and was a centrepiece of the store. People would come up to him and want to interact since he could talk. He was a draw for people coming in as customers could feed him, say hello, and he would say hello back. He had a couple of his wing feathers clipped, meaning that he couldn't fly for more than a couple of seconds.

One day, someone came through the door and Benji saw a golden opportunity to hop out. He had sat there on his perch hundreds of times as the door opened and closed and never moved. But this day he did. He swooped out of the door and I stared in disbelief as Benji, who was worth about a thousand pounds in today's money, flapped awkwardly out of my sight.

He was the most expensive asset I had. I ran outside after him, but he was gone. There were about 10 cars outside and some buildings. I looked around thinking he must have walked somewhere. He couldn't have gone far. I searched around the cars and the immediate area but couldn't find him.

The business was already struggling, and I now had to go home and tell Heather that £1000 just flew out the door. I went to bed that night and couldn't believe my luck. You better believe I prayed for Benji to come back to me.

Early the next morning I had a knock at our door. It was our neighbour. 'Do you own a parrot?' I had just woken up and was struggling to try and understand what was happening… 'Yes, I do actually,' I responded.

They told me that there was a parrot in the hedge outside our house. I could not believe it. We were 13 miles away from the pet shop and it was not as though Benji had ever been to my house. I went out and sure enough, it's Benji. He made another attempted run for it and tried to run through the hedge, but I caught him this time. I was so happy we were reunited. I'm not sure he felt the same. I looked him over and saw oil on his tail and realised what had happened.

When he had fled the pet shop he had crawled underneath my car and climbed into the engine compartment. He must have seen the zebra car and felt his homeland calling. It was amazing to think out of all the cars there, he had chosen to crawl into mine. I had done deliveries that afternoon that he had gone missing and must have covered about 50 miles, with Benji there the whole time.

He had then escaped in the night and then got caught in the hedge. The local paper wrote about my story; then it made it a national paper too. After a couple of years of running the pet shop with all its losses and troubles, I closed Dr. Doolittle's and never wanted to have a pet again.

Next I had an opportunity to move the original business to a new garden centre, taking on a franchise to sell conservatories (garden rooms). I remortgaged our house and seized the opportunity to take my business to a better location. It was a very exciting million pound development and I believed that this would bring the breakthrough I needed.

It launched and for the first 12 months my business did phenomenally well. I had so many orders coming in that I couldn't do it all myself anymore, so I took on a salesman and adapted as it grew.

One day, I came in to open up one morning and I couldn't get in. Two men in suits were standing outside with clipboards in their hands. They told me that the garden centre had gone into administration. I explained to them that my business was on the site, and I needed to get in to take sales. There were no telesales back then, no internet business, if I didn't have customers coming in, I couldn't make any money.

'Sorry, we cannot open the gates, and for now you will have to wait to see if we can find someone to take on the garden centre.' Trying to find a buyer for the garden centre business, the big umbrella that we were under, went on for months. Our cashflow disappeared overnight. I was still supposed to be making payments to the bank, but we couldn't make the sales we needed.

When the garden centre did finally open under new ownership, they tried doubling our rent. Our reputation had also been tainted by the garden centre administration. People did not want to put up the money for a £3000 conservatory in case they never saw what they paid for. I would explain again and again that it was not my business that had gone into administration but the premises that I was operating from.

Even though my doors were now open again, we were still in serious trouble. I decided to take some emergency action. I got off the site and made a deal on getting a factory in Leominster and taught myself how to manufacture windows. I found out what machinery I needed and invested even more money into that. With this move, I could cut out the middleman and improve my profits. We opened the factory and started manufacturing.

———————

Over all the time it had taken to get back into operation, I had built up quite a debt. We started getting orders in, but I couldn't make money fast enough to keep up with our repayments. This went on for three years, with things gradually getting worse and pressure ever-building as I was trying to make it work. I built up the debt to £70,000. I had already re-mortgaged my house and had no other way of getting any more money. Working evenings and weekends became my normal. As well as selling windows and making windows, I was fitting them too.

The ongoing strain of this pressure on us as a couple and me personally was incredibly stressful. It felt like I was constantly treading water to try and keep my head above the waves but never able to escape to dry ground.

The bank was not happy with my progress of repaying the loans I had taken against my house and they made the decision to recall them. They wanted me to repay the full amount that they had borrowed or they would sell my house to cover the debt.

I was out of options. The banks were threatening court action. I had people calling our home phone, debt collectors who were intimidating and aggressive. I got help from a Christian lawyer who told me that I needed to act before things got ugly. They advised me to file for bankruptcy. I would lose everything, but it would prevent people forcefully taking things from our property.

If you know anything about business, you will be wondering why I didn't set up a limited company, instead of a sole trader, but I never knew such a thing existed. Everything for the business had not just been in my name but in Heather's too: the worst possible scenario. If it has just been in my name, they would only be able to take half of what I owned. But they were coming for everything. I took away the bankruptcy papers and I felt in the pit of despair. I had failed.

We had built the house we were living in and had named it 'the House of Promise', a miracle that God had made a way for us to partake in. And now we were going to lose it all. I felt a failure as a father and as a husband. I had four sons and Heather was pregnant with our fifth. We were now going to have to live in council housing as we lost our house. I also felt the failure as a pastor and leader; how could I go on to lead a church when my personal life was shattering before me?

The sheer weight of this situation crushed the life out of me. The night before I was to submit the bankruptcy forms I was overcome with depression and grief, mourning the business and the litany of failures that lay behind me.

I had totally lost hope and lay on my bed contemplating over and over the mistakes that had got me to this place, and dwelling on my failures. Heather had seen enough by this point. I don't ever wallow or feel sorry for myself, so she knew that I was in a serious mess.

She called a friend of ours named Julie Anderson who had a prayer ministry. Heather told her everything that had happened on the phone and the state I was now in. Julie prayed with her, and then told her to share a message with me; 'Tell Gary to get up and get his fight back.'

Heather came into the bedroom and told me that she had called Julie. She told me, 'It's not over, you've got to fight'. I was numb. My first response was to think, 'All I have done for the last three years since the Garden Centre went into administration was fight.' But the truth is that even when you have given everything, there is still more fight left within you. As Heather continued to speak, it began to land in me. Fresh hope was being awoken after feeling so dead inside. She prophetically spoke to the faith that was within me. The fire inside began to revive.

This transaction has happened again and again throughout our lives together. In family, in business and in church building, her faith has sparked the tenacity in me to keep going, to believe for more than we see. Heather may not have always been the one with the microphone, but she has done more to build this church than many will ever understand.

Over the years of pioneering together, God has used her voice to shape our culture, bring balance to my leadership, and display His heart to countless people in our church family. She has always been my greatest cheerleader and armour bearer, and this night was one of those times that the spirit within her changed everything.

Something changed within me as she spoke. I was able to sleep that night. I got up the next morning and threw the bankruptcy papers into the bin. I got in touch with an advocacy organisation that would talk to my debtors on my behalf and we proposed paying a certain amount back if they would agree to giving me more time. We put together a new business plan and presented it before a judge who would decide if our plan had enough potential to work.

Our fourth son Isaac was three years old at the time, and we took him along to the hearing. His name means 'son of laughter' and he laughed all the way through the proceedings.

The judge looked over our plan with caution and thoughtfulness. He said, 'I think you have got something here. There's a chance this could work and I want to give you that chance.' He made the decision that the banks would have to give us the opportunity.

It came with conditions. We would have to sell our vehicles, get rid of the factory and sell all the machinery that I had acquired. I had to sign over our house, which meant that if we defaulted on one payment then they could seize our house in 28 days without going to the courts. It would be automatic. It would not matter if I had paid the first 20 months, and then missed the 21st month. The agreement was that I would have to pay back the debt every single month without fail.

I was allowed to start the business again with just £1000. They would let us keep the house for now as we would need somewhere to live. But I was forbidden to sign a lease, so I had to find a business premises with a landlord that would let me pay and stay on a month by month basis. I used our cash to buy a desk, a phone and our first month's rent. I then advertised and sold four windows to a customer.

I bought them, went and fitted them and made some profit. I used that cash to buy the windows for the next customer, and so on. It was an extremely sensitive and fragile operation: one mistake or unforeseen challenge had the strength to make my business fall like a house of cards. Every single month I had to pay the debt then make enough money to support Heather and the four kids and pay our mortgage.

This went on for two years and 24 payments. We had that date fixed in our minds, we prayed towards it and worked so hard for it. The day finally came, where we had paid off the payments over two years and finally got free of our debt. The elation and celebration that we felt was overwhelming. Through God's grace and goodness we had done it! We met with the administrator, who congratulated us. 'There are few people that make this work. You rose to the challenge, you've come through. In fact you have done such a great job of paying this off, that we want you to do another year.'

It was like a punch in the stomach. 'How can you do that? That was not what we agreed.' It was hard to hide my indignation. 'Well, you have to understand we have had some extra legal fees that we have incurred through this process.' They had me over a barrel. I couldn't do anything about it, no matter how much I argued. They had the right to enforce this upon me. I had to gather myself, and take on another 12 months of payments. I took a deep breath and put my faith and trust in God once again.

During this repayment time, our friend Clem was in town once again and he was praying for us. 'If you remain faithful in building God's house, He will build yours. God wants to bless you with a bigger house.' I'm there thinking, 'We have hardly been able to keep hold of the house that we already have'. Clem spoke again, 'Even now, you are doubting the purposes of God. Even now, you're thinking, 'I can't keep what I have.' But God wants to bless you with a bigger house, and it's time to believe.'

I wrestled with it, but I received it. If God wanted to bless us that was great, but he would have to do the work.

Not too long after this, I was measuring up for a customer who was after some windows. He asked me 'Would you like to buy a plot of land I'm selling?' There aren't many plots of land available in Leominster, so I was confused and asked him what he meant. He pointed over to where an old building was, and told me he was selling it as a plot of land. I said 'But it's not on the market?' "Oh no, I'm not selling it publicly. But I want to sell it to you.'

I hadn't said anything about property, I was just there on business, and yet somehow God was knocking at my door with opportunity once again. I asked him how much he wanted, and he offered to do a deal if I deducted the windows off his asking price. It had planning permission for a six bed house. I now had five sons and our family needed more space than we currently had.

I later found out that he had already been offered the price he was asking for by his neighbours but had turned them down because he didn't like them. I told him that I was interested, but I didn't have the money for it. He told me to go away and see if I could sort something out and raise the finance I needed.

I went back to Heather bewildered and excited and told her what had happened. I got the plans from him to look them over. We pinned them to the back of our bedroom door and prayed over them again and again, dreaming of what God may do. We couldn't see any earthly way of raising the funds we needed, but we had a prophetic promise and a heavenly opportunity and so put our faith into action and our trust in God's goodness.

In the months that followed, I pushed every door I could find to raise the funds. Selling the house that we already had gave us most of the funds to purchase the land while we moved into rented accommodation. However we had a short fall. It took some humility to turn to Heather's father, a frugal (saying it kindly) old Scot. He didn't like the idea of parting with any of his money. We only needed a small amount from him, but after some considera-tion, he agreed to it. We had the land!

Now we needed money to actually build on it. I went around every bank looking for someone to give us a mortgage. Because of our previous debts tainting our credit history, each one turned us away. But we would not give up. I had one more contact to reach out to and pitch the viability of our project. We went in all prayed up and they said yes! They would not loan us enough to finish the house, but God continued to bless my business and the profits covered the shortfall.

We had been on the brink of bankruptcy, looking into a dark abyss with all hope depleted. But God had turned things around so radically that we not only survived our grapple with debt, we had come all the way to the other side victoriously, claiming the promised house that God had for us.

My business never struggled again. We made every payment, were free from the debt and transformed through the process. In the years to come as the church grew, I sold my windows business and took up property development to be able to continue to support ourselves and also to allow the entrepreneurial part of me to continue to fire. I know now that there is a sharpness and resourcefulness it brings to me. But as the years went by the business became less, so our ministry could grow.

16

GOING THROUGH THE STORM

God was stripping away my perception of what success was. I had lain on that bed feeling like a failure as a husband, father, pastor and businessman. I felt that success was having a great business, but God removed that from me. 'You're going to find your success in me,' he would say repeatedly to me over the years. God confronted some of my fears, challenging my definition of success and the real depth of my trust.

It is so tempting to measure ourselves by our achievements, but God taught me in this season that He cares far more about what is happening within me. My identity should be found only in Him, my Father, who can lead me through any situation I face. However, I must make the choice to put all of my life into His hands and follow His direction.

In fact, I believe that Jesus was the one that brought this storm to my door; it was not of my own making. Through it I was stretched to the absolute brink of what I could take, but in that stretch is where my faith grew. In Matthew 14, Peter had a collision with a Jesus storm too.

> 'Immediately Jesus made the disciples get into the boat and go on ahead of him to the other side, while he dismissed the crowd. After he had dismissed them, he went up on a mountain-side by himself to pray.

Later that night, he was there alone, and the boat was already a considerable distance from land, buffeted by the waves because the wind was against it. Shortly before dawn Jesus went out to them, walking on the lake.

When the disciples saw him walking on the lake, they were terrified. 'It's a ghost,' they said, and cried out in fear. But Jesus immediately said to them: 'Take courage! It is I. Don't be afraid.' 'Lord, if it's you,' Peter replied, 'tell me to come to you on the water.' 'Come,' he said.

Then Peter got down out of the boat, walked on the water and came toward Jesus. But when he saw the wind, he was afraid and, beginning to sink, cried out, 'Lord, save me!' Immediately Jesus reached out his hand and caught him. 'You of little faith,' he said, 'why did you doubt?' And when they climbed into the boat, the wind died down. Then those who were in the boat worshiped him, saying, 'Truly you are the Son of God.'

Matthew 14: 22-33 NIV

Jesus 'made' the disciples get into the boat, at night time, without Him. Immediately my alarm bells would be ringing. Jesus is 'making' us go out by ourselves for a night boat ride... I have been out on the water in a storm and it is an eerie and scary place to be. No wonder that when they see a ghostly figure headed toward them, they are terrified.

In the midst of this fear, when Jesus calls out to them, Peter responds with courage. He makes this audacious statement that he will join Jesus out on the water. Taking that step was huge. It is representative to all of us that getting out of the boat means putting our faith and trust in Jesus.

The boat symbolises our manmade security, our safety. The reality is that following Jesus means getting wet, but many of us want to stay dry. To stay dry is to be predictable and dull; to step out is to embrace the adventure.

I can't help but think that this is a set up. Jesus had orchestrated all these circumstances, making the disciples get into the boat. Then He waited till the dark of night, when the wind was howling, waves were crashing, to walk out on to the water to meet them.

Don't tell me He was surprised by their reactions. He could have done this any time, he was often in a boat with them. It would have been nice to do it on a sunny day, put a foot onto the water and see the disciples react. Probably would have made them laugh in wonder!

No, Jesus does it at a time when fear has already set in. They believe Him to be a ghost and start crying out in panic. I think Jesus planned to test them. And sure enough one of them was brave enough to believe in Him, to step out of the boat, walking onto the water. I think all of the disciples would have had a try at it on a nice sunny day, but the faith and courage that Jesus wanted to bring out could only be mustered in the midst of a storm.

Jesus was not in the safety of the boat but in the wildness of the storm. And that's where Peter wanted to be. There is a moment where we all have to make the decision to get out of the boat. There may be a storm brewing in your life right now that Jesus has generated, wanting to see if you will get out of the boat and put your faith in Him.

A number of years ago, I went white water rafting on the River Nile. An important part of our training was to practise capsizing before we went on to the white water. I thought the point of being in a boat was to stay dry! But we did capsize because it was inevitable with water currents that powerful and knowing what to do when you were in the water, how to get back into the boat, was essential.

It is the same for our Christian walk. There is an inevitability to our capsizing. We will 'fail' many times, but how we deal with that failure is so important for the rest of our journey.

Storms are a part of following Jesus. I don't think we tell new Christians this enough. We all need to know what to do when we capsize. Where do we think the storm came from that was on the lake? It was from Jesus. It was all a part of the plan, to create the environment that he wanted to put the disciples in.

When Jesus got back into the boat, the storm stopped all of a sudden. That could have happened when Peter took his step out of the boat onto the water. Jesus could have turned the sea to glass and the winds to stillness. But that would not have been true to life. Jesus called Peter out during the storm, to trust and believe and endure through the waves.

Storms hold the greatest potential for growth in your life. Can you imagine how difficult it was for Peter to step out of the boat for the first time, taking that initial step on to the water, leaving the safety of the boat to the amazement of his companions?

How do you walk in a storm? Keep taking one more step towards Jesus. Just one more step. If you are in a storm right now, the best thing you can do is to take just one more step toward Him, fix your eyes on the Saviour.

Doubts are also a part of following Jesus. If you have not experienced a moment of doubt, then you are probably playing it too safe. Have courage and confidence to move through your doubt. Doubt will sink you, but faith wants you to take another step.

Don't feel condemned because of your doubts. Your faith in Jesus is not intimidated by your moment of doubt. Your faith will penetrate your doubt. Sometimes the enemy would have us believe the opposite, that our doubt can eat away at our faith. But faith is far greater and more powerful than doubt.

Peter could never have depended on Jesus in the boat. There is an independence and security that the boat offers. But when you step out of the boat, even if you doubt, you throw yourselves into dependency on Jesus. Surely that is far greater than your boat with all the safety it can offer you.

One of the things that captures my imagination is to think of the walk back to the boat. They must have been a little way away. They must have walked back on the water together, with the arm of Jesus around a soaking wet Peter. Then everything stopped as they climbed back in. There were 11 dry disciples and one that was drenched. One that had exercised faith, taken the risk, and seen a tremendous miracle.

If you want the miracle, if you want to step out on the water, you will have to embrace the risk of sinking too. But Jesus will be there to lift you up in your moment of weakness, and I can assure you that it will have been worth every step.

GOING THROUGH THE STORM QUESTIONS TO CONSIDER:

- What comfort is God challenging you to leave behind right now?
- What are the doubts that hold you back?
- How can you overcome those doubts and jump out of that boat?

17

A NOT SO GOOD FRIDAY

The threat of bankruptcy was just one storm we had to weather. More came our way.

On the morning of Good Friday in 2005 we had just got home from church and were reflecting on the day that our Saviour gave his life. We had some friends over for coffee, and it was a warm morning so we sat on our patio round the back of the house.

There was an unexpected knock, and I opened our front door to find two police officers on my doorstep. I thought this must be routine, a door-to-door thing, or maybe that they had the wrong house. But they were exactly where they intended to be, and this was no routine visit.

They told me that they were here because of my 17-year-old son, Luke. He had been involved in a fight in the middle of Leominster the night before and they wanted to arrest him and take him to the police station to charge him with assault. They went up to his bedroom to collect clothing that they believed would have the victim's blood on and confirm that Luke was indeed the perpetrator. I asked them if they had the right to come and take it, but they said 'Do you really want us to go and get a warrant?' I decided that if Luke had done something then he needed to own up to it.

Unbeknown to us, Luke had got more and more influenced by his friends. Over the past years he had been drinking and getting involved in football hooliganism, where you go to a football game, not to watch the sport but to make your own sport by picking a fight with the opposition's fans.

Drinking had led to drugs, making him more withdrawn, and more violent. He had ended up seriously hurting some men in the middle of town, and they were pressing charges. Heather and I knew that Luke was going through some troubles but had no idea the extent of this. As the police made their way up to our son's bedroom with evidence bags, looking for blood spatter on his clothes, our hearts broke.

As a Christian and as a pastor you don't envisage the police coming to arrest your son and take him away. It was an incredibly difficult day for Heather and I after all that we had poured into him, all that we had given into the church. It felt like our world was caving in.

I was well aware of the verses in 1 Timothy 3 about the qualifications of a leader.

'He must manage his own family well and see that his children obey him, and he must do so in a manner worthy of full respect.'

1 Tim 3:4 NIV

That had been well and truly broken. I met with my leadership team at the time and offered my resignation. We had got the fire started, but maybe it was down to someone else to keep it burning. Once again, that feeling of failure crept over me. I knew Luke had been in a bad place, but I had no idea about the drugs and violence. How had it come to this? How had this been allowed to go on right under my nose and I had not been able to see it?

As I began to reflect on the last few years, I thought about how much I had been doing to build the church: the evenings out, the meetings. The ministry had, at times, come first. Maybe if I had been there more I could have stopped Luke from going down this road.

My eldership team refused my resignation. Luke was almost 18 so they said that he was able to make his own decisions, and I couldn't take all the responsibility upon myself. They urged me to go on leading the church. I felt heartbroken and didn't know how I would get up and preach the coming Sunday. They prayed for me and gave me the fresh strength that I needed and the belief that this didn't have to be the end.

It wasn't long before the police were knocking on my door again. I could see their fluorescent jackets through the frosted glass and I opened the door with an expectant: 'What's he done now?!' They told me he hadn't done anything.

Luke had left the house early that morning and was headed to a football match, but he never arrived. Luke and the three others that he had been travelling with had been involved in a serious car accident. The police told us an air ambulance had been sent to the scene, and were taking two of the four to specialist hospitals where there was more access to the special care needed. The other two had been taken to Hereford hospital, 13 miles away from where we were.

The police didn't know who had been sent where or how serious each of the injuries were, just who had been involved in the accident. We knew with them mentioning a spinal clinic and air ambulances that things must have been pretty traumatic.

They recommended that we travel to Hereford and go from there. As we quickly drove over to find out more, we prayed for our son, our hearts pouring out pleas to God,, begging God for his life and his health along with the other boys too.

We found out later that Luke's friend who had been driving had slid on the road and crashed into a house. Three of the lads were seriously injured, one breaking his back, another shattering his entire side of his body, and the third sustaining a serious head injury, needing to be resuscitated on the scene, which led to brain damage.

Luke was in the front seat as the car went bonnet first into the house. After he came round from being unconscious he woke to the sound of the others in pain. Adrenaline fizzing through his body, he knocked the remaining glass out of the passenger side window and crawled out to look for help before collapsing on the side of the road. The only damage he sustained was a fractured collarbone, which was like a graze compared to the other lads in the car. It was a miracle, particularly given his position in the impact, that he had not been killed.

As he recovered, Luke was signed off from his work as an apprentice carpenter and used the time to go visit my old friend in the States, Clem Ferris. He attended a youth conference while he was there and one evening an invitation was given to receive the Holy Spirit.

Luke was not interested, his heart was hard. It's not that he didn't believe in God anymore, he just didn't want to live the life that he knew came with following Jesus. The person he was sitting next to wanted to go out to the front, so Luke, being the polite Englishman that he is, stood in the aisle to let the guy out.

As he did so, someone from the church, who must have thought Luke was responding, lay his hand on him to pray for him. As the hand touched his shoulder, Luke hit the ground like a sack of potatoes. He came round to see people praying for breakthrough for him.

When Luke came back and told us what had happened, we thought that this may be the catalyst for change, but almost as soon as he had returned, he was out again with his old friends.

One thing that was different with Luke after his car accident was that he became darker, more sad, even depressed. He felt a weight of guilt. He questioned why he had been allowed to walk away with such little impact when his friends had such life-changing injuries. From an outsider's perspective, it may seem that someone should have more gratitude because of going through something like this, but sometimes our failure to accept God's grace can allow guilt to crush us.

Luke carried on in this dark state, drinking, taking drugs, pursuing violence. Things were spiralling out of control. Sometimes he would leave the house and we didn't know if he was going to come back. It had only gotten worse after the events of the past months.

Now that we knew what was going on, Heather and I did more to try and stop this behaviour from happening. Some time later Luke was arrested again and his drug-fuelled behaviour became more and more difficult in our home. We contended in prayer for him on our knees, crying out that God would change him and redeem him. It was a deeply upsetting time for Heather and I, seeing Luke plunge deeper and deeper into darkness.

I felt that I had to make a stand with him, so I gave him an ultimatum. I told him that he either needed to abide by the rules of our house and family, or that he needed to move out. This made his blood boil. He was livid. He came right up to my face and told me that he would be gone as soon as he could find somewhere to stay. He stormed back to his room and slammed the door.

I had been afraid to take this hard line with Luke. What would it do to him? Where would it send him? I couldn't bear the thought of him leaving our family: our little boy, ending up in some dive taking drugs, with no value for his own life. And with Luke's reaction, as aggressive and angry as it was, it seemed my worst fears were about to be realised.

With a sadness and heaviness of heart I continued to pray for him.

Later that same night, I headed out for the evening to a church meeting. Luke and I hadn't spoken since the argument. Heather had gone away to stay with some friends. I came home a few hours later, it had just gone 10 o'clock at night and I found a letter waiting on my bed. I thought to myself 'He's gone, and this letter is Luke's way of telling me what he really thinks of me.' I braced myself for more pain.

Dad,

I have thought alot about moving out. And thought it was a good idea. Since we argued the other day I havent been sleeping properly because I feel depressd and angry. I just want to cry but cant. I'll just be sat there doing something then all of a sudden just want to cry. I cant go on like this. It is because I dont have a relationship now with you, or God I was lay in bed and all of a sudden it was like I had a blindfold taken off me and I could see what was happening, what the devil was doing. But I did not feel that I could do anything. And I know that If I moved out, the bad things I do would only get worse and worse until I end up in prison, hospital or even worse. I am not going to let my pride and anger stand in the way of me saying I am wrong, and I cant be reasponsible to live without Gods rules. I am So sorry I have let you, myself, God and everyone down. I hope I can make a change to my life for good. I want to meet you half way if you will.

I was amazed. Luke would describe it to me later, that when he was in his room, it was like he had a veil lifted and could see the truth for the first time. That God was saying to him that he can still make a decision on what he wanted for his life, but he had to choose with all the facts revealed. God wanted him to understand where his destructive life choices were taking him. Luke understood that it was all or nothing.

This was the breakthrough we had been praying for. We had been in a battle, and it had taken us right to the edge. I was relieved, heart-broken, joyful, tearful and thankful all at once. On reading it, I realised that Luke must still be here, in his room right now. I went straight to his room, and opened the door.

Luke is a big lad; six foot two, broad shoulders. But as he lay there in his single bed, all I could see was a little boy. My boy. I put my arms round him and he wept, and we just hugged each other in the dark of his room. Through the tears I told him, 'Luke, I love you. It's going to be alright. We're gonna make it'. As I held him, I could see how the mess of sin and darkness had ravaged my son, the drugs, the violence, the hate, the depression. But in these moments, Jesus was beginning to heal the wounds.

There would be a long journey ahead. Luke needed to separate himself from the friends that had become such a strong influence, but we were in a small town and that wasn't easily done. There would be moments of relapse, times where we would take two steps forward, one step back, as Luke struggled to resist the temptation to go back to his old life. But this was undoubtedly a turning point for him.

Eventually the latest charge that he had been arrested for came to court. Luke already had four convictions by this point, and had been seeing a probation officer. The probation officer had written on his documentation that after the amount of charges that he had received that 'Custody is inevitable'.

Luke braced himself for probably six months in prison. When he was in court before the Magistrate, the Magistrate was confused as to how he got there. He told him that he didn't fit with the people that he sees come through the system.

We had arranged for Luke to have a character witness, our friend Karin Cooke, who was a social worker at the time. She stood up and gave a heartfelt account of how Luke had done some bad things, but he had turned his life around, had stopped taking drugs, had been on a mission trip and was involved in serving in our church. She testified of his change and how he needed another chance.

The judge himself welled up with tears and was clearly moved. The judge considered their decision and left us with bated breath. They gave Luke 18 months probation, avoiding prison altogether. We were so relieved and so grateful. God had intervened and heard our prayers once again.

His old friends had come to 'support' and were watching on, sniggering at the court proceedings. We left the court, and instead of taking his friends up on their offer of a drink at the pub, he came home with his mum and dad. That was the second victory of the day.

We have gone through some difficult things through the years of leading church. Public criticism, private criticism. Accusations, discouragements, slander and anything else the enemy could throw at us to try and throw us off course. But the battle in our own household for the life of our son was the most intense and painful that we have had to fight. Heather and I fought in prayer together, cried together and saw the triumph of Jesus together. It's the ones that you love the most that the enemy can use for the most pain.

A few years later Luke still needed to go and find his own space and get away more than just living 13 miles away from his old life. He had the opportunity to move to Australia and serve in a church on the Gold Coast.

His journey would eventually take him to NYC, working for a church through serving the homeless. He ran feeding programmes and back-to-school programmes in some challenging neighbourhoods, giving children new shoes and the equipment they needed for school through the projects he coordinated. He even established a prison ministry. We are so proud of him, and I am so thankful that he didn't move out that day, but it's only through the miraculous saving grace of Jesus.

It could be easy to look at our lives and the church now and think that we have got it all right. A lot of people don't realise the prayers that have been prayed, the tears that have been shed, and the battles that have been fought that at times have looked like they were lost. People see our five sons within the church, all following God, and ask us about our wisdom and how we did it. It is by God's grace that we see all of our sons following Jesus today.

I know there are things that we did right, but there were things that we missed, ways that I failed as a father. I was still making mistakes and with two of my sons over 18, I was still learning about fatherhood. Even reflecting on it now, I wonder if things could have been different if I had not allowed myself to be driven by ministry. And yet despite those failings, God has blessed us and been faithful.

This was a huge lesson for me, and even as I lead other pastors now and speak counsel into their lives, one of the things that I will always try to encourage and to protect is the importance of family. Husbands should be there for their wives; sons and daughters should know they are valued and prioritised by their mothers and fathers.

If we put ministry before our family, it can embitter them towards the kingdom, and our family should be the jewel in the crown of our fruit and discipleship. If we are pouring ourselves into someone else's son, but neglecting to lead and pour into our own, we have missed the calling of stewardship to our families.

I recently called one of our pastors and told him that it was time for him to step down. He was doing a fantastic job. The church was growing and going forward, people were being saved, discipled and growing closer to Jesus. But the place he was ministering was so expensive to live in that he was away five days a week to work and sustain their lifestyle. It was beginning to have an impact on his wife and children.

> 'Unless the Lord builds the house, the labourers who build it, labour in vain.'
>
> Psalm 127:1 NIV

We have to trust that He is the builder, not us. He is the saviour, not us, and if we keep this in mind, we will not allow family to be sacrificed on the altar of ministry.

18

CONTENDING IN PRAYER

The key factor of the restoration of our son was the power of prayer. I have had to believe, petition and pray for things right through my life, but there is nothing like the battle for your own child to teach you what it really means to fight for someone in prayer.

A lot of Christians are so reasonable in what they ask for in prayer: they make well-behaved, polite requests. They may pray for something a few times, but when they don't get the answer they wanted and it affects their faith, they don't ask again. Or maybe they just don't want to bother heaven too much.

As the relationship with our son became so difficult, it would have been easy to be discouraged and to give up praying for something that had become so painful. He was in turmoil, our relationship was in ruins. Why would God not answer our prayers as quickly as we wanted?

God was bringing us closer and making us more dependent upon Him as we pursued Him in prayer.

> 'Ask and it will be given to you; seek and you will find; knock and the door will be opened to you. For everyone who asks receives; the one who seeks finds; and to the one who knocks, the door will be opened.'

Matt 7:7-8 NIV

But who gets what they ask for on the first time of asking? Only a spoilt child. Who plays hide and seek then finds the other player first time, every time? Who knocks on doors and they open immediately each time? We Christians have often taken the verses above and interpreted it to think that one prayer is enough.

Our faith in action needs to become persistence in us. Jesus told the parable below to bring to life this idea:

> Then Jesus told his disciples a parable to show them that they should always pray and not give up. He said: 'In a certain town there was a judge who neither feared God nor cared what people thought. And there was a widow in that town who kept coming to him with the plea, 'Grant me justice against my adversary.'
>
> 'For some time he refused. But finally he said to himself, 'Even though I don't fear God or care what people think, yet because this widow keeps bothering me, I will see that she gets justice, so that she won't eventually come and attack me!"
>
> And the Lord said, 'Listen to what the unjust judge says. And will not God bring about justice for his chosen ones, who cry out to him day and night? Will he keep putting them off? I tell you, he will see that they get justice, and quickly. However, when the Son of Man comes, will he find faith on the earth?'
>
> Luke 18: 1-8 NIV

The widow did not come begging, she was not just hoping for mercy. She knew her rights and demanded justice be done, and that is a whole different posture. The widow was making a 'plea' to the judge. A plea is 'a formal statement backed up by the power of the law.'

How many of us Christians often beg, when we should be putting a demand upon the promises of God? We have a God-given right to an inheritance, not just scraps or leftover blessings. Jesus teaches us to make a plea before him, confident that what we ask for is backed up by the power of the law of the cross. We should be expectant for answers, anticipating that something will happen.

Even though the judge is evil, he gives way to the determination of the widow. How much more then will God who is good and loving give to us?

It is conditional: *if* we 'cry out to him day and night'. Many of us don't want that. Not in our convenience-warped, on-demand, Amazon-Prime-next-day-delivery culture. We want to write it in a prayer journal one time and hope it's done. We want to utter a whisper as we drive the car and believe that was it.

———

Our endurance and perseverance in this generation has been significantly impacted by our environment. But we must find that long-suffering patience, that ancient faith to 'pray without ceasing' as in 1 Thes 5:17. The key is knowing our position and His promise. The promise that we have a right as his children, that his word is powerful, and that it cannot return to him void as Isaiah 55:11 states.

> *'But how much of that kind of **persistent** faith will the Son of Man find on the earth when he returns?'*

Luke 18:8 MSG

Jesus is looking for the persistent prayers, those that will not give up: those that will not be deterred, no matter what. That they will keep putting faith in him, again and again. Our plea or prayer and our persistence must be coupled together to be effective.

How much are we believing for? How much will we practice fasting with our plea and persistence?

There is another parable that Jesus tells about persistence. Late one night, a man has visitors to stay. He wants to be hospitable, so he visits a friend's house, bothering him and insisting that he get up in the middle of the night to give him some supplies. Jesus finishes it with this:

> *'I tell you, even though he will not get up and give you the bread because of friendship, yet because of your shameless audacity he will surely get up and give you as much as you need.'*

Luke 11:8 NIV

When we start getting unhindered in our prayers, things really start to happen. When we stop trying to behave ourselves, get some shameless audacity, start believing, then keep on believing, we start to see impossible things in front of our eyes.

May the Christians rise up, get out of our formal queues of polite requests and start ferociously banging on the door of prayer, demanding for breakthrough. Unrelenting, fearless, persevering. God's truth over their current reality. Shameless audacity opens doors.

We have not because we ask not. There's no answer, because we gave up too early. Whether for your marriage, your child, your health, or your finances, get your faith again and do not relent in asking and asking.

The cycle of persistence is this:

Faith.

Action.

Expectation.

Repeat.

Faith gives birth to action. This is followed by the posture of expectation, which in turn feeds our faith. This cycle produces persistence and continues until we see the breakthrough.

Imagine what could happen if you only kept knocking? You need to not give up, hold onto the promise, start getting loud, and put a demand upon the promises of God. Whatever you are facing, keep knocking.

CONTENDING IN PRAYER QUESTIONS TO CONSIDER:

- What words would you use to describe your prayer life?
- What habits can you develop to become more consistent and persistent in prayer?
- What could change if you developed that persistence?

19

A SIGNPOST FROM THE NORTH

It was the early 2000's and we had seen our church community in Brook Hall go from strength to strength, we were growing to be a respectable community church. We were running a mums and toddlers morning, had a thriving youth group and had even opened up a day-nursery to connect with the community at another level. The church was the strongest it had been; even financially the money given was covering all of our costs comfortably. We had built a nice, safe, predictable fire.

There was something in me that was disturbed: in fact it was the unhappiest I had ever been. On the face of it, everything looked great, but I hadn't started a church to be respectable but to be radical. In theory, what we had should have been satisfying to us, but I could not escape the fact that there was a world to reach and we were barely scratching the surface. I couldn't stand the thought of staying where we were, and knew that God had called us to so much more.

At that time across a number of churches in the UK, there was a movement away from more community-style church, to a more relevant and dynamic approach. I had begun to question the way we were doing everything. What did our name 'New Life Community Church' really mean to an unchurched person?

One of the churches that was leading the way was Abundant Life Church, (now Life Church), then led by Pastors Paul and Glenda Scanlon in Bradford. Some of the churches in Hereford had begun to hear about the amazing things that were happening in Abundant Life as they embraced a new style and approach. They were running conferences to help other church leaders learn how to build more effectively. I am not really one for conferences, but there was something in me that felt I had to go.

I attended a leadership conference called 'Stronger' with our team and it had a huge impact on me. I was inspired by the vibrancy, the youthfulness, and the life and passion in every aspect of the church, from the building itself, to the worship team with so many lights on stage! God used it to strengthen my burden for relevance. I was so convicted that we had to ensure what we were doing was relevant to the people we wanted to reach, including young people. I was seeing my own sons become disinterested in church, and I was passionate to draw them in and see them take their part in building the kingdom.

Paul Scanlon shared in one of the sessions on how he had 'crossed the church over'. The majority of his leadership team had been trying to protect the way things had been done and to ensure that things didn't change.

But just as Joshua crossed the Israelites over the Jordan to enter the promised land, we as churches needed to make changes to cross over into the new for the next generation. As I heard this, and saw everything the church was about, it clicked. This was why I had felt so burdened, why I had felt something needed to change, why I couldn't be satisfied with where we were. We had to keep moving.

One night in the conference Pastor Tommy Barnett from Dream City Church in Arizona, USA spoke. We were sitting on the back row, taking it all in. He talked about the mustard seed of faith in a compelling and inspiring message. He had handfuls of mustard seeds and said if you want that seed, come and get it. Many people started filtering through the aisles towards the front, and there was so much response that movement was slow.

I had this fire stirring in me. 'How desperate are you? How hungry are you? How much do you want this?' It was as though God was on the stage, saying, 'I have this for you, but you need to respond.' The room was full of pastors and I am not an extravert. I would naturally filter slowly along the queues, but I felt God say to me, 'Have you got a way to get to the front?'

I looked at the crowds in the aisles, and I looked at the rows and rows of chairs in front of me and responded, 'Yes, over the chairs.' God prompted me, 'Then go.' I wanted that seed for the next season, so I started climbing over the sea of chairs, from the back to the front. I looked round and one of our team, Chris Cooke, was following me.

There were so many down the front that Pastor Tommy began to call people up to stage to make more room. I had clambered my way to the foot of the stage. 'Is that enough God?' He says to me again 'How much do you want it?' So I climbed on to the stage, and stood right next to Pastor Tommy Barnett. That night as a whole group of us received prayer, it was not only about me receiving something, it was testing my heart. Was the fire still there to be consumed for the call of Jesus? It was.

'He jumped overboard and swam towards Jesus'

20

WHO LOVES JESUS THE MOST

That night that I started hurdling over the chairs, clambering my way to the front, there was an emotion in me that I knew well. Jesus, I love you and I will do whatever it takes to show you that, even if it makes me look the fool.

I feel a kinship to Peter in this way. I love Peter because I can easily identify with the guy who jumped in with both feet but often got it wrong.

At the last supper Jesus tells the disciples that they will all fall away from him. Peter is hurt and responds that even if the others fall away, he never would, he would rather die. Later that same night, he infamously denies Jesus three times.

One day after the resurrection, in John 21, Peter went fishing. I think he was feeling depressed. Fiercely loyal, Peter had promised to never leave Jesus and then broke his word by denying his Saviour. When we break our own moral codes and promises, it often results in self-loathing. Peter was blessed with friends and brothers, the disciples, who went with him.

In these low moments he returned to the thing he knew he was good at: catching fish. Then he didn't catch anything all night.. How about that for feeling like a failure. Maybe this is an insight into what Peter was considering. Peter could go back to his trade and give up on the call to preach the gospel. Maybe we would never have heard anything more about him.

Then Jesus appeared on the beach. The disciples did not recognise Him. He shouted out to them: put the net on the other side of the boat. Peter the fisherman knew best about how to fish.. Would he be willing to listen to someone else, a stranger to him?

Maybe you're reading this and you have failed, but Jesus is calling you to put your net on the other side. Give it a go. Trust Him once again. Put your faith in Him over yourself and your circumstances.

Following Jesus requires us to lay down our pride and recognise that where we thought we knew a lot, we actually don't know much at all.

All of a sudden they had a miraculous catch, a net loaded full of fish! John recognised Jesus, and told Peter that it is the Lord. Peter had an awakening moment. He couldn't wait a moment longer, so he jumped overboard and swam towards Jesus.

They were only 100 yards from the shore, but to wait for the boat to sail in was too long for Peter. He had to be with Jesus immediately. The other disciples sailed towards Jesus towing the catch. All are heading towards Jesus, but one is a swimmer and the other sailors. One is a man who does irrational things to be with Jesus. He was the one who threw his dignity aside: the only disciple arriving dripping wet and dishevelled in front of Jesus. The love that Peter had for Jesus drove him to jump overboard.

I am someone who has determined to be a swimmer, not a sailor. I am raising up a generation of swimmers. Those who would leave the rationality and dignity of their boats because they are so madly in love with Jesus that they cannot bear to be without Him for one more second. I pray that even now this would stir your heart to be a swimmer, to throw yourself overboard.

Interestingly, John describes himself as the disciple whom Jesus loved. He was the disciple that reclined against Jesus at the last supper, such was their closeness and friendship. But John was not the one jumping into the water, it was Peter.

In this moment, it was not about the one that Jesus loved the most but the one that loved Jesus the most. Peter was the one that would lead the church through their early years and take responsibility for the direction of the followers of the Way.

As a leader, maybe you have denied Him, maybe you fished all night and have not caught a thing. In verse seven, it says that before Peter jumped overboard, he wrapped himself in his garment. He embraced his covering: symbolising how he re-embraced his covering in Christ.

We know from Scripture that when they placed the nets on the other side, after having caught nothing all night, they immediately caught 153 large fish. The catch represented food, provision, finance and success. But when Peter saw that it was Jesus on the shore, he cast all of that aside to be where Jesus was. Sometimes we can get too obsessed with what we are doing rather than being focused and consumed by who Jesus is and who he calls us to be.

There is something beautiful about the urgency of Peter to get to Jesus. The first command Peter received from Jesus was to follow Him and that same call was what overwhelmed Peter's heart once again here. If only we as the church would have that response to Jesus, that we would move aside from our common sense, our reason, and go after Jesus wholeheartedly, unashamedly, wherever He was calling us to. Would not the world be set alight with the hope of the Gospel as we were consumed with urgency to be with Him?

After Peter arrived at the shore, he displayed some Herculean strength to pull in all 153 fish onto the beach himself, and then had some breakfast. Jesus withdrew from the others to spend a moment with just Peter. He asks him:

'Simon, son of John, do you love me more than these?'

John 21:15 NIV

It was important to Jesus that Peter loved him the most. We should be desiring to love Jesus the most. We can think that when we pray and sing out worship songs that we all love Jesus the same. We can presume that it is black or white, but it is a far more colourful scale than that. Jesus selected Peter as his rock despite his mistakes and despite his failures, all because he was so in love with his Lord.

Jesus is asking you the same question, even now, do you love me the most?

Jesus asks Peter two further times whether he loves him and Peter confesses his love. Jesus is healing the brokenness of Peter's three denials by asking Peter the same question three times. He also responds each time with a command to take care of His sheep, or to feed his lambs, referring to the people, His church. Jesus is teaching Peter that he cannot just love Jesus, but to love Jesus is to love his church.

The two are intertwined. That is why so many who want to love Jesus but have turned away from the church are trying to do something impossible. You cannot love the bridegroom but despise the bride, for they are one flesh. If Jesus is the head of the Church and the Church is a body, you are walking around with a decapitated head in your arms. Christ and his church are one.

That's why an overboard love for Christ outworks itself in an overboard love for your local church.

WHO LOVES JESUS THE MOST? QUESTIONS TO CONSIDER:

- What factors in your life can stop you from jumping out of the boat?
- What would that reckless, fearless, running towards Jesus look like in your circumstances?
- Do you feel that you could identify yourself as one who loves him the most? What needs to change so that you could give a simple 'yes' to that question?

21

LEAVING BROOK HALL

This love for the church was the driving force for my decision making. I had this conviction that there was more. I knew something had to radically change in the way we were doing church. There were big, brave decisions ahead of us. I prayed and sought God about what He wanted us to do, and he said: 'It's time to sell the building.'

I wrestled, 'But God, we are set up so well, established in the community, we have everything we need to build the church here.' We were comfortable, but God convicted me. It was time to make things uncomfortable, disturb the status quo and jolt the church out of it's predictable routine. It was time for another journey of faith.

As I accepted this was what God was saying, I asked him, 'Well what's next? What do I tell the people the plan is?' He responded very clearly to me, 'You don't need to know that yet, just be obedient to what I have told you. You need to leave Brook Hall, otherwise the promise will become your prison.'

God had provided for us to go to Brook Hall in a phenomenal way. It had been the biggest breakthrough of our church: a modern day miracle. God warned us that if we were not willing to let the promise go, it would eventually become a prison.

GARY SNOWZELL

We have to receive a miracle with open hands and trust God with it, not hold on to it and let it start defining us. When God provided food miraculously in the desert for the Israelites, he sent them Manna, a bread that would appear on the floor every day. But if the Israelites tried to keep some bread for the next day, it would become rotten and maggotty. They always had to look to the next miracle and not hold on to yesterday's. I wonder how different the church would be if we were more willing to chase after and embrace the next miracle, instead of clinging to the former glory that God has previously revealed.

We had been in Brook Hall for seven years, but this promise had an expiry date on it. Brook Hall was not the final destination, it was just a step, and a huge lesson in our understanding of faith.

I began to make enquiries with the estate agent to find out what they thought about how long the building would take to sell. Taking into account that it was over 400 years old, had a very unique layout, and was a government listed building, (which imposes building restrictions on it) he said it would most likely take a lot of time to find the right buyer in a small town like Leominster.

He estimated that he thought it would probably take a year if we were being optimistic. A year would give me the chance to take the church on the journey and work out what we were going to do and where we were going to go next.

It sold within two weeks. I got up in front of the church and told them we had sold the building. Obviously, questions were asked. 'Well where are we going to go?' All I could say was: 'I don't know yet'. We looked around and found a leisure centre, called Bridge Street Sports Centre, on the outskirts of the town where we could meet.

The sale of Brook Hall went through with no problems. We wouldn't have the space for a lot of the things we had accumulated for our church building, so we did a big auction and sold everything off. We went back to a set-up and tear-down model after seven years of having our own space.

We tried moving the nursery there for a while. It didn't last long though, which meant that we had to shut it down after building it up over all these years. Our mums and toddlers group also had to end, after years of our bril-

128

liant mums running it. We had gone from being a respectable, grown-up, established church to being back on the uncharted seas. Some of our people hated it. I thought it was exciting.

As we began to meet in the Leisure Centre, there was a freshness to what we were doing. It was stripped back and less complex. God was beginning to speak to me about culture and who he was calling us to be. I set about speaking into our people messages that would begin to transform who we were as followers of Jesus and therefore, who we were as a church.

I knew the importance of media for the future of our church even though in my business I still used paper and pen and was uncomfortable using technology. As a leadership team we decided to take a big chunk of our yearly budget and buy two Apple Mac computers and a video camera. I had no idea how to even turn them on! But I gave them to some of our young people who had shown an interest in media and encouraged them to step out in creativity.

They set out on the classic mid-2000's creative church expression of Church News, making the boring bits of church, the deadly 'notices', a bit more interesting. Our young team would go on to find every single way possible of saying 'groups next week' through stop motion, foreign films with fake subtitles, using an upside down head and a squeaky voice to create 'Mr. Chin'. They even would sing the notices!

Some of these were terrible, but some of them were hilarious and some even genius. We had begun to engage the creativity of our young people, and they had made church more wacky - yes but a lot funnier. There should be joy and laughter in the church; we should actually enjoy going. Our 'respectable' tag was really starting to become tattered.

Many church leaders have asked me about how we were able to move our church across from Brook Hall. How did we get our people to follow us through this transition? My approach was not to convince everyone. The price of true change means that you must not be afraid to lose people. If you try to keep everyone happy, you will never make the decisions that God is calling you to.

The people that were critical of the move were reluctant followers anyway. They wanted to be part of the church but only on their terms. I was determined that God has not called us to build a church for the people we had, who wanted things their way but for the people we wanted to reach, including the next generation.

I have seen so many pastors abdicate their leadership so they can purchase favour with their people. If you carry on trying to win the ten people that don't want to follow you, you may miss the hundred that are around the corner.

Of course we want to do what we can to take people with us who are willing. But be bold in your obedience and fearless in your leadership, even when faced with opposition from the people around you, and watch how God will honour that faith you place in him.

As we began to meet in Bridge Street, we started having people join us from Hereford (13 miles away), connecting to us from a wider area, which was a big deal when you are in a small market town like Leominster. We saw key families joining us and bringing their children, like our great friends the Cooke's.

I knew that the Sports Centre was only a temporary solution and that we would need another facility for our growing church. I found a warehouse on the Industrial Estate and thought this would be a great next location for us. We had paid off our loan from Brook Hall and had money leftover to invest into a new facility. I went through negotiations and put in an offer, but over a 12 month period it would not go through. It seemed like no matter how much we prayed, we were not seeing the breakthrough with it. God was about to reveal that he had something else for us and this closed door was exactly what we needed to prepare our hearts for it.

22

CHANGELING

When I look back at our decision to leave what was so familiar, to take the risks that we did, it was through embracing a quality which I have long come to value. This principle has been so important for me, empowering who I am and what I do. It is something that we have put in the fundamental identity of our church. It has given us the power to 'move on', to keep fresh, to stay relevant.

In all the earth, it is a gift that God only gave people. **Change**.

We have a resolve to not get bogged down in routines, structures, and one way of doing things. As well as being powerful for us in building church, it has also been transformative for people personally:

It's an answer to depression.

It will move you from complacency to progress.

It fuels the fire of your destiny.

It saves marriages.

It saves us from our history.

It is an antidote to a bland and boring life.

Zacheus is an example of being a 'changeling' (Luke 19) Zacheus was sinful, he was outcast from Jewish society because of his profession of being a tax collector. Most people don't like paying their taxes, but it was worse than that. He was working for the enemy, the occupying Roman forces. He was also charging his fellow countrymen more than they owed so that he could pay what was due to the Romans and take a cut himself, becoming rich in the process. But there was a yearning in Zacheus for change.

We all know what it's like to be in a pattern of a sin, and in certain moments we have this urge to get out of that life. The desire to leave it all behind. You're overweight, but for the most part you're fine with it. It's just the way life is. Then one day, something snaps. You put on an old shirt you haven't worn for a while and it doesn't look as good as it once did. Cue the Googling of fitness plans and weight loss programmes as you get this overwhelming need to change everything! But for many, it never evolves past those internet searches and you carry on as you were, quickly getting rid of that shirt (you never liked it anyway).

Zacheus hears of Jesus being in his town, and that same desire surges within him: to change. He is surrounded by crowds of people, and as a shorter man, he cannot see. This is the decisive moment. Will he give up because he comes up to a seemingly immovable barrier or press through and find a way? Zacheus makes his choice: overcome. He lets this inner desire for change take over, casting aside his dignity by climbing up a tree so that he can see Jesus.

When Jesus accepts Zacheus, he has an immediate response: he wants to repay all that he has gained from others, three times the amount that he took. His response was to change. That willingness began in the moment he started to climb the tree.

In contrast, we have the rich young ruler who asks Jesus how to gain eternal life. He has acquired everything else and he wants more. But instead of gaining, Jesus tells him to give away everything he has. The rich young ruler walks away, not willing to change the one thing that will lead him to eternal life.

We never know the name of the rich young ruler, but we know the name of Zacheus. Zacheus was willing to change any and every part of his life as he interacted with Jesus. The rich young ruler was still holding on to parts of his life as he made his offering before Jesus.

The ones who are willing to truly change are the ones that will change the world.

Here Jesus isn't simply teaching us about money but about priorities. The thing most precious to the rich young ruler's heart was what he owned, and that is why Jesus challenged him. It was also his identity: we are introduced to him according to his wealth, his heritage and his title, rather than by a name. A rich, young ruler. Jesus is looking for those who are willing to change.

———

I refer to them as a 'changeling': someone who is willing to change anything and everything in their life to become more like Jesus and grow closer to Him. A non-changeling is someone who is unwilling to part with something of their habits, behaviour, possessions or identity, preserving it for themselves. When you're a changeling, everything is on the table. When you're a non-changeling you are offering some cards and keeping others in your hand.

Look at the disciples: they were changelings. Jesus sought them out and approached them because he could see this capacity for change in them. Jesus was magnetised to the fisherman on the shore, drawn to an isolated tax collector, people whose lives were wrapped up in their family business. Their identity was in what they previously did, but when Jesus came calling there was a willingness to lay it all down for Him and His kingdom.

We have seen many people come in and out of our church through the years. Those who are attracted to the worship, the teaching or the community. But there comes a crunch point for so many where reservations are revealed; there is something that they hold back and refuse to put on the table, a lack of willingness to change. This is often where we see them move on and go somewhere else, walking away just as the rich young ruler did, because what they hold on to they deem to be too precious to change.

———

Generally, there are many people who don't like their life, or their church but feel like it is out of their power to change things. We all need to take responsibility for our own lives. If you don't like it, change it. If you are a pastor and you want to do things differently, then be courageous enough to make the changes you know need to happen.

One of the biggest barriers to us becoming changelings is blame-shifting: looking to people and circumstances around us and placing blame on them for our life or the way that we are rather than taking responsibility to implement the change that we desire. Blame-shifting is something we learn right from when we are children and something that can poison our God-given gift to change right through our life. When we blame someone else, it removes our responsibility and our power to take authority over our own lives and change them.

> 'I guess what I'm trying to say is, that if I can change, and you can change, everybody can change!' Rocky in Rocky IV.[2]

Rocky knew it. And He didn't even have the power of the Holy Spirit. I believe in the transformative power of the gospel, which means that no person and no character flaw is off limits. If we're willing to apply the ointment of change, it will work upon every single one of us.

Through over 30 years of building church, however stubborn, difficult, angry, depressed, religious or whatever else people may seem, I always believe that they have the capacity to change. There is hope, and my job is to help them see it and to empower them to do it.

You may be reading this now and thinking of those areas that need to change in your life, but there will be a temptation to delay. 'Maybe I could think about that next month because I won't be so busy.' I can tell you now, it probably won't happen. Being a changeling is about single-mindedness; it's about having a determined mind. 'I WILL make these changes, I WILL pursue who God has called me to be without compromise.'

Zacheus had that single-mindedness. He didn't think about change or take lots of time to ponder on it; he did it. He didn't have a prayer meeting about change. He didn't do his accounts to check whether he would indeed be able to pay everyone back. He made a declaration that he would do it. He was determined that this would be a turning point in his life. When we deliberate and delay, we pass up our God-given power to change.

Zacheus could have received salvation and forgiveness from Jesus in that moment, and he would have been made right with God and could have left it there. This changeling quality brought a revelation to Zacheus though: He realised that because of salvation, because of forgiveness, he could change his ways. Not tomorrow, not possibly, but now. Now is the time to change.

I can't tell you how many people over the years have told me, 'That's just not me', 'That's just the way I am,' debilitating the power to change by the confession of their mouths. But as they have begun to change what they believe, that has gone on to change their whole life. They are set free from the shackles that they and others have placed around their identity and who they think they are.

Change can be fun too. Get a new haircut, try a new outfit, go somewhere different for date night. God has created change in our seasons, always giving us freshness and reminding us of how he has designed things to continue moving forwards.

Let us draw inspiration to be more like the seasons and keep moving. We get stuck and tired of the same old way of doing things and the same old thinking, but there is so much life in the new. There are nine verses in the bible that call us to 'sing to the LORD a new song' Psalm 96:1 e.g.

God wants us to keep it fresh. It's time to cast aside that old melody and find a new rhythm, a new beat for this season. Change is good for the soul, although it might seem strange at first. Many people may comment about it. Humanity always glitches a little when someone doesn't conform or changes something about themselves, but it is so worth it.

Not one of us gets saved and becomes the full package of what it means to be a Christ-follower overnight. In Matthew 5:48, Jesus says, 'You therefore must be perfect, as your heavenly Father is perfect.' I know, we will never be perfect until the day we get to eternity. That means each one of us needs to strive, to pursue, to persevere in change constantly to pursue the perfection that we are called to.

I believe one of the great masterstrokes of the enemy has been to deceive people into thinking that they cannot change. I have heard believers praying for God to change them, when he has given them the authority and the power to change themselves. Confused Christians who are 'more than conquerors' (Romans 8:37) live as though they are weak, accepting where they are rather than daring to rule over themselves and make new decisions about their lives. There are those waiting for change to happen to them as though they are waiting for their lottery numbers to come up, hoping with everything in them that 'their day will come'. But it is far better than that, it is a gift that we can seize hold of and utilise as much as we desire.

One of the huge obstacles that can stand against change is our pride. Our inability to accept or even see our deficiencies or imperfections can then spill over into stubbornness and unwillingness. Humility is the key to change. We must accept that we are far from the perfection that Christ called us to, but have the faith and boldness to believe Christ has given us the power to change and the resolve to implement it.

Change can come at a huge cost, especially when you are leading a church, but how many churches have died over the years, disappearing into irrelevance because of a failure of the leadership to change? It starts personally, then it must be applied to the way that you lead and structure the church. Give the church the life it so desperately needs through the power of change.

CHANGELING QUESTIONS TO CONSIDER:

- When were you last overwhelmed with the desire to change? What did you do about it?
- What area(s) of your life do you feel God is currently drawing your attention to and asking you to change? What is your next step?
- Where can you identify unwillingness to change in your life? Are there any areas you consider off limits to God, or feel that you are simply unable to change?

23

REHEARSAL TIME IS OVER

The call to change was knocking at our door. We were meeting at Bridge Street Sports Centre, and we had our old friend back in town from America, the Prophet Clem Ferris. He spoke over us and said, 'God wants you to know, rehearsal time is over.' We had been doing church for 18 years at this point! On first hearing, it was discouraging to hear that everything that had passed had been a preparation, a run-through before the real battle.

Clem continued, 'You are going to be a regional church. You are going to be a hub with spokes that reach across different locations.' I had heard this word before spoken to a church in Hereford over a decade ago, and I knew at that moment that God was calling us to reach Hereford. Clem confirmed, 'This word has been given to others, but now it has been passed to you.'

My whole mindset shifted from Leominster to Hereford. I began to think regionally instead of locally, and it was as though God breathed into the balloon of my vision and mindset, expanding its volume and shape.

After this night, the thoughts of getting a permanent home in Leominster were over. I could see it now; the reason that he had moved us from Brook Hall was to move us into Hereford to reach the region. It was so clear!

Heather questioned me about it at first. We had poured almost two decades into this little town, Heather had personally invited half the town to church - at least! She said, 'If we go to Hereford, we have no connections there, no presence, and we are risking all that we have fought for and built in Leominster. Do we really want to go back to the beginning and start again after 18 years?'

It was wise to consider this, but I knew what we had to do. We had to take the fire to Hereford.

24

PROPHETIC DIRECTION

As you have seen through this book, the gift of prophetic direction has been a valued guiding light to our personal lives and to the progression of our church. It has challenged us, awoken us, caused us to dream bigger and imparted faith and courage. I cannot imagine where our church would be now had it not been for the embracing of the prophetic gift through these past decades.

The church as a whole needs to wake up and honour the gift of prophecy in the way it was intended. Has it been misused over the years? Absolutely. But just because you see a bad marriage doesn't mean the whole idea of marriage doesn't work. Sadly, this is a lot of the attitude I have seen from the church in its posture towards the prophetic, treating it like the crazy relative at the party who you try to avoid.

Do we need to weigh up and measure what is given to us prophetically before throwing ourselves headlong into its direction? Of course! That's biblical, (1 Thess 5:20-21). As much as we have been shaped by the words that have come to us, there are those that we have never fully understood or seen come to pass. And that's okay! It's less of a science and more of an art. That's why so many of the prophetic books are written in poetry.

'Follow the way of love and eagerly desire gifts of the Spirit, especially prophecy.'

1 Cor 14:1 NIV

We are taught to eagerly desire the gift of prophecy by Paul, but much of the church is more in the 'If I happen to bump into it, I'm open' category. That's far away from what God's word instructed us. We need less complacency and more holy curiosity.

What would the Church, or even Christianity as a whole, look like if we began to genuinely desire the gift of prophecy? Yearning for these words that would speak life, hope and encouragement from heaven.

'So Christ himself gave the apostles, the prophets, the evangelists, the pastors and teachers'

Ephesians 4:11 NIV

We are familiar with a number of these listed, but the prophet has faded away for many and is assigned only to the church of the past. The Old Testament is full of prophets, but the New Testament has them too. Jesus was a prophet Himself, even prophesying his own death. So the spirit of prophecy is the spirit of Christ. Can prophecy make us uncomfortable sometimes? Yes. Confused? Yes. That was often the reaction of the disciples to Christ Himself as he would prophesy about what would happen to Him or the end times that are to come.

Having and exercising the gift of prophecy does not make someone a prophet. Just as if I was to apply a bandage to someone's injury, it would not make me a doctor. The 'office' of the prophet, the position of authority and weight that speaks powerfully and directively, is something that Clem Ferris has held in our church for many years. He was there before we even began and continues to speak in, to this day, in a significant way.

We have also raised our own prophets too. When the prophetic comes, it is always done under submission to the apostolic oversight of our church, not superseding but coming under, as an offering. This is where the prophetic gifting has caused confusion through the years: when it has taken higher authority than the apostolic authority that is in place to safeguard, direct and lead the church.

The Word prophecy in Greek is: 'prophéteuó' which means 'the gift of communicating and enforcing revealed truth'. How many of us want to hear more of God's voice and his direction for our lives? Yet we often discount and discourage the ancient medium that he has chosen for humanity, the prophetic gift. The prophetic is often rejected when it is received in the mind rather than the heart.

> 'Do not neglect your gift, which was given you through prophecy when the body of elders laid their hands on you.'
>
> 1 Timothy 4:14 NIV

Prophecy equips and imparts gifting to the church, which we need in order to realise the calling that is upon us. How many Christians are there in this world that have never heard a prophetic word? That have never received prophetic impartation? Far too many. The body of Christ needs to be equipped, then released.

The most powerful and effective delivery of the prophetic that I have seen through my years of leadership is through the local church. The prophetic is meant to be a part of the body of Christ, as we see in the church in Corinthians 12:12-31. There have been many gatherings through the years where the prophet has operated in isolation, out of the oversight and foundation of the rest of the body of Christ. That is often where problems can lie, even with money being exchanged for prophetic words.

Now is the time for the church to reintegrate the prophet and prophetic gifting into the body and see the impact of it as the Holy Spirit speaks and prophecy is redeemed.

We see in the scriptures that when there are prophetic gatherings, the church is often driven to reach out and to plant churches. That's what happens in Acts 13:1-3 when Paul and Barnabas are set apart and sent out. That's what the Holy Spirit does through the prophetic: it draws us to take the steps that He is calling us to.

What about this from Paul, (again to his young disciple Timothy):

'Timothy, my son, I am giving you this command in keeping with the prophecies once made about you, so that by recalling them you may fight the battle well, holding on to faith and a good conscience, which some have rejected and so have suffered shipwreck with regard to the faith.'

1 Timothy 1:18-19 NIV

Paul is not just encouraging Timothy but commanding him to recall his prophecies in order to give him strength for the fight. Prophetic words are not just to be heard and disregarded but to be valued and remembered. They help us hold on to the faith we have and direct our conscience. All prophetic words need to be tested against the word of God. If you cannot find a basis for it in scripture or it opposes His word, then it needs to be rejected.

The pivots, the revelations, and the challenges that have come through the prophetic have been so life-giving and exciting in our church journey. We are committed to raising up a prophetic generation that speaks out what God is saying with great boldness and a love for the bride of Christ.

PROPHETIC DIRECTION QUESTIONS TO CONSIDER:

- Where have you experienced God speaking prophetically in your life? Have you ever received a prophetic word of direction or encouragement?
- Do you feel that you are personally utilising this part of our faith? Are you confident to step out and obediently deliver prophetic words to others?
- How could you grow in that confidence?

25

PLANTING IN THE PUB

The prophetic was calling us out of our comfort zones. I had this ongoing conviction that not only did we need to be a church that was regional, but we also had to get out from our four walls and make more of an impact, truly reaching people, seeing them get saved and become disciples.

We had a home group who were already meeting in neighbouring Hereford, a group of people who traveled over to Leominster each Sunday as they felt called to be a part of our church community. I called some of this group together, along with our leadership group and told them the news. We were going to be putting together a Sunday night outreach into the city of Hereford to reach local people and take responsibility for being more effective in our region.

The decision was met with some excitement, some uncertainty, and some tears. As the weeks progressed we developed a plan. We would buy a trailer, load all our sound equipment and take it to Hereford after our morning church meeting in Leominster.

We would do things differently, more creatively. We didn't have to have worship, notices, and then a sermon in the way we had always done. It would be unpredictable, youthful, gospel-centred, passionate and fun. We found a venue. The Herdsman was a local pub with an affordable event space. It was sticky-floored and grungy, had space for about 100 people and was used at weekends for gigs. Apparently they used to do a good Metal night.

We also found a name. Freedom. My favourite film is Braveheart, and the mad cry of the Scot to inspire the name of our new outreach seemed appropriate. It was simple and easy to understand and didn't sound 'churchy'. I knew I needed to get the young people of our church owning this vision, so I met with them and told them how we were going to reach into the city of Hereford and do church in a pub. Some of the adults had really struggled with this new concept, but the young people got it: they were passionate, they wanted to be involved. They could see how this could make a difference, so I started involving them in the planning of this new exciting thing that God was about to do.

At one of our planning meetings, one of our team walked in with a Firetrap t-shirt. It had a lion holding a banner and it gave us the idea for our logo. We took a photo of it, had it edited and made our own with the words 'Lion of Judah' over the banner. We wanted to be driven by the lion, and make Jesus the centre of this emerging venture.

We took out a city-wide advertising campaign on buses with graphic posters that said 'Looking for something?', targeting people who knew there was more to life than they were living.

We came up with a plan for our first event in the Herdsman. My son Josh and his future wife Rose started a band with some of our young people. Josh had grabbed hold of the idea of passionate worship and was determined not to be playing any acoustic worship hits from the early 2000s'. It had to be grittier, more edgy, and be sung from the heart. He dug out songs from the band Delirious, some that were fantastic to sing congregationally and some that were less good.

We came up with some creative videos to make people laugh but also to use media to show visuals of who God is. We even threw a few creative expressions in the mix, having an eight-year-old girl read scripture over a violin track as we drew all the lights down. We put together a video with some scriptures about the sword of the spirit and the kingdom of God being seized by violent men and got one of my sons to swing a replica Braveheart sword round on stage to some epic music. We had a testimony interview and a short sharp gospel message.

There was lots of interest in what we were doing, with rows of visitors on the opening night. We were buzzing with excitement to see what God would do.

When our young worship team took to the stage, they led us in some songs. But no one knew what to do in this pub environment, with its traditional decor and sticky floors. We had round tables down the side of the room and people just sat there watching our worship team try and do something new. We learnt from this, and soon started bringing people out to the front at our events and worshipping in a mosh pit. Rows of chairs gone, sticky-floored sweaty worship was in. Our young people pushed towards the front as our older members seemed to get closer to the back door.

We would hold prayer meetings in shut down toilets at the back of the pub, pleading for God to move and praying for the people that were attending that night. We started to have people wander into the back of our event space from the adjoining bar, with a pint of beer still in their hands, wondering what was going on.

This was shaping up to be different to any church events we had done before. I was speaking with Chris Cooke after our event, celebrating and analysing how it had gone and I noticed a teenage girl standing there by herself down by the stage. I asked if Chris knew who she was, (he knows everyone), but he said he had no idea. This might seem common to you, but for us, this was a big moment. We were having people, and young people, come into a church environment, and we didn't know who they had come with or how they had got here. This had never happened in Leominster. It was a sign of things to come.

Over the coming months we would see people with no church background at all coming in and meeting Jesus, and getting saved in the pub. It was amazing! There was such a buzz to it, with our young people involved right at the centre. We would run our New Life Community Church service in Leominster in the morning, and then pack up our trailer, travel 13 miles to Hereford and set up in the pub for the evening. It was easy to see that there was more excitement around the Freedom events than there was with our old church format in the mornings.

One of the problems that we faced initially was that as we had made our Freedom events about the gospel, we delivered short sharp messages that people would respond to, but we then lacked the ability to grow them and see them discipled. They would return to hear another gospel message week after week.

After almost nine months of running both events on a Sunday, it was clear to me that we needed to combine the two models. We would fuse together the depth and the teaching of our morning service with the dynamism, creativity and youthfulness of our Freedom events. We would change the name of our church completely to Freedom Church. We would meet in the mornings and leave the sticky pub behind to appeal more to families and accommodate children better.

But this big decision meant that we would stop meeting in Leominster altogether, building only in Hereford. I wrestled with this. I remembered the prophetic word earlier in the year we had received from Clem: '18 years of rehearsal time is over, now it is time to begin.' I must be the slowest learner ever! 18 years of our lives! 18 years and we haven't even got started?!

It had hurt to hear that, but there was truth in it too. In my spirit I knew what he was saying was right. But how could we shut down what we were doing in Leominster? How could we turn our backs on a town that we had been pouring into for 18 years? It had been such a painfully slow journey. Could we really start again? How would people respond? What would people think of us leaving Leominster?

As I was praying into it, I attended a conference and a friend approached me and said: 'God wants you to know that it's alright. Whatever it is that you are considering, it's going to be alright.' This was the green light I needed.

So the move to Hereford was on. We would be a regional church to reach out from. Around half of our church was already travelling from Hereford to Leominster anyway: this move would mean a shift so that our people in Leominster would be the ones to travel. We didn't expect that of them though, and gave them the opportunity to find another church if they didn't want to travel over to Hereford with us.

A portion of our church decided they wanted to stay in Leominster and so we prayed for them, thanked them and blessed them as they moved on. Strangely, some of the people that had been travelling from Hereford to Leominster were not happy. They would rather things stay as they were, continuing to travel to Leominster and back. We were undeterred. Quickly finding a new venue in a Hereford school, we began to meet there in October 2006.

By the time those struggling with the new vision had left, and those that wanted to stay in Leominster found other churches, about 70 people remained. We had shed those that didn't want to come with us, and now had a unity and excitement through the church. All kinds of potential-packed people started joining and the church began to really grow. It was in this season that many couples joined us who would go on to become the pastors that we would send all over the world.

26

RISK TAKERS

Shutting down what we had built for almost two decades and moving the church to a new city was a massive risk, but I believe that taking risks is what we are all called to do. We are called to take risks that activate the faith that is within us, to make our way out of our sheltered Christianity, contending for the more that God has for us. When we don't take risks, it's amazing how self-reliant we can become. When embracing risk, you ultimately put faith in the driving seat. It makes for an exciting ride.

A story that I have always identified strongly with is that of Gideon. I see myself in this young man. He didn't believe in himself at all and yet God called him anyway.

> 'The angel of the Lord came and sat down under the oak in Ophrah that belonged to Joash the Abiezrite, where his son Gideon was threshing wheat in a winepress to keep it from the Midianites. When the angel of the Lord appeared to Gideon, he said: 'The Lord is with you, mighty warrior.'

Judges 6: 11-12 NIV

Gideon is threshing wheat in a winepress because the Midianites had been ravaging the land of Israel for seven years. Every time they would sow crops, the Midianites and others would invade and ruin what was planted. Livestock would be destroyed. The Israelites were being squeezed and strangled through starvation, so this food was precious. Gideon was scared that it would be seized, so he was preparing it in hiding.

Then the angel of the Lord does something very surprising by calling Gideon a mighty warrior. Gideon is bemused. Here he is, not with a sword or any battle experience but hiding from his enemies in a winepress. This is not the block-buster 'Gladiator' or 'Braveheart' hero that we associate with the words 'mighty warrior'. It's a perfect example of how God calls out what is within us, far beyond our own perceptions.

When looking at Gideon, you have to remember what he has been through. Think about the seven years of enemy invasions that would have impacted him. Seven years of hunger, seven years of living in fear. Gideon was now being called to break out of this deep-rooted fear to defeat the Midianites. The exchange continues:

> 'Pardon me, my lord,' Gideon replied, 'but if the Lord is with us, why has all this happened to us? Where are all His wonders that our ancestors told us about when they said, 'Did not the Lord bring us up out of Egypt?' But now the Lord has abandoned us and given us into the hand of Midian.' The Lord turned to him and said, 'Go in the strength you have and save Israel out of Midian's hand. Am I not sending you?'
>
> 'Pardon me, my lord,' Gideon replied, 'but how can I save Israel? My clan is the weakest in Manasseh, and I am the least in my family.'
>
> The Lord answered, 'I will be with you, and you will strike down all the Midianites, leaving none alive.'
>
> Judges 6:13-16 NIV

When Gideon dares to challenge the angel, it is ignored. The Lord turns to him instead and rather than dwelling on Gideon's question, presses into the call. How many of us are asking questions that God has no intention of answering? I think back to our story. What if we had been so consumed with asking the Lord, 'Why are things not accelerating in Leominster? Why have we not seen all the breakthroughs we want to see?', when God was wanting us to ask different questions altogether?

For Gideon, the Lord refuses to be drawn into explaining the past seven years but is intent on leading Gideon and Israel towards the future. What are the things that God is ignoring in your requests right now because you are asking the wrong questions?

What I love about our God is that he ignores our cynicism and calls us anyway. Your limitations and your faults cannot shake off the calling on your life. It still remains! God doesn't look at Gideon and say, 'I need someone who is going to have a more positive mindset' and then go on to find someone else. He persists with Gideon, despite his self-doubt. Gideon has self-esteem issues, stating, 'I'm from the worst clan, and I'm the weakest in my family.' Not a great self-sell, but the Lord continues to call Gideon, reminding him that He has everything he needs, as it's not about Gideon's strength and status; it's about God's.

———

Before God delivers the Israelites, there is something that God must do with Gideon and his family. Gideon has to deal with the altar in his own household that was erected by his father to a false God, Baal.

> *That same night the Lord said to him, 'Take the second bull from your father's herd, the one seven years old. Tear down your father's altar to Baal and cut down the Asherah pole beside it. Then build a proper kind of altar to the Lord your God on the top of this height. Using the wood of the Asherah pole that you cut down, offer the second bull as a burnt offering.'*
>
> *Judges 6:25-26 NIV*

The Lord commands Gideon to take a specific bull who is seven years old, to represent the seven years of the oppression of the Midianites, and sacrifice on a new altar, one dedicated to the Lord. We have to deal with our own back garden before we can take on the world.

I feel that is what God did with Heather and I through our 18-year 'rehearsal'. He was deconstructing and reconstructing, building deep foundations within us for what He desired to build.

The Lord wanted to birth a complaint within Gideon. How could it be acceptable to have this altar to a false God in his backyard? He needed to get a complaint, instead of being compliant.

How much of the world has been changed and transformed because someone got a complaint? Think of Martin Luther King Jr with his complaint about civil rights, or of William Wilberforce with a complaint about slavery, or the suffragettes with a complaint for women to have equal voting rights. Complaint can be such a negative word, but when a complaint is morphed to vision, it compels us to do wild things and take big risks. We will face the consequential challenges with guts and determination.

In our own way, a complaint had formed in us to go and reach this world in a more engaging way. We wanted the church to be relevant and to see young people fall in love with the bride of Christ. That complaint birthed vision. What are the complaints that are stirring up within you, even now? What vision can they become to see the change that this world needs to see?

'So Gideon took ten of his servants and did as the Lord told him. But because he was afraid of his family and the townspeople, he did it at night rather than in the daytime.'

Judges 6: 27 NIV

This wasn't just the family altar, it was known as Gideon's father's, but it was used by the whole town. Gideon was so afraid that he did it at night while everyone was asleep. Everyone wakes up, finds out what happens, and is furious. So angry, in fact, that they want Gideon killed.

Gideon takes a huge risk in burning the altar; he would have known how badly everyone was going to react. He knew that he was taking his own life in his hands in desecrating what was seen as a holy place by his family and all his peers. Even though he is afraid, even though he can only bear to go through with it at night, he does it. He risks everything to honour what God asks of Him.

How many of us have resisted what God says because we are too afraid of what we put at risk? But it would have been a far greater risk for Gideon to have denied the Lord's request. When we lose the perspective of who God really is, we lose the value of what He asks us to do. I think even though Gideon was undoubtedly afraid of losing his life that day, he had something that drove him onwards: a 'fear' of God. Not being afraid, yet fearing God is a huge principle of the scriptures.

———

One of the best ways I have heard to explain this principle is this: not to be afraid to be with him, as Adam and Eve were in the garden of Eden after they had sinned but fearing to be without Him. That is the fear that keeps us safe and keeps us close.

Gideon risking everything to be obedient to God inspires me. If he could risk his life, I could risk everything that we had built in Leominster. It was all on the table as we chose to trust God's call rather than trusting what we had already gained.

Some of you reading this need to find a way to break out of your 'winepress' where you are hiding, just as Gideon did, standing up and taking the responsibility for the call that is upon your life and risking it all to unleash the complaint that God is birthing within you.

———

RISK TAKERS QUESTIONS TO CONSIDER:

- Can you identify any areas in your life where you might be asking the wrong questions of God? Gideon wanted to know why his last few years had played out as they did, but God wanted to show him more of his future.
- What righteous complaints is God stirring in you?
- How can you begin to tackle it?
- Gideon stepped up in obedience because he understood the healthy and powerful fear of God in his life. Do you feel that you are living in the fear of God? How can you cultivate that more to keep you growing healthily in the direction He has for you?

27

HARNESSING YOUTH

I think of the risk of starting a fire: you don't know if it will catch, maybe you'll get burned. Fire is not always safe, it can be unpredictable and wild.

Almost as risky as starting a wildfire is unleashing young people within the church.

One thing that made church different and so exciting was putting young people front and centre. It put a lot of noses out of joint, but it was essential to us finding the new thing that God wanted to do.

As we moved church meetings from Leominster to Hereford, the young people went into a bit of Sunday morning mode. I always find it so sad when I see young people sitting on the back row of the church when they should be right in the mix. So one Sunday when the school hall had been set up, I came in early and reserved the two front rows of seats, writing 'VIP' on them. When church began, I invited the young people to the front to come and claim these seats. I told the church family, 'I don't believe that youth are just the church of tomorrow, I believe that they are the church of today.' I wanted to let the young people have the best seats in the house.

Having them at the front changed the energy of worship, and their youth and enthusiasm built the response to the message. It was a game changer. They owned those front seats and set the tone for our whole church.

This was the final push for some of our old guard. They had been with us for a while and hung on through all the change, but this prompted their decisions to leave. They were irritated by the clapping and shouting of the young people. The untamed passion pressed unseen buttons, and they spent time on the back row with their arms folded. Instead of seeing it as making space for the young people, they felt pushed out.

———

It's amazing how powerful perspective can be and what damage it can cause when not kept in check. Even though it was tough seeing people leave who had been such a crucial part of what we had done before, we had to build the church on the new thing that God was doing. So our young people took ownership of our church and held on to their new place up front. By this point we were having young people lead worship, give creative input into the meetings and contribute media and design. It was a lot of fun!

Sometimes as leaders, we want to make peace to keep people on-side, to try and win their approval. But instead of peace, we need to make war against religious mindsets, entitlement and control. You have to go to war against that spirit that wants to stagnate things through legalism. The apostolic wants to release and empower. That's what the conviction within me was leading me towards. Many of my previous leaders and pillars of the old church had now left, and we were left with these young people that were not big givers, though they showed incredible generosity from the small amounts of money they did have. They were not experienced, nor holding any leadership roles, but they were the ones that I was fighting for and wanted to see given opportunities.

'There was a fight and irreligious love for Jesus and his kingdom that was just waiting to be unleashed"

RAISING UP BARBARIANS

To get the fire burning strongly in Hereford, we were going to need something different. We needed a new radical approach with our young men.

With everything that had happened previously with Luke, one of the most perplexing things had been that I had no idea what was really going on with my own son. He came to church every week, when all of the drinking, drugs and violence was happening, and would sit there (though not exactly cheerful), listening to me preach.

I knew that he was going through a dark time and was away from God, but the depth of his troubles were unknown to me. I thought that as Luke was sitting there in church, God would eventually convict him. There was a playact going on. I couldn't stand the thought that we would be turning up at church, 'playing Christians' and then going back to our lives. It was everything I was against.

I didn't blame Luke for this, I blamed the culture I had allowed at our church. I knew it had to change, and this would ignite in me again when Jonny Powell asked me for my time in 2006.

Jonny was 17, a country boy and farmer's son and had not long joined our church. He had grown up in the same Brethren denomination chapel as Heather, and in fact, his mum and dad had been Heather's youth leaders.

Jonny came to me and told me he was hungry for more of God and asked if I would meet with him to disciple him. These are not opportunities you should pass up when God sends them your way. I met with him a few times and spoke into his life. At the time I had also been reading a book by Erwin McManus `The Barbarian Way.'

'Barbarians wake to live and live life fully awake. To be filled with the Spirit of God is to be filled with dreams and visions that are too compelling to ignore.'

The book defines 'barbarian' as being uncivilised by Christian culture. There was a fight and irreligious love for Jesus and his kingdom that was just waiting to be unleashed. This book resonated so much with what I believed faith should be about: untamed, full of faith and fire, really believing that Jesus IS who He says He is.

I thought about how hungry Jonny had been to pursue more of God. What if instead of pouring into just one young man, I could pull a group of them together? If they were hungry and desiring it like Jonny was, then I could work with them.

So after a Freedom event in the evening, I did an invite only event for twelve of our young men and we all went back to Chris Cooke's house. I called it Barbarians (thanks Erwin) and got them all together and asked them, 'What do you think it means to be a Barbarian for Jesus?'

The amazing thing was that they already knew the answers. The seeds of living an untamed life, a passionate life, even a radical life for Christ were already inside of them. They just needed someone to water and nurture them. We had a time of prayer at the end and the room really lit up. The oldest was my son Josh at 19, and the youngest was Chris's son, another Josh, at 13.

Chris and I knew that we had just stumbled upon something that was going to become special. There was an expectation and a zeal in these young men every time we gathered them, and it quickly became their favourite time of the week.

Barbarians was a radical rescue mission. There are so many young men whom the enemy desires to ravage through his weapons of sin and shame, fighting to steal their lives away. This was our fight back. Having seen my own son almost get tragically robbed, I was disturbed into doing something for the next generation. I wanted to ensure that I had done all I could to inspire them to live lives full of passion for the kingdom of God and to love Him with every fibre of their beings.

One of the principles that I built into this group was honesty and integrity. I shared with them that living a life of no compromise was what we were called to. I remember teaching on the power of confession. We opened it up to the room after the teaching and asked the guys to share what was the greatest thing that was coming between them and their relationship with Jesus.

As the first guy shared, he shifted in his seat, nervously looking around. He had a choice to make. Did he say that he is struggling to read his Bible and to pray? Or did he share from his heart about the porn addiction that had been causing him shame, frustration and compromise?

In this environment, we managed to cultivate being real. We were brothers, and this was not a place of judgment. So he gave us the answer that hurt, not the answer that cost him nothing. This set the tone for the rest because it's very hard to give your cheap answer about 'being more disciplined' when someone has just poured their heart out about their own pain of sin and owned it.

It was so much more than a group for confession. It became a group that was about real, raw and honest worshipping of God. Not long after we started, we began meeting in an empty office space that we had leased. No natural light, fluorescent bulbs only. It was not ideal for setting an atmosphere, but these kinds of problems became irrelevant as these young men were not coming for a great show but to encounter the presence of God.

I remember my son, Josh, leading us in worship with an amplified bass guitar as he couldn't play the acoustic and one of the other lads playing a snare drum. It sounded horrific. I think eardrums were bleeding. But boy did we worship, heartfelt, stripped back, no pretense, crying out from the depths of our souls for more of Jesus in our lives, adoring him with everything that we were. There was no big track to jump to, but we were bouncing victoriously to the rhythm that our drummer Fin would play. He would play so hard his hands would bleed.

In the heat of the environment, they'd go King David style and whip off their shirts, singing with their arms around one another. Then they'd be on their knees, and then taking off their shoes as one of them sensed God telling us this was holy ground. It was raw, it was unpredictable and it was full of the Holy Spirit. We would often finish by praying for one of the guys, encouraging the others to lay hands on and share any word or scripture they had with authority. Lives were changed in these moments as we dared to use and promote the gifts of the Spirit.

I remember a special forces soldier joining us for the first time, (as Hereford is home to the SAS). He came in and was a part of our wild worship and heard a word that challenged him about being a man of God. We prayed for him at the end, and as we did, he began to weep. He had never been a part of or seen anything like what was happening as God was moving amongst us so powerfully. He began to pray out and thrust his arm into the air as he declared the sword of the Spirit to be in his hand. The young men in the room hit the floor with their knees. It was an incredibly powerful moment.

That special forces soldier would go on to leave the army in the years to come, move back to South Africa with his wife and four children, and lead one of our church plant teams to reach the people of his nation. But this was a huge marker in his journey of living a radical life for Christ, building in him the courage and conviction to pursue all that was ahead.

29

CONINGSBY STREET COURAGE

A few years went by, and what had started as a sparky fire was now becoming roaring flames. There was new confidence and fresh momentum. We had been obedient in taking the step to come over to Hereford, and God began to give us an upgrade. There was renovation happening in our worship, our leadership and our vision.

We started to have prophetic input again from Clem Ferris and he kept prophesying things directly and indirectly that said: 'Freedom Church is going to change the world'. He had never said this before in all the years of ministering into our church. Now he was repeating it again and again.

It was as though the prophetic was opening up the global call that was upon us. We had been leading for 20 years by this point, and had never heard such bold statements about what God was going to do through us. We were ready for it; we believed it! God was shaking us and preparing us, as He was about to do something powerful through this small church in Hereford.

As the church grew, and after years of hiring spaces for church, we knew that it was time to get our own building again. We searched through the properties of Hereford to find something that would fit our tribe. Chris and Karin Cooke were a part of our leadership team at the time, and lived in Hereford, so they offered to take a lead on the hunt for a home. Karin is an ex-rugby player, a passionate Welsh woman with short and spiky blonde hair and a colourful wardrobe. When Karin is on the hunt, she is going to find what she is looking for!

———————

After months of praying into it, Karin was walking down Coningsby Street where she saw a warehouse, an old Plumb Centre. She could see a man measuring it up and caught his attention through the window. She found out that he was measuring it up so that it could be leased out. She told him not to put it on the market, and to send her the details instead. It was an empty shell and needed a lot of work to be usable. No heating, no natural light, no insulation, and we would later find out there were some serious drainage issues.

We had taken the money we had left over from the Brook Hall sale and invested it in order to multiply it. We now had £200,000. We would need to invest all the money into this old warehouse to make it work. We needed to put in a second floor through half of the building, to create offices, a media room and kids spaces.

It had such amazing potential, but there were a couple of big risks with it too. We would have to change the planning permission on it, as it was currently defined as a commercial property, and in the UK that is complex.

We decided to see if we could get the permission changed and put in our application with the local council. That's when the next challenge arose. Hereford city centre was undergoing a major redevelopment with millions of pounds being spent on a new shopping centre, restaurant strip and access roads. The development group was called the Edgar Street Grid (ESG). The access road to change the traffic system of Hereford was going right through the building that we were trying to get planning permission for.

The director of the ESG had all the planning documents for the city centre across his desk, and when he saw ours he called me and arranged a meeting. When we met together in his executive office, he was very clear with me, 'Stay away from that building.' He showed me the plans for the city and how they intended to build a new road right through this old warehouse. He then took me out of his office and showed me two buildings that we should go for: one was a car wash and the other a converted house used for selling carpets. They were both a quarter of the size and very poorly placed.

I told him I preferred what we already had our eyes on. He got a little more serious then. He warned me, 'We can force your landlord to sell the building to the ESG, as we have a governmental and local mandate for the regeneration of the city. It's called a Compulsory Purchase Order (CPO). If you make all these renovations, you would lose everything you had invested into it.' I told him that I would go away and pray and consider what he said.

Maybe you are reading this and thinking the answer is obvious: find somewhere else! But we had been looking for a long period of time and this place was affordable, strategically placed and had lots of space for our growing church.

It was an incredibly difficult decision. Once again we were contending for a property, and I was leaning into God more than ever. One of my leadership team was against the idea. He told me that this was too great a risk to take and that taking this building on would be biting off more than we could chew.

The council came back and gave us a temporary planning permission for 12 months while they looked at it in further detail for the long term. I am not one for just doing my own thing and wanted the backing of those with me. I shared the journey with the church so they could be praying and standing with us.

One of our small group leaders came to me, serious and earnest. You could tell that he had something important to say. 'I want you to know something. If we go for this, and we take the lease on the building, make all the renovations to it, and spend every penny we have, then they take it from us - I will still back you. I will still believe in you and the vision God has given you'

I was stunned. Sometimes you get stirred and encouraged from the places you don't expect. But it gave me the courage I needed. I prayed, I sought counsel and I still felt the same conviction that this was the building God was calling us to. Despite the limited permissions of just a year, and regardless of threats of a multi-million pound, government-backed organisation, I had to follow what God was leading us to: to step out on another journey of faith and sign for the building. So we sailed into uncharted waters once again and trusted God.

We set our people to work on clearing out the dirty, tired old place, and it was a picture of joy. People with sledgehammers and smiles, covered in dust and dancing as they worked! God had given us land in the city, a place of our own. It would be a staging ground for invasions all around the globe to advance the Gospel.

We managed to find a steel mezzanine floor on Ebay from a closed down tele-marketing firm that had gone into administration. We sent up an articulated lorry to the north of England with a few of our guys to dismantle the whole thing and ship it back to Hereford. This alone saved us tens of thousands of pounds. We managed to do the whole conversion for less than we anticipated, which never happens.

We used cheap materials but modern design with lots of colour and IKEA magic everywhere. Heather was key in styling our new look and giving us freshness and a relevant vibe. In just six years, we had come a long way from the damp, old-looking Brook Hall. We now had a building that people always complimented when they came through the doors.

We moved in March 2009, and it was an incredible time of growth. There was a buzz about the place, another fresh wave of momentum as we opened our doors. I decided the only way to open my sermon was with a zip wire, so when it was time for the message I zipped from the balcony down to the stage. We were building the kingdom passionately, but we were going to have some fun along the way too!

We opened up our building for the community and made it available to chari-ties and organisations that would want to hire the space. We used it for parent and toddler groups, drama groups, dance groups. It was vibrant and always filled with different people using it and enjoying the spaces we had created.

After about a year, we had a booking from the ESG. They were using it as a meeting place for one of their planning meetings. I saw the director of the ESG, and he asked to meet with me again. I was intrigued to know what was going to happen next. Was he going to make his move to force us out?

He looked at me and said, 'You didn't listen to me, did you?' I grinned, still wondering what he was thinking. He continued, 'Well, we love what you have done with the building. It has become a real centre for the community. The ESG isn't just about commercial regeneration, it's about community regeneration, and what you have been doing is an amazing example of what we want to see.'

I tried to restrain myself from punching the air and bellowing the name of Jesus. He went on to tell me that they had redrawn and restructured the entire access road to allow us to stay where we were. They no longer had plans to knock down our building and saw us a key part of regenerating the community. The change had cost them lots of money. God had rewarded our faith once again even when it felt like the odds were against us.

3 0

HEART OF AUDACITY

Through the Coningsby Street miracle, God affirmed that audacity within me once more.

Do not limit your faith in what God can do! What God has for you is always going to be beyond what you can imagine or think. Yet so many of us live a boring and predictable Christianity that looks the same year on year.

That is not what God awoke you from the dead for. To live with limitations, wrapped up in your own preferences, was never His plan. He called you to a far greater dream of faith that is streaming from heaven. It disturbs me when people short sell their faith. It's like having access to a bazooka and choosing a water pistol instead. I pray that something of this story pulls the rug out from underneath you and awakens you to what God destined you for: to live audaciously.

Audacity looks like ordinary people living with boldness.

What are you going to do with the faith that you have? Will you be like the servant that buries what they are given in the ground (Matthew 25:24-25)? I think that many Christians treat their faith like a child's comfort blanket. It's a bit smelly and wet, It makes them feel more at ease, helping them go to sleep.

To live with audacity is nothing like a comfort blanket. Instead of comforting you, it can terrify you. Of course our faith should comfort us at times, bringing peace. But not without the audacity that God designed us for, that believes and asks for things that might seem ridiculous to others.

When I think of audacity, I think of a young shepherd boy taking on a giant. The story of David and Goliath personifies this shameless audacity that we are called to.

> Goliath stood and shouted to the ranks of Israel, 'Why do you come out and line up for battle? Am I not a Philistine, and are you not the servants of Saul? Choose a man and have him come down to me. If he is able to fight and kill me, we will become your subjects; but if I overcome him and kill him, you will become our subjects and serve us.'
>
> 1 Samuel 17:8-9 NIV

On hearing this, the Israelites were terrified and fled the battle line. No one wanted to face him. This went on for 40 days. Two countries at war but no one actually fighting. The Israelites dressed up in their armour each day, took up their battle positions and unleashed their war cry.

All noise and no action.

Then David arrived at the camp with his supplies. He was a young shepherd thought to be around 16 with no battle experience whatsoever, but he was incensed by the Philistine's insults. He began to ask what would be done for the man that kills Goliath?

David's own brothers heard him and were furious with him. I cannot tell you how many times I have seen audacity in others be quashed by those who are too afraid to act that way themselves, fearing that they will be embarrassed by someone else's boldness. David was serving his father's request by being the lunch delivery boy. Audacity starts with humility and willingness to serve. Audacity doesn't have to be boastful or arrogant.

David is sent for by King Saul after Saul hears of this audacity. David manages to convince him to let him represent Israel against Goliath. Saul was moved by the heart of boldness that David possessed.

David approaches the Philistine but not with traditional armour or weapons. He instead uses his slingshot to kill the giant and proceeds to take off his head. It is an incredible victory that is as famous with non-Christians as it is with Christians. Through this story highlights a dramatic overcoming of the odds because of the heart of audacity in a young man.

We see the humility of the sandwich delivery boy coupled with the confidence of a warrior. As I mentioned, confidence can be misunderstood as arrogance. We cannot stop others' judgments, but we can ensure the humility of our own hearts that only God can see.

God loves for the downtrodden and forgotten to rise up. It's the ones that others reject, but God calls out, so that they would take up the confidence that He has called them to.

Reading this you might think this kind of audacity is just for the young, but I would show you Caleb, who at the age of 85 was still audacious enough to believe he could go into battle and seize the land that God had promised him:

> 'So here I am today, eighty-five years old! I am still as strong today as the day Moses sent me out; I'm just as vigorous to go out to battle now as I was then.'
>
> Joshua 14:10-11 NIV

It has nothing to do with age and everything to do with our mindset.

Audacity plays to win. Paul wrote that we should run the race in such a way as to win the prize! (1 Cor 9:24). So let's start demanding more from ourselves, calling brothers and sisters to a higher standard. Let's become the cheeky, audacious, faith-inspired lot we were called to be!

When we were faced with the threat of the eviction of Coningsby Street, I could either crumble underneath the pressure or defy the giant that sought to intimidate us. I made a choice to seize hold of the vision that God has for us, holding on to his promises rather than believing the loud taunts of the enemy.

To be audacious, you have to take a stand. When all around you are complacent, when it is easy to just go with the consensus, you must have the boldness to be different. I want to tell you that all things are possible in your life through the power of the name of Jesus.

This is dangerous stuff that can get messy, but it can also bring down giants. Will you shake off the passive nature that so many of us have inherited and embrace the call of audacity?

HEART OF AUDACITY QUESTIONS TO CONSIDER:

- Not many of us need to face down a literal giant in our lifetime, but there are many spiritual giants, intimidating scenarios and battle-like circumstances we are called to triumph over. Where is audacity required of you in this season?
- How can you represent the unshakable, victorious nature of God in that arena?
- Where has intimidation set in, and how can audacity and boldness rise up in you again? What do you need to dwell on, read, remember, or who can you speak to that will remind you of the God-given audacity within you?

Relentless Reaching

First and Best

Heart and Soul

Punching Above Our Weight

Warrior Poet

Wildfire

Live Full, Die Empty

Changeling

Everything's A Gift

Raise The Next

We Will Elevate

Relevant To Our Time

31

AMERICAN MUSCLE

Our Coningsby Street days were really very special in our journey. We saw lots of young people coming into our church. When we used to hold baptisms in Leominster there would be 3-4 people. In Coningsby St, we now had 17-20 people, three or four times a year. Things were gaining radical momentum, and we were seeing our dreams come to life as a generation was rising up to claim their place in the Kingdom.

We had a group of young leaders, a number of them just leaving sixth-form college, who were sold out for the church and ready for more. They didn't want just to turn up at church next week, they wanted more input and shaping. What were we going to do with them? I wanted to give them a better foundation than I had had at Bible College. It had to be more engaging, more equipping and transformative.

My daughter in-law Rose was 22 at the time and was a part of our Eldership team. She had been thinking on a plan and strategy, along with Chris Cooke, on how we could get the most out of these young people who wanted to give us their time.

Rose got together with my eldest son Josh, when she was 16 and he was 17. To many they would be seen as just kids at this point, but we always valued them and took them seriously. Rose grew up on a farm in the south of Herefordshire, and each week she would get a lift into Hereford with her parents, then catch a train to Leominster and stay with us for the weekend. As the months went by, Rose and Josh knew they had found love and wanted to get married. Amazingly, Rose had grown up in the same small Brethren country-side chapel as Heather.

Rose loved the community of her church and had great friendships there but didn't have much of a consistent relationship with God outside of the hymn book and the youth group. As she came along to New Life Community Church, she encountered an expression of praise and worship and a passion that was provocative to her. She liked it, but it was tough for her to engage with. One night we prayed for people to receive the Holy Spirit for the first time. We prayed for Rose and she cried so much she didn't have a tear left in her.

She came away with us on a family holiday to Spain, and after the rest of the boys had gone to bed, we stayed up with Josh and Rose on the veranda, talking to them about prayer. Rose had been coming to our church for about a year at this point and been in a Christian environment all her life but had never prayed aloud. It was such a battle, but inside Rose was a gifted communicator, prayer and teacher.

As soon as the move over to Hereford began, we got Josh and Rose involved in the transformation of our church, from the design, to the creativity, to the strategy and to helping win their generation. By 2009, Rose had spoken at the church, led worship, led our weekly prayer meetings and become a part of our leadership team. Rose and Josh both have a gift of leadership, and God had warned me off discounting my own family just because we were related. So Rose had grown up in, and led through, the vital transformation and crossing over of our church and had been raised in this new and dynamic culture that we had created.

She had vision for these young leaders and with the support of Chris Cooke, put together a programme for half a day's teaching over a nine month period. It was called the 'Freedom Internship.' We set it up in one of our conference rooms in the Freedom Centre on Coningsby Street and taught the students about the Church, the five-fold ministry, the gifts of the spirit and church culture. It was successful and gathered momentum as the year went on.

Rose and Chris had been teaching a lot about our way of doing church, but Rose had a conviction that we needed to go and see what others were doing and learn from them. We looked at various options, but we'd just started looking at some of the video and creativity coming out of Elevation Church, and it was super inspiring. That had led us to the teaching of Pastor Steven Furtick and through him we also found another pastor that we loved, Pastor Perry Noble at Newspring Church. Elevation had only been going for about four years but was already, along with Newspring, among the fastest growing churches in America.

The two churches were less than two hours apart, and there were a couple more we wanted to visit in the area too. Rose led us towards Elevation and Newspring in North and South Carolina, and it would turn out to be a prophetic decision with colossal impact. We booked the trip with Chris Cooke, Josh, a pregnant Rose and nine interns heading out to go and learn from these megachurch power houses.

It was late May 2010 when the team turned up at the airport in Charlotte, North Carolina, most of them visiting the USA for the first time. A huge, white Ford E Series was the vehicle that would transport them around the Carolinas.

The first thing that impacted them was the size of everything. Big cars, big roads, big houses, big microwaves! The team were on a high, all getting to travel together and to see what God would do. They got in their rooms at the Econolodge for the night and got into trouble for jumping in the pool after hours.

In high spirits, the next day they went to Elevation Church's Matthews Campus. There was an assumption at how they would be received at Elevation. Lovable Brits on tour with interesting accents - what's not to love? But when moving through the sleek, modern, impressive building, they were to find out that this trip was not just going to be a cute Q and A. It was going to be intense at times and deeply challenging.

Larry gave them a tour of the building and spent the next four hours with our team. Josh told me that the four hours that they had with Larry, though brutal at times, was the best outside input that he had ever received. No message, no podcast, no book, no conference had given as much challenge and application as those four hours with Larry.

Elevation Church was making waves and headlines as a brand new church that had become thousands in just a few years. They had attracted visitors from all over the world who were hoping to try and glean their secret from them. Some of these visitors would inevitably waste their time, be critical, religious or consuming. This meant Larry was a kind of gatekeeper to the church to protect them but also to ward off people who were there to be difficult.

That day, Larry shared some invaluable wisdom from the Elevation treasure trove of how to do ministry. We learnt about volunteering systems, about how to train volunteers effectively and to raise leaders that represent the heart of your church. They shared their resources and their manuals with us, and it was like gold dust. We had never heard or seen church being done so excellently. Larry told us about their VIP team, a team of people specifically in place for welcoming first time guests with a VIP treatment that would mean that they were cared for, valued and loved from the moment that they drove into the parking lot.

The most important piece of strategy that they shared with us, that would be transformational in the way that we built the church, was capturing the heart of church values and identity in their DNA. This was a set of values that defined and communicated to new people coming into the church, and that served to remind ongoing members about what the church stood for and who they were.

We knew who we were as a church; we had plenty of personality. We even had 'Commitments' - statements that kind of did the same thing. But Elevation had taken the idea from ING bank, to package your core values with creative names, simple statements and striking icons. When the team got back, we knew this was for us as a leadership team and went to work straight away on repackaging and communicating who God had called us to be in our newly formed DNA.

Within just eight weeks we were sharing them with the church. This was so important to us: to get people used to our DNA and integrating it throughout our church, so that we could replicate who we were. Over the years we have developed and refined our DNA, but these are the current descriptions of each one:

Wildfire

Expressing outwardly, the work that God has done inwardly, our faith and love will not be contained. We have a contagious passion for Jesus that is raw, real, and unapologetic.

Warrior Poets

We reflect the creator by embracing and expressing creativity. The colour of our lives becoming a revolt against the mundane and ordinary. We communicate the Gospel with the life and vibrancy in which it was intended.

Relevant To Our Time

We will share an ageless message that engages the next generation and is easily understood by unchurched people. We will adapt our methods and lay down our preferences for the times and cultures we are called to reach.

Changeling

We are on a constant journey of transformation and personal freedom to become more like Jesus. We refuse to get stuck in our ways, taking individual responsibility for our learning and growth.

First and Best

We will serve God and our church with all that we have, giving sacrificially to the one who gave us everything. We won't just go through the motions or do the minimum. The best of our talents, time and resources will be used for the Kingdom.

We Will Elevate

We freely give honour to everyone: women, men, all ages and all races. We reveal God's value for each person by opening our homes and our lives. We honour leaders who serve us. We honour God when we build a culture that honours people.

Punching Above Our Weight

With audacious faith, we set impossible goals, take bold, confident steps and watch our God move. We are giant-killers who refuse to limit the Holy Spirit.

Relentless Reaching

We persistently share the hope and salvation of Jesus with our family, friends and communities. We won't stand by and be silent about the truth and love God has for this world.

Heart and Soul

We take personal responsibility for the vision and unity of our church. We are committed to making God's Kingdom the central cause of our lives, no matter the cost.

Everything's A Gift

We intentionally celebrate and give thanks. We shake off complacency and entitlement to overflow with gratitude for God, our lives and one another. Practicing thankfulness gives us a joy that will sustain us.

Live Full, Die Empty

We are adventurers, who take risks and grab life by the horns. Our joy stands in opposition to lifeless religion. Dancing and laughter mark our lives, and we are determined to release all our potential before we die.

Raise the Next

We lovingly disciple, we release leadership, we inspire kingdom influencers and plant new churches. We share the truths and opportunities given to us, changing the world through a legacy of multiplication.

These DNA have allowed our church to replicate who we are, wherever we are in the world. It has been an invaluable tool that has creatively expressed the heart and identity of our church.

32

AN UNLIKELY FRIENDSHIP

Next up on the group's agenda was a visit to Newspring Church in Anderson, South Carolina. Anderson is a small city of just 30,000 people, it is a rural place, similar to Hereford, not the most promising. And yet in the year 2000, Pastor Perry Noble started Newspring as a Monday evening Bible study group, and in the next decade it grew to a State-wide church of 20,000 people.

It was an amazing and remarkable thing, and at their peak Newspring was the second fastest growing church in America. Our team turned up in their big white van, after stopping for a Chick-fil-A on the way down from Charlotte and couldn't believe their eyes. In the middle of what seemed like nowhere, on the outskirts of the city of Anderson, were the huge campus buildings of Newspring. The parking lot alone was big enough to get lost in.

Chris had arranged to meet someone at the building to see inside. They met a young woman with a sticker on her jumper, stating her name and her volunteer area: 'Tour guide'. The church was making such huge waves domestically and internationally that they had trained a group of volunteers to specifically give tours to all of the people that were pouring in from around the country and across the world.

So many people were getting saved and finding an authentic church community at Newspring that it had grown exponentially. It was staggering for the team to see the contrast. Coming from our story, which originated in Leominster, had taken us 22 years, and at this point we were still under 200 people. As the tour guide took the team around, it was clear that there was excellence running through everything that Newspring was doing and that their facilities must have cost tens of millions of dollars.

It was hugely inspirational and the team later got to spend time with some of the leadership team, asking them questions, and trying to absorb and learn from them as much as possible. The experience at Elevation had been so valuable, but it had been very clear that there was no chance of getting to meet Pastor Steven. This made it an even greater surprise when the team were introduced to Pastor Perry in the Newspring 'Green Room' before the 6pm service.

They had a great time and laughed at the differences in culture. The group were shown to their seats in a huge auditorium that had the capacity of 3000 people and were taken to the front row, feeling incredibly honoured and humbled.

The worship began and the quality, musicianship, and sound system was of the highest level. Our team didn't know any of the songs, but this didn't stop them from worshipping, and they were exactly how they always are: passionate, singing, shouting, jumping, dancing.

Pastor Perry had been watching from the balcony as it was his third service of the day. He saw something was different about our group. He had felt energised by being around them before the service had begun and had seen their passion as they worshipped, unashamed in front of 3000 people. He spoke and was cheered on by our team, shouting 'Amen' and 'Come on!' as he delivered his message.

The room cleared out, and one of Pastor Perry's staff came up to our team, 'Could you stay here a moment, Pastor Perry would like to pray with you before you go.' As the room was emptied, Pastor Perry joined our guys from behind the stage, and they huddled together as he prayed. He thanked God for them, prayed a blessing on them, and expressed how he was also moved by them.

182

The team finished their trip and came back full of inspiration, strategy and passion for what was to come. We began to implement the DNA into our church and came up with training programmes for our volunteers to take our church to a whole new level of intentionality and excellence. It was a fresh wave of excitement and enthusiasm that swept us up as we discovered these new ways to walk out our identity.

Just a few weeks after the team had got back from the States, Pastor Perry posted a blog about how his heart had been stirred for the UK, and he planned to hold a roundtable conference at a church in Milton Keynes. A day to teach and to connect to those that were interested. It was open to anyone who wanted to come from across Europe, with no ticketing and no costs. This was to be my first opportunity to meet Perry and the Newspring team for myself, so when September came, we travelled to Milton Keynes.

We had been praying into a connection and relationship that would spur us on and help us go to the next level as a church. Since the early days of planting the church out of my parents church in Hereford, we had been pretty isolated. In the mid-nineties my parents had handed on their church, and after about 12 months it had amalgamated with another congregation in Hereford.

I was a part of some joint-pastor groups in the county for a number of years, but this felt more dutiful than relational. We were a part of a church network which for a season was really helpful, until I realised that the churches and pastors this network was planting and raising were completely different from the church that God was calling us to build and to the leader that I was.

We had pushed some doors to other relationships, but none had opened. We didn't have a big network or a lot of friends within the Christian world, so after praying into it for a number of years, we really felt that God was wanting to connect us in relationship with another church for input and accountability. At this mini-conference day, along with Newspring, there would also be other pastors for us to connect to. We went with an expectation of forging a relationship.

I travelled with our whole leadership team and some of the interns that had travelled to the USA. We were all excited about what God was going to do that day, but we didn't know what to expect. There were about 50 people who had shown up from across the UK, and even a small band of teenagers from Estonia that had slept in the airport as they had been so keen to come and learn from Perry and the Newspring team.

Perry is a giant of a man, at 6'5', and uses his dinner-plate size hands to talk a lot. He has a strong southern accent and loves to crack the jokes, especially if they make the religious squirm a bit. Perry shared about church building and gave leadership lessons to the group, allowing for some Q and A too.

One of the most striking things about the day was how Perry opened himself up about his own struggles with pornography and depression. He was vulnerable and honest in a way I had never seen a pastor be before.

I thanked Perry, not only for the day but for hosting our interns when they had visited the church, and he lit up as he recounted their visit. 'We loved your team! We had so much fun with them. After speaking with them, it was what made me want to come over to the UK and see how I could assist the church here.'

We continued to converse, and three times Perry said to me, 'If there is anything we can do to help, just let us know.' Once is polite, twice got my attention, but a third time made me realise he was serious and really meant it. No one ever offered to help us. We were like the desert rats, from World War II, we had dug in, we had backbone, we knew how to fight our corner. I had learnt to not rely on others, we had to take responsibility for ourselves.

But here we were in Milton Keynes, with this southern-talking, giant, American, megachurch pastor and he was offering help, earnestly and authentically. He meant it. It baffled me. I thanked him and said that I would be in touch. As we travelled back to Hereford, I had an excitement in my spirit, believing that God was going to do more through this connection. A dose of Ephesians 3:20 'more than you ask or imagine' was at play in what God was going to do through this new friendship.

At this point our leadership team had been dreaming big about our very first church plant out of Herefordshire. We had looked at the surrounding cities and decided upon the capital of Wales, Cardiff which was about an hour away for us. We went on the journey of researching how it would look to plant a church and search out a venue. We went to one of the most iconic venues in the city, 'Cardiff National Museum', and looked at the 300 seater Reardon Smith Theatre and decided that this was the place for us to begin. It had a greater seating capacity than our current church in Hereford. And yet we believed that this old lecture theatre, right in the heart of the city and located so close to the University, was where God was calling us to go.

I had been thinking and praying about what Perry had said to me. 'If there is anything we can do to help, just let us know'. As time went on, I believed that this was not only about offering to pray for us. I decided to put it to the test, and envisioned my son Jordan, who at 19 was our Creative Director, to make a video that would communicate our vision for planting a church in Cardiff.

Jordan came up with a video of him and Josh Cooke, in military jackets, leaning over a world map on a table, lit by a desk lamp. In the video, they were talking about the continents of the world and the great and mighty works that God was doing. They talked about the movements of revival coming out of South America and the sounds of worship leading the church to lift up the name of Jesus like never before coming from Australia.

They passed through all the continents until they came to Europe. A barren wasteland of religion and former glory that was symbolically covered in dust on the map. The two young commanders blow the dust away and beckon fresh awakening in Europe, in the UK, and declare that an outpost of hope will be set up in Cardiff.

After this dramatic telling of our church plant venture was done, the video went to me talking about our heart to plant church, throwing back to the old Welsh revival of 100 years ago and talking about our hearts yearning to plant church and see salvation multiply in the UK. It was an invite to Newspring to join with us and partner financially in helping us get this church started.

We sent our video over to Newspring and sent a lot of prayers up to heaven.

We heard back from Perry a week later to say that they had played their video in their leadership meeting that week and all been blown away by the power and faith of it.

We had been really convicted to put one particular line into what we shared in our 'pitch'. I stated that we believed God had called us to do this, and He would make a way, with or without Newspring. We were not begging for their help but offering them the opportunity to be involved, 'but we're going anyway'.

Perry told me that really struck them as they get a lot of requests for finance from all over the world. But a lot of people will imply that if they don't get help, then it won't happen. It was an audacious statement of faith in God and who he had called us to be rather than a cry for help.

Perry shared with me that when he had been at seminary, he had been given a small booklet about the Welsh revival and had read the whole thing: it had fascinated him. That seed had been planted years and years ago but had prepared Perry for our conversation and connection, so that he knew Wales, Cardiff and the significance of the Welsh Revival.

Chris Cooke took a call from one of Perry's leadership team. He then called me to let me know what it was about. I had been out driving with Heather, so we pulled over into a lay-by. He let me know that after discussing it with his team, Pastor Perry had said that they would cover the first six months of our rent.

I immediately rang Pastor Perry and after thanking him and Newspring, we put the phone down, got out of the car, and started running around the lay-by together, laughing and crying: 'Someone actually believes in us!' It was great that they were going to help us financially, but what it represented was even more powerful to us. We had relational backing and belief.

We were so grateful, full of joy and hope. God had gone before us and made an incredible connection with Newspring. We were riding on a high, the church in Hereford was flying, we had unrelenting passion, unprecedented unity, unfaltering momentum. But the enemy was about to throw a stick in our spokes that would shake us and try to break us.

33

HITTING THE HEADLINES

Two weeks before the momentous launch of our first ever church plant out of Herefordshire, we had a call from the only newspaper in Hereford which had a large readership at the time. In a small city and county with no competition, they were very influential. They called us to say they were going to be doing an article about our church and wanted to get some quotes in response to some of their content.

Karin Cooke, part of our leadership team at the time, answered their questions. I didn't think that much of it. From the nature of the questions that had been asked by the journalist, I expected a bit of criticism perhaps but nothing to the extent of what was to come. We waited for the day to arrive, and picked up the freshly delivered copies late on a Wednesday night ready for its sale the next morning.

Tens of thousands of copies were being delivered to every petrol station, news agent, and grocery store across the county. Accompanied with the A frame that would carry the leading headline from the newspaper that would be on streets, forecourts and in shop windows all around us. We had made the front page.

'Church or 'CULT'?

There is not much worse that you can say against a church. The word cult brings an immediate and powerful picture to all who hear it (and in capital letters to emphasise the point). The article was shocking, it was tabloid stuff, with lies and exaggerations, the kind of gossip that would sell like hotcakes in a small place like Herefordshire. The article was based on the accusations of three people. We knew though:

'Our struggle is not against flesh and blood, but against the rulers, against the authorities, against the powers of this dark world and against the spiritual forces of evil in the heavenly realms'

Eph 6:12

This was an out and out spiritual assault on our church, which had been causing far too much disturbance for the enemy's liking.

We had been accused of three main things in the article: brainwashing, mass baptisms and running a fight club

First of all, what church doesn't want to be accused of mass baptisms?! It was fantastic, we had been baptising up to 20 people every three months and were seeing amazing things in our relatively small city. There were about 25-30 in just one school that had all been hugely impacted, got saved and been baptised, becoming a part of our church. They were having their own prayer meetings at lunchtimes in the school together. It was staggering: we had never seen so many teenagers coming to Jesus at one time.

In Acts 2:41, 3000 people got baptised: now that's a mass baptism.

There was some basis for their third accusation of our fight club. We had put on a charity boxing night to raise money for our charity, 'Heart for Africa,' some months before. It was two minutes of sparring between some of the guys in our church. We thought it was brilliantly funny and posted it to Facebook. We were naive with some of the things that we had posted online, never imagining how much things could be taken out of context and used against us.

The front-page article had a picture of a woman looking at our building, with a torch lit underneath her chin to make her look like she was getting sucked into the cult. It also featured a picture that they had lifted off our website of my son Jordan. We had been to a men's conference a few years before and on the last night, had bought a load of blue face paint and gone full Braveheart style, decorating our faces with Celtic war paint. We had an absolute riot and started painting people all over the conference, including the cameraman. We had taken a couple of pictures and put some on our website that talked about our mens' group: 'Barbarians'.

But now this picture of my son, Jordan, with his blue face paint on, mid-roar, was being used in the context of us being a cult, and we looked completely bonkers.

Looking at this article, it really was unbelievable. They had really gone to town. They even accused us of not empowering women, even though we had a woman acting as our spokesperson.

———

The biggest cost to us immediately was our children and teenagers in schools and colleges who began to get bullied. My own son Isaac was called 'cult-boy' which was upsetting. Chris and Karin's daughter Ffion had so much abuse levelled at her that she came out of school for a few days until it died down.

I'm not one for taking things lying down, so I called our leaders together to make a plan. It was the injustice of it that was so infuriating. These lies had been told about us, then printed and distributed all over the city. I wanted to call the church together to do a march and get our church on display to show that we were real people, families and teenagers, children, teachers, business-men, mums, builders. Normal Herefordians, not this mysterious, dark, brain-washing cult as we had been portrayed.

I was pretty fired up: I wanted to do a burning barrel and burn a load of their newspapers! We even had some banners printed to hang on the front of the church about the discrimination of the newspaper against Christians. But after 24 hours of cooling off and getting some counsel from the rest of my team, it was clear that perhaps this would not be the best reaction; though something in me still wished we had done it!

We put together a video response that we could at least get our voice heard in some way. We started off by poking a bit of fun at the ridiculousness of the whole thing. Our video genius, George Downes, got hold of a plastic brain, and as the camera rolls he is distracted with his work, with a cleaning spray and a cloth, 'Oh sorry, didn't see you there! Just doing a bit of brainwashing...'

He cracked a few more jokes and then the video came over to me and our leadership team to talk a bit more seriously about the allegations that had been made and the reasons why it was not true. We had thousands of views on the video, and it was a lift to us to be able to fight back in some way. But the thousands of views was nothing compared to the ten of thousands that read the newspaper.

Chris and Karin arranged a meeting with the newspaper to challenge them. We talked about the impact it had upon the children of our church. The editor and the journalist were completely indifferent. They then proceeded to ask Chris and Karin some questions to which they responded 'Hold on, are you doing another article?' The Hereford Times put us on page one again the following week about another thing they had taken issue with. Then week three came round, and they had printed another article about us on page three. The editor had even said: 'At the end of the day I'm here to sell papers. And this sells papers.'

This was a targeted and intentional smear on our church. It had sold lots of newspapers and been the talk of the town. I was told: 'Today's news, tomorrow's fish and chip paper,' but I think these people didn't realise how a place like Hereford can talk and also that the internet can't be made into chip paper. It would pop up for anyone looking for our church on Google, and it still does.

In the years to come, we would have a further four articles written about us. Things changed almost immediately. We had seen huge traction with youth and students, but most of them were stopped from coming by concerned parents who were worried that their child had got mixed up in a cult. Sadly, people didn't come to see for themselves but made their decision from what they had read and heard.

Since our move to Hereford, we had a constant flow of new people coming in, visiting and staying. Our VIP (first-time guest) count hit rock bottom as new people through the doors dried up. It robbed a lot of confidence from the people that had been doing the inviting, bringing friends, family and neighbours to church. People felt awkward and embarrassed to talk about our church that was perceived to be a cult, some even not wanting to be associated with us. Our people had been so proud to call us their church. But now some were fearful, second-guessing how people would respond to them when they found out they went to 'that Freedom Church.'

It was surprising to us that it served as an encouragement and inspiration to some of the other churches. They said that they would love to be causing a disturbance like we were. They said they wished it was them on the front of the paper! But the ripples continued from the article, with a brick being thrown through our church window, the front of our church being graffitied and people making threats to burn down our building.

One of the positives is that it cemented the bond between Perry and I. He moved in like an older brother in a school punch up, offering prayer, support and talking through our response. I remember him discouraging me from trying to take on the newspaper in a legal battle, saying: 'It's like getting in a fight with a pig, you both get covered in mud, but the pig enjoys it.'

We had made plans to visit the USA before Cardiff was to launch, as NewSpring were holding a church leaders conference and had invited Heather and I to attend. The timing of it was a week after the article had come out and a week before the Cardiff campus opened. We had an amazing time continuing to build our relationship with the Newspring team and Perry.

34

THE BRIDE

One of the hardest things about the article was seeing something so precious to us and to God getting trashed publicly.

When I was a young man, there was a scripture that breathed life to me. It gave me a revelation. It has become one of the most meaningful and important scriptures to me and ignited a passionate love in my heart for the church.

> *Husbands, love your wives, just as Christ loved the church and gave himself up for her to make her holy, cleansing her by the washing with water through the word, and to present her to himself as a radiant church, without stain or wrinkle or any other blemish, but holy and blameless. In this same way, husbands ought to love their wives as their own bodies. He who loves his wife loves himself. After all, no one ever hated their own body, but they feed and care for their body, just as Christ does the church— for we are members of his body. 'For this reason a man will leave his father and mother and be united to his wife, and the two will become one flesh.'This is a profound mystery—but I am talking about Christ and the church.*
>
> *Ephesians 5:25-32 NIV*

Paul writes about the global family of Christians being a bride, with Christ our bridegroom. If this is Christ's heart towards the church, how can so many believers treat her with such indifference, or as a necessary duty or chore to get to Jesus? Is that the way you would want your spouse to be treated? To be used to get to you?

The bride's preparation is a big part of the wedding day. The hair, the make up and of course, the dress. That she should be presented without spot or blemish. That is what we should be committing our lives to do. We are those who get this bride ready for the bridegroom, preparing her, ushering her towards her destiny. We're not just allowing the hand-me down dress to be acceptable but giving her the best, preparing her with holiness and righteousness through 'the washing of the word'.

Our lives as Christians should be wrapped up in preparing for this great and eternal wedding.

It is impossible to love Jesus and hate his Church. We cannot divorce the two, they are wrapped up within one another. But so many believers have nothing to do with his Church.

How can you talk about the bride of Christ with disdain when you are part of that very bride? 'No one ever hated their own body,' and yet that is what we do when we dishonour and disrespect the Church. When we criticise and voice opposition against the church, we criticise ourselves. It is like publicly criticising your own wife, 'Oh yeah, we are married. But she disgusts me, so we stay in different rooms.'

I want to encourage and implore your heart to love the bride of Christ. You were made to love Jesus and His church. It is within you. Perhaps you have been hurt by those that have carried the name or authority of the Church, some who were not truly a part of the bride, but she has taken the flack for their wrongdoing. Hurt has caused many to look at her with disdain or bitterness.

However, she is beautiful, she is the one that Christ died for. You yourself, if a believer, are a part of the bride of Christ. You cannot therefore hold offence or hurt against her and be distanced from her. How can you divorce a part of your own body and find it despicable?

There are those that treat the bride of Christ like a prostitute. Using her whenever they need gratification, dropping a bit of money into the pot, and then not showing her any affection until they need something again. There are many that have abused the bride, treating the wife of Christ with ill-will, and we need to repent.

We can read Ephesians 5 and think that marriage is being used as a picture of Jesus and His Church, but actually Jesus and His Church is the original design, the eternal picture. Marriage has been given to us as a symbol to represent Jesus and His Church, not the other way around. Do you want to fully understand it? You can't. It's a 'profound mystery'. I'm in love with the bride. We often say, 'We love our church.' We express this by the way we live, the way we speak to one another, and the priorities that we have.

Jesus' life and whole purpose is totally wrapped up in the bride. He came to save us, to be our ransom and to purchase the bride with his blood. But the wedding has not taken place yet. It is what Jesus so eagerly desires, to be united with His bride. He waits for her to be prepared. He waits for this Gospel to have maximum impact, to see as many souls saved as possible.

When he returns, he will be coming back for his Church. In 2 Corinthians 3:18, it says that we are 'being transformed into His image.' So we are becoming like Jesus. To be like him, we must also give our life for the bride, to love her just as He does. He does not force us against our will; He gives us the choice. He is calling people around the world right now to love His church. We are building towards a crescendo as we head towards that great wedding day.

As Christians, we must be more conscious of this truth: history and creation itself are collaborating together for the sole purpose of preparing the bride for His return, creation's ultimate purpose.

When the printing press was created, was that so that we could just enjoy the beauty of human literature? No, it was so that the Word of God could become accessible in a way that it had never been before. The first book to be printed was a Bible. It was for the bride.

If we think of the air travel that humanity now has access to, was it so that we could have nicer holidays? Better Instagram backdrops? Or was it to be able to mobilise the bride of Christ in a whole new way to be able to answer the call of the great commission to 'Go' into all the world?

When we see the rapid development of technology, is it just so that we can post our relationship status? Or is it so that we can put the gospel into hands all over the world without even being there physically through the mediums of pictures, video, text through the power of the internet? It's all for the bride.

It is amazing, the unawareness that we have that credits mankind for these innovations. Where do we think we got the ideas? God is depositing specific breakthroughs at specific times for his bride. Even now, there are God-whispered technologies that are being created that will allow us to be able to reach more people than ever before. There are world-changing advancements being made every day. It's like the increase in pace in the build up to a wedding day.

We are caught up in the momentum of history and creation, heading towards the most amazing wedding imaginable. Let this give you confidence and assurance that when you have not seen those prayers yet answered, when your friends have just left your church, when you are in that difficult season: the wedding is still inevitable.

The bridegroom will return for the bride, and we must attend to her, prepare her, give our lives for her. The church needs to keep praying, keep believing, keep preaching and keep serving in anticipation of His arrival. Then that momentous day will come when Jesus, the bridegroom, is united with his Church, the bride, and there will be a great feast. (Rev 19:6-9)

In light of this, the bride is not secondary but should be the very epicentre of your life. If you are a businessman, then I believe that you are a businessman to raise money for the bride of Christ. Everything we do should stem and flow to and from the bride. A businessman who just attends church, without making it the centre of his purpose, has not yet had a revelation of the bride of Christ.

Your family should be about the bride. If your family is about little Johnny being the next football superstar, it will reflect in your priorities and choices of your time, i.e. skipping church for football practice. And how would you justify it? You'll say that this might be little Johnny's opportunity! Wait and see how that pans out, when little Johnny grows up, having failed to make it as a footballer and has no value for the bride of Christ in his life.

Many would detach themselves from the church community in pursuit of a job in another city to further their career. Would we move somewhere for the Church? We should. The bride being the epicenter means making decisions that centre around the Church. This includes decisions about our finances, our holidays, our jobs, just as it would in a married relationship. If you joined the army without telling your wife, what would that say about the place that she has in your life or the way you value her? It would be hurtful and self-absorbed.

Jesus laid down his life for the bride. What drove him on through the utter pain and agony of the cross was the joy that was set before him. The joy that kept him going was you, it was me, it was the believers that make up his bride. There is a convergence happening as we head towards our destiny of that great wedding day. Let each of us be prepared! When He does return, he won't come for a bride who is hanging on by her finger-tips but a victorious, overcoming church that has prepared herself for that great day.

There are many Christians who want to batten down the hatches and await the return of Jesus instead of accelerating towards the finish. As the wedding day draws closer, there will be glory around the world for the bride. There will be miracles; there will be an increase in signs and wonders. Our King has a passion for the bride. Will you love her like he does?

THE BRIDE QUESTIONS TO CONSIDER:

- What do you love about the Church? How is that love seen in your life?
- Are there things that need to be forgiven? Grievances or offences caused by people within the Church that affect the way you see her

now? How can you lay those down and move on healthily, serving her as Jesus asks you to?

- There is no claim that the Bride, the church, is already perfect, but there is an invitation to us to help prepare her. How can you play your part in that work? What does it require of you?

CALLING THEM UP

We had an amazing unity in our leadership team with Heather and I having Chris and Karin and Josh and Rose alongside us. There was a sense that we could do anything together.

But we needed more hands to the plough to pull off the vision that God had put on our hearts. We needed people that were going to rally behind the vision, to shoulder this call to church-plant alongside us. We also needed pastors and leaders.

So in October 2010 we had a leadership away day. We planned and strategised for 2011 but put aside time at the end of the day to invite this next tier of leaders to join us for the evening. These were couples with young families who loved our church and had greater capacity and leadership than they were currently walking in.

As the couples arrived at 5pm on that Saturday afternoon at a converted barn in the countryside of Wales, they were not expecting the call that was about to come their way. One of the mums came in and couldn't hide her feelings: 'Who puts on a meeting at 5pm for people who have small children?!' One of those half jokes. Oh dear.

We were not deterred and set about praying together and putting some questions to them to answer as couples about where they were at, what their vision was, and what they felt God was speaking to them. They went off together as couples to talk things through and get some answers. You could see some thoughtful and intense conversations happening across the room.

We then called them back together and unveiled our plans for 2011: we would be planting a church in Cardiff in the new year. The group was stunned, excited, speechless and full of enthusiasm. You could see the vision come alive in them as we had shared it.

We had our first pastors that we would send in the room: Dave and Saz Thomas, who were in their mid-twenties. Dave was Cardiff-born and raised. They didn't know that we were going to send them yet, but we already had them in our hearts as we had prayed and prepared to share the news.

But that was not the only church that we would be starting in 2011. Cardiff city was over an hour away from Hereford. But we were going to do something even more radical and daring.

We had been reaching out to Kampala, Uganda since 2005 when I had been to a conference there. I had seen the desperation of poverty and had an amazing connection with a pastor who had been assisting as my interpreter. His name was Deo and he had an extraordinary testimony, growing up as a street fighter to getting radically saved and later becoming a pastor.

We struck up a friendship, and I got to see his church, 'Word of Life Ministries', which was based in an area called Kosovo in Kampala. It was named after the atrocities of what happened in Eastern Europe as some terrible things had happened in this area too, with many people being buried there.

When I had returned to Hereford, I mobilised the church around doing what we could to support this vision. We set up a charity 'Heart for Africa', a child sponsorship programme, helping children to get an education. We also undertook specific building projects to support the church's school. We took a number of trips over to Kampala, doing missionary work and assembling playgrounds and constructing classrooms.

But each time we had been we had come back overwhelmed with the sheer volume of need. What we were doing was a drop in the ocean. I would hear more and more about government money being given to a specific road or sewage works project and then the work would never be done. There was so much corruption. We were attacking a wildfire with a water pistol.

A burden grew in me for the need of a relevant church in that nation. There were churches which were full of religion: churches that were selling 'holy rice' to the poor (and still do) at a hugely inflated price because it had a blessing spoken over it. There were good churches too, but there seemed to be so much need that we should do something more.

I had been thinking about how we had been serving the poor and having little impact, and reflecting that what the country needed was change at the very top of society. We needed to see transformation and integrity within the leadership of the nation: teachers, doctors, business people, politicians.

What if we could plant a church nearby one of the most influential universities, not just in Kampala, or Uganda but the whole of East Africa? Imagining the impact that this could have brought a fire to our leadership team. It's never enough for us to just plant a church. We want to see nations changed. It was audacious, and we had no experience, but we were confident that God could do it through us if we believed in Him.

———

So that evening we presented the vision of not just planting a new church in Cardiff, Wales but also in Kampala, Uganda. It was crazy, it was wild, it was us. If we are going to do something like church planting then let's jump in with two feet! God was about to do a whole new thing within our church, He was moving, and as we planted there was a choice for these couples to come with us on this wave. We urged them to not miss what God had for them. I even gave a warning that if they did not catch this opportunity, there will be others that come on their heels and replace them, who are willing and who want to fight for the vision. God had called them, but it was up to them to respond.

A lot of these couples were doing fine, but they were not personally operating at the leadership level we would need to pull off such a daring vision. So I shared this scripture:

> 'If you have raced with men on foot and they have worn you out, how can you compete with horses? If you stumble in safe country, how will you manage in the thickets by the Jordan?'
>
> Jeremiah 12:5 NIV

We put the challenge to them, and called to the leadership within them. Some of them were 'worn out' from running with soldiers, but God had given them the capacity to run with horses. A number of those couples came with us that night and stepped up, chasing after the vision, owning the calling along with our leadership team, and counting the cost personally as they committed to GO to the ends of the earth.

It was a profound, landmark night for us that springboarded this group forward into the heart of our church vision and strengthened our unity. It set in us a momentum that would drive our church forward in the years to come.

But there were some that attended that night that soon left the church. As the call came to step up, in an unsaid way, it also came with an opportunity to get off the train before it took you somewhere you were unwilling to go.

36

CONQUERING THE CAPITAL

When planning the launch of our Cardiff location in 2010, we developed the method of multiplying our locations but retaining one church, one culture and one vision. Josh suggested that we plant churches using a multi-site model with video messages.

This may sound obvious now, but at the time, as far as we were aware, no one else was doing this in the UK. It had been proven to work in other parts of the world, but could we make it work here? We had only just begun filming and capturing our messages at a broadcast quality after putting some significant investment into cameras.

I had such a battle becoming a speaker. I had hated learning to speak publicly, and it was the necessary pain required for answering the call on my life. It had become easier over the years, but I would still get nervous and have to fight off self-doubt before preaching. When the idea was put forward about being recorded and then played somewhere else, it was my nightmare coming to life. I reluctantly came round to the idea though and accepted that if we were going to expand, it would have to cost me too.

In the run up to Cardiff campus launching, we had taken to the streets of the city and handed out thousands and thousands of flyers. We took three Saturdays to take a team of about 25-30 volunteers who would travel and hand out flyers in the city centre, having as many conversations with people as possible and working at it 9-5. We would also do 'interviews' with a camera and presenter and ask people for conversations about faith.

It was early March, and it was a cold time to be standing outside all day trying to get strangers to have a conversation with you. We had a strapline 'Church like you've never seen before,' inviting people to see that church could be different to their previous experience or current expectation.

We got posters printed and pasted hundreds of them in the middle of the city. As well as our pastors Dave and Saz, who would move down in the months after our church launched, we also sent a group of four others to go and help our church get started. One was Sian, the eldest daughter of Chris and Karin, and another was Jordan, my third born son. They were both 19 and moving out of home for the first time to live in another city to go and plant a church.

After three Saturdays of handing out flyers, it came to the week for us to launch. We were doing a run-through early in the week, and two of the ushers in the National Theatre overheard some of our team talking about the article that had come out in Hereford. They reported it back to the trustees of the building, and we were told there would be a meeting to investigate this further and make a decision over whether they would permit us to use their premises.

They met, and we prayed. To our relief, they let us know that they would honour our contract. They had been friendly and could not do enough to help up to this point, but after this, things changed, and it was clear that we would not be welcome long-term.

We drove down from Hereford with droves of people who all wanted to be a part of this first miracle night. After all the flyers we had put out in the city, would anyone actually show up? Who actually likes being stopped for a conversation and a flyer when they are in town anyway? I was really nervous about it. I thought: 'What the heck am I doing?'

But I was so proud of our church. When I saw our guys moving there, our musicians setting up their equipment, and volunteers getting ready to welcome new people in, it had a huge effect on my heart. I love our church. This picture of them all owning and running with the vision in a city that was not their own was a beautiful thing. I felt that this was not my vision, this was God's, and I felt privileged to be a part of it.

We held prayer meetings as we got closer to opening our doors. We prayed for those who were wrestling with decisions, that they would make it out of their homes and come and hear what we had to share. We prayed that they would get to know our Saviour and we would see salvation that night. 6pm came and groups of 2-3 people started coming through the doors. About 60 people came who were not a part of our church in Hereford!

We were stunned, amazed, filled with thanks and excitement of what God might do through this. We had a big creative opening sequence with video, some huge drums, and lights flashing. I preached live that night, and as I stepped out onto the stage it was so moving. I wasn't used to preaching on such a large stage, I was out of my comfort zone and it was humbling. People responded: our first fruits in this great city. Just the beginnings of the marriages that would be saved, the teenagers that would find identity, the lives that would be transformed.

The cafe area in the basement of the theatre filled up with people afterwards and our church set about loving on them, speaking words of encouragement and sharing who we were as a church. When the last people finally left, we celebrated with huge smiles on our faces, thinking about the amazing thing we had just seen.

As we drove back, it wasn't lost on Heather and I that just five years before we had been doing Sunday morning services in Leominster, and now we were travelling back from having launched a church in the Welsh capital!

Worship teams, production teams, kids teams and volunteer teams would serve in Hereford in the morning and then travel down to Cardiff in the afternoon to set up church in the Reardon Smith. It was a time of momentum and excitement; we believed God could do anything through this new church.

Our weekly late-night stop at McDonalds on the way home became legendary and was all a part of church planting. The teams who had just served twice, in two different cities, packed down and were now travelling separately would regroup for a cheeseburger and milkshake after a day of doing church.

Our willing soldiers were teenagers, mums, business people and students, all of whom had an early start the next day. But all of us look back on it now as one of the best times in our lives. I think we often don't want to put on people or ask too much of them, but in reality it is these kinds of vision-packed experiences that give people the opportunity to grow in loving the church and building character. We have to keep on giving people the permission and opportunity to serve with their time, energy and effort.

37

ACCIDENTAL APOSTLE

I want to rewind a moment and tell you about my first experience of firestarting outside of Leominster, before we ever even dreamed of Cardiff.

Back in 1997, a young woman who had been a part of our church in Leominster moved to Belgium to do a Christian training course. She met a guy while she was there and fell in love. They were going to get married in Brugge, Belgium. We were invited, though she said to us there was no pressure to come because she knew we had a young family and it was a big commitment. We had every reason not to go, but we wanted to support her and represent our church family, so we decided we would make the journey across the English Channel.

She kindly sourced us some accommodation with someone from her fiancé's church. We travelled with another couple from our church and arrived at the address that we had been given in a small seaside town called Knokke Heist in the north of Belgium. Two families that had offered to accommodate a British couple each. As we pulled up to the drive, we hadn't decided which couple would stay at which house: it was a lucky dip.

Heather and I made the call to go first, and went in and met the family we would be staying with. Their names were Jan and Marleen Blondeel and they had three children, Tim, Lieke and Eva. Jan was a businessman and Marleen was a teacher, they were incredibly hospitable and we got on really well despite Jan not being able to speak English. Marleen acted as the translator between us and we had a few conversations over the few days we were there, just getting to know one another.

We attended the wedding and it was a lovely ceremony, with Jan and Marleen serving as a part of their church community there. On the last day, Heather and I had decided to take a day to enjoy our surroundings and not talk about church. Church life was intense at this point and we wanted to switch off and have a break, enjoying the luxuries of Belgian chocolate and Belgian beer. What a place!

I was keen to make the most of our break from the kids and from business too. But our host, Jan, had other ideas, 'Tell me about your church, Gary!' We were quite a contrast to the Christianity they had known and experienced. When Jan opened the door to greet us he had expected a tired old English minister, and instead he got Heather and I.

The church Jan and Marleen were in was very different to our church. Speaking in tongues had been banned there, and they were unfamiliar with the practice of the prophetic or the apostolic. There was a very limited expression of the Holy Spirit.

Jan had a hunger for more. As I shared about our church and talked about the Holy Spirit, he was coming alive in front of me; 'Tell me more, Gary!' It was like his soul had been crying out for more of the Holy Spirit, but he had not known it. He could see Heather and I had something different and he was fascinated by it.

I often think of it as a frequency. If you hit a tuning fork, the notes from that fork will set off others in the room. That's what it is like with the Spirit of God. There are certain people that you get around, and as that frequency goes off within you, there is a resonation and connection beyond just conversation. It is at a spirit level. We had this frequency and this connection firing off with Jan and Marleen as we stayed with them, despite the language, despite different cultures. It was stirring something far beyond what we could see or understand.

Jan and Marleen were in a bigger church than Heather and I had built. It was more resourced and experienced, and yet it was dying from the inside out. So were they. Jan saw some of the life, vision and power of the Holy Spirit within us and knew he wanted that.

He had already set retirement in his sights and was earning enough money to make things very comfortable for him and Marleen when they finished working. They had a plan to buy a house in the south of France, live in the sun and drink red wine every day. A great dream. Then we showed up in their lives seemingly 'by chance' and vision got birthed in their hearts. They knew that they were born for more than just to live out a great retirement plan. Their hearts burned within them as they felt the call to centre their lives around the kingdom, and to love and build the bride of Christ. As we talked about a life consumed by Christ, living in a Kingdom-centred way, Jan was moved to tears. Destiny was crying out within him. All this was happening despite us communicating via Marleen as the translator. Not even the language barrier could stop this prophetic awakening that was happening. It was a deep work of the heart and a transformational encounter.

We laid on hands, praying for Jan and Marleen. This was a commissioning to the work of God's Kingdom. We had gone with no intentions, no plans, and by accident raised up some leaders that would go on to impact thousands of people. How that would happen was totally unclear at this point; we didn't know. It might have been an accident for us, but the Holy Spirit had orchestrated every detail. As we travelled back towards the ferry, Heather and I reflected on our trip in amazement about how God had used us once again. We knew that surely we would return, that God had more for us in Belgium and more for us with Jan and Marleen.

———

Jan called me shortly afterwards and said that he had not been able to stop thinking about the things that we discussed. 'It's like God has shaken up our world'. Jan and Marleen invited us to return to stay with them for a holiday, so we made plans to head back to Belgium that summer with our four boys.

As we arrived and saw them again it was like seeing friends we had known for a long time. We had so many conversations that week, so many long hours into the night, talking vision, talking about the Holy Spirit. Jan was like a vacuum cleaner determined to suck out every bit of juice he could get from me. It was clear to all of us that there was only one thing for it. They were going to have to leave their current church so they could start a new church plant in Belgium.

I shared with him many things about church building, one of them being the power of accountability and leadership. He asked me if we would cover them, becoming that accountability for them. I had never overseen or really inputted to anyone else before. It felt like I was only just learning what to do myself. I said I would pray about it and discuss it with the other leaders in my team. When I returned to the UK and talked it through, we all agreed that God was calling us to support them. It wasn't to be our church, but we would support and give leadership when needed.

How we had managed to get involved in helping to plant church into Belgium from little Leominster, England is something that still amazes me today. But it was truly a sign of things to come.

In just a few months time, we would send a mission team, doing street outreach to share the news of this new hope coming to town, and to help Jan and Marleen get started. 'Nieuw Leven' was born, our Belgian sister church. Jan learnt English fluently in 12 months so that we would be able to converse directly. Jan and Marleen would go on to build the church there for the next 14 years.

They tried everything in those 14 years to help it grow, starting in Knokke Heist and then moving the church to the historic city of Brugge later on. They had a huge heart for the lost and came up with many creative ideas to evangelise. The church had done really well at certain times but had also come across huge struggles, very similar to our own church.

As we went through our crossing over period from 2005-2011 and we began to plant church into Cardiff and Kampala, Jan was attracted to the momentum he saw. He wrote to me in 2011 and asked me for help in Brugge. Would we be willing to send them 5-6 young people that could make up a worship band so that they could take things to the next level?

Our church was about 200 people at the time, and had already sown into two other cities in a huge way that year. So I said no, that we didn't even have the young people to send. I wanted to do something to help though, so I invited him and some of his team to come and see what God was doing in our church.

He spent some time visiting our freshly planted Cardiff campus and came to observe what was happening in Hereford too. We had been talking about church for over 10 years and they had visited many times. They could see something was different now. We had tapped a youthfulness, a passion and relevance that was really impacting people.

After seeing our churches, we had a meeting where we discussed the future of the church in Belgium and I had a suggestion for him. After building into the nation for the last decade, we had a heart for Belgium. How about laying down what they were doing and becoming a Freedom Church location?

———————

Jan is such a visionary; he would always be coming up with new ideas and new strategies to reach people. So I knew that if they were going to come under our vision, then he would have to lay his down. I used more brutal language than that, as I didn't want anything to get lost in translation. 'Jan, you will have to kill your vision, let everything go that you have built all these years.'

I repeated this about three times to make it unmissable. If he wanted in, he would have to come under the authority of our vision and submit to my young leadership team, some of whom were less than half his age. It hadn't been that long since they had managed to get their own building in Brugge, which had cost them a lot of energy and effort. I warned him that if it didn't fit with our vision and strategy that we would make the call to let it go and find some-where else.

It was all on the line and was not a decision to be taken lightly. We agreed that it would be good for Jan and Marleen to think and pray before coming back with an answer. Would they be willing to risk everything they had built, to sacrifice it all, for the chance of something more fruitful and effective?

They had a cycling holiday planned after their trip to us, and Marleen tells me they covered a huge amount of miles for Jan to think and think and think. He hardly spoke for the coming days, the words kept swirling around his mind 'kill the vision.' We had been working with them to build their church, but it had been alongside them rather than over them. We therefore had limited authority. But this was completely different; it would be directly under and fully submitted.

Jan came back to me after three weeks and said that they wanted to lay down what they were doing, to 'kill the vision' and become a Freedom church. They had a core of about 25 people. I began planning with him about how we would teach them our church DNA and vision, taking them through a course of transformation and preparation to become a Freedom location. They would lay down their old church identity and fully embrace the vision of our church.

In January we sent over Academy students and mission trips to re-launch the church in Brugge as a 'Freedom Church' campus. They would use our video messages from Hereford that would be subtitled on a weekly basis. Our church had gone from 200 people in Hereford to five different locations in the space of 10 months (we had planted into Bristol, England too in October 2011 which I will share more about later on). It was amazing and surreal all at the same time.

The church gathered some momentum and grew to a solid and committed group. But within six months, in the summer of 2012 Jan and Marleen shared with me what God was stirring in their hearts. Their son Tim had travelled and then worked in Cambodia in South East Asia, ended up meeting a girl, falling in love, marrying her and staying.

Jan and Marleen had visited and had their hearts stirred for the people there. I didn't even know where the country was. They told me they felt called to go and plant a Freedom Church in Cambodia. This was difficult for me. We had only been going six months in Belgium, even if it had been 15 years in total for them, and it was still very early days. But on talking to them further, Marleen said: 'If we agreed it was right for us to go, I wouldn't even bother to go home and pack, I would go straight to the airport'.

What had happened to this reasonable, sensible primary school teacher with the retirement plan? The call of God had got hold of her. She had found the pearl that was worth selling everything to grab hold of.

So we made a plan for them to transition out of Brugge, raising up one of their leadership couples in their place. They would take some of our academy graduates with them to Cambodia, some of whom had already been involved with our other church plants, and start a campus in February 2013.

They were going to be heading to a city famous for its Buddhist temples; 'Siem Reap'. They had a relationship with a local pastor in the city there, who had agreed to loan us 20 of his people to help get the church started.

———————

Jan and Marleen moved there in September 2012 and went about preparing things on the ground and teaching these local volunteers about the culture and vision of Freedom Church. It was like a rerun of their previous 12 months, but instead of their homeland, they were on the other side of the world communicating through interpreters.

The rest of their support team from our church in the UK arrived in January, and they went out on the streets to promote our new church coming to town. They handed out thousands upon thousands of flyers in the searing heat of Siem Reap, a Freedom Church record to this day. There was a totally different culture and response in Cambodia. People wanted a flyer, and would even line up to get one. They would stop in the traffic - there was a real interest in what we were doing.

We had booked a 700 seater building called Rosana Broadway. It was a theatre that housed a show for 'ladyboys' who actually lived in part of the building. We had already got caught out booking big venues before and seeing congregations dwindle down and down, so we were unsure whether this was the right direction.

But we are suckers for some big vision, and Jan is a visionary for sure. He told us that we needed this huge venue and that we would fill it. It was a controversial place but was the only one that had the size that Jan believed we needed and was regularly available on Sunday mornings. So we agreed to it, and Jan was not wrong. 700 Cambodians turned up on our opening Sunday, most of whom had never been to a church.

It was complete chaos. As they kicked off their event, the place was buzzing with people wondering what they had come to. As Jan began to speak through an interpreter, there were people walking around the theatre and others taking phone calls, and friends in conversation with another. Nobody knew how to behave in church!

Then midway through Jan speaking, one of the people who lived there was wandering about behind the stage and tripped in their heels, kicking out and bending the plug that was powering our sound system. Jan was trying to then shout out from the stage to keep people's attention, but it was incredibly difficult.

Meanwhile our team were trying to unbend the plug to get it back in the socket! By the end of the event, Jan gave an opportunity for salvation. We had around 100 people come forward! After an attendance of 700, and 100 responses you would think that Cambodia was about to spark into revival. But none of those that responded came back and the church dwindled down to a small group.

Once again we had a huge theatre with very few seats filled. We changed venues to a hotel and began to build slowly and steadily. The things that we have seen there over these last years have been truly amazing. The church is now training up dozens of people every year as leaders through our Academy programme, and we have outgrown the building that we have, taking the church to two service times. Now local Cambodians are leading the churches, seeing many people saved including former Buddhists, even some who had been monks, coming in and getting radically saved by Jesus.

Jan's story was not dissimilar to my own: 14 years of seeing hardly any fruit as he and Marleen plowed their lives into Belgium. Then they answered the call and have seen God do more than they ever could have imagined. They planted their first church out from Siem Reap into another Cambodian city, Battambang in 2018, planted into the capital Phnom Penh in 2019 and have a plan for the following year too. Each of these new church plants are led by Cambodian nationals that have been saved, transformed and trained within the Siem Reap church. Their church is currently the fastest growing in our movement. They are raising up so many leaders and are already self-replicating.

Here is a story of just one couple out of the many who have been impacted by Jan and Marleen's decision to move to Cambodia:

Lyta was an 18-year-old young woman who had been born and raised as a Buddhist. After feeling unwell, she went to a doctor and found out that she had cancer of the blood. She felt shattered, and the fear of death began to envelope her. Her condition was so serious that the hospital became her new home. She was given three months to live, her life seemingly over before it had even really begun.

Her parents, desperate to help their daughter, began financing visits to other hospitals in the surrounding countries of Vietnam and Thailand, but no doctor could do anything to help Lyta. The situation was hopeless. Medicine was failing her, so she turned to Buddhism, worshiping spirits and inviting them to heal her. But there was no answer.

Amazingly she went on to live for another two years but remained incredibly unwell. That was when Lyta's brother invited her to a church small-group. That evening she heard the Gospel and gave her life to Jesus. Lyta fell in love with the church. She got involved in serving and attended all the meetings she could. Her life was transforming week by week.

Her new found community prayed for her and declared healing in Jesus' name. Some time later, she had an appointment with the doctor to check on her. They were shocked. As they tested her to see the cancer's status, they discovered a miracle. There was no evidence of any cancer in her whole body!

She had been healed by faith. She was elated with excitement and joy, and relief swept through friends and family who had supported her through these years of ill health. They all celebrated along with her church family, in bewilderment and awe. Given months to live, with no medical solutions, Lyta confounded doctors by making a supernatural recovery.

It was around the same time that she began a relationship with Visal, who had been at the small group the night that Lyta had come into church for the very first time. Visal has an extraordinary journey of his own. He had grown up as a Buddhist and had become a monk with an orange toga and shaved head. But that life could not satisfy Visal; he was looking for something. He found it in Jesus.

Visal and Lyta got married. As they thought of their future, it was weighed down by one thing. Lyta had been on heavy medication for the treatment of her blood cancer. One of the consequences of that was infertility; she would be unable to bear her own children. This was a hard time for both Visal and Lyta. They made a choice though, to believe who God was rather than the realities of what the doctor had told them. They began to fast and pray with serious intention. Never giving up, never deterred from believing for another miracle. This time in the form of a baby.

After praying, waiting and contending, Lyta got her next miracle. What had been pronounced impossible had become possible in the hands of God: she was pregnant. Baby Maya was born, a beautiful little girl that will always remind Visal and Lyta of God's greatness and faithfulness.

The story doesn't end there though, Visal and Lyta through their journey of faith became prominent leaders and examples for our Siem Reap campus. Jan and Marleen saw their potential and began to train them as pastors. They were raised up and sent out to plant a new church into the capital city of Cambodia, Phnom Penh. The month that they said yes to the call to Phnom Penh, was the month that they fell pregnant.

Jan and Marleen could have followed their dream and ended up in the South of France, but the roar of the lion had a different plan for them. Now they're in their sixties, consumed by a different life than they ever imagined and starting roaring fires across South East Asia.

They are in love with the people of that region and have set their hearts on doing everything they can to see as many saved as possible. It's a far greater retirement plan that impacts eternity. When you are willing to give up your dream, God will give you something far better.

38

EMBRACING APOSTLESHIP

To not only be a firestarter myself but to help others get fires burning too, was going to need me to embrace my call as a leader at another level.

I have not always felt like a leader. For many years I suffered with an almost crippling lack of confidence and have never seen myself as particularly academic. The classroom was not where I thrived and I hated exams. In fact, I once took the same exam three times, just because I was so convinced that I had failed. I found out after checking my results years later that I had passed all three times.

I have always been an ideas person. I have always had an adventurous spirit, the heart of a risk-taker, and the mind of an entrepreneur. Leadership is far more than book-smarts and eloquence. God uses those traits powerfully in some, but I have realised that the way we view leadership has been far too narrow.

In Ephesians 4, Paul gives a much broader understanding of the sorts of leadership required to equip the Church. He lists five different 'graces' given to us for the building up of the body of believers, some of which we still use frequently in our church language today. Others seem less familiar.

> 'So Christ himself gave the apostles, the prophets, the evangelists, the pastors and teachers,
> to equip his people for works of service, so that the body of Christ may be built up'

Eph 4 v 11-12 NIV

Many of us will be familiar with the role of pastor or teacher in the church. We have an understanding of the work of the evangelist, and depending on our background, we may have encountered prophecy in our churches too.

The least understood of these five seems to be the apostle, perhaps because it is so rarely referred to in the church today. It is a vital part of God's plan for the church and for the world.

These five offices were given for a purpose. Ephesians 4 goes on to describe the unity of faith, the knowledge of Jesus, the maturity, steadfastness, discernment and love that will be produced in the Church when these leadership giftings function together, as directed by the Holy Spirit. To simply lean into the safety of good teaching and the love of faithful pastors is not enough for the global church to grow stronger and complete her mission. We must develop our awareness of all of these giftings.

As I have wrestled with my confidence and grown understanding of my personal leadership over the years, God has exposed an apostolic function in me that has been fundamental in the progression of our church to this point.

To take it back to basics for a moment, our word apostle comes from the Greek apostolos, which means 'sent one'. It has been used throughout history to describe an ambassador, one sent on behalf of a higher authority with a specific purpose. In the Roman empire, these ambassadors were sent into conquered territories to build infrastructures and systems that reflected Rome itself. Governmental changes were made, irrigation and road systems improved, law enforcement practices altered, all so that this newly won land would eventually resemble the empire that they were now a part of and its centre, Rome itself. They were strategists and leaders, called to move a society forward.

Biblically, the apostle has a different mandate but the same role. We are those sent and tasked with bringing our home land to this new land: to bring heaven to earth. That will mean changing some systems of thinking, of living, and calling for God's standards of love, justice and peace to be the governing factors in our lives.

We are all tasked with bringing heaven to earth in our own way, but the office of the apostle is necessary to keep the church on track in that.

The term apostle is also used to refer to the admiral in charge of a fleet of ships. An apostle is one entrusted with the authority to represent the wishes, and the character, of the sender.

Hebrews 3:1 recognises Jesus as the chief apostle, sent to represent and administer the heart of the Father. We're also familiar with the term as it was used to describe the 12 disciples, or as Revelation 21:14 calls them, 'the apostles of the lamb'. We even accept a post-ascension apostle in Paul.

But when did we stop seeing this function as one relevant for today? We still need prophets, evangelists, pastors and teachers, so why not apostles? I would argue that not only are apostles still vital in the church but in fact that the lack of them is detrimental to our mission of spreading the gospel.

Apostles are sent: they build foundations, and they govern. We only need to look at the life and teaching of the apostle Paul to see how strongly the apostles can express themselves and the heart of God in leadership. They keep people focused on the goal of bringing heaven to earth, and they take bold, audacious steps of faith, encouraging faith in others as we work together to fulfil what has been asked of us.

Many of us are tasked with leadership in different ways. These gifts are a grace given to us by God. That means that we didn't earn them. They are not distributed based on merit or skill, but they are freely given for the benefit of the Church, His bride, whom he loves so much. As no one person has all the gifts that God has available to us, we need each other. We are designed to function in community, not just to love and care for each other but to access the fullness of the gifts given.

I have noticed that in Freedom Church, my apostolic function brings out an apostolic grace in others. The shape and design of a leader will often impact the whole church. It's not just because like-minded people will often be drawn to your leadership style but also because God operates in team, using your leadership gifts as a covering that others can operate under as they follow you.

You can probably think of examples yourself, where the nature and call of a particular church leader influences the whole experience of that church. Evangelists will preach, teach, and encourage people to focus on reaching. Those with a strong pastoral gifting will build church in a way that prioritises care, community and involvement in one another's lives.

———

Not everyone in our church is apostolic, but there is an apostolic grace over our church. God has called us to an apostolic, sending, church-planting function because of the bold, adventuring, faith-filled nature that He put in me since before I was born. That's not a boast in myself. We each have giftings deposited within us and roles allocated to us to bless others with, but the apostolic happens to be one of the more overlooked.

Where there is awareness of this role, it is so often limited to one outlet of church planting. In reality, the apostolic grace that sits so evidently in some people's lives can look like far more than just church planting. It is a spirit of pioneering that stretches into so many arenas of life: business and entrepreneurialism, creativity, and cultivation of the new, unseen things of God, the ability to replicate and release the potential in others, and the desire to break new ground and to take risks with new approaches.

Embracing the apostolic in myself and in the church has helped us to go from one location to many, in different continents and cultures of the world, and yet maintain one heart and one vision throughout. It has enabled us to raise up leaders and church planters and see them released into their calling.

That is not to say that operating apostolicly is always easy or comfortable. Sometimes the leadership structures we have are for a season, and change is required. As our church grew and we answered the call to 'Go', it became obvious that we needed to have an apostolic leadership team. In our local churches, we need the gifts of pastors and teachers to the fore, but to oversee this developing church planting movement, I needed true apostolic gifting around me.

This meant making some bold decisions to restructure our leadership team. It's not easy to make those kinds of decisions when it concerns people around you who are faithful, gifted and sometimes even family. We need the bravery to take apostolic authority and the humility to realise that every leadership role we have is borrowed and ours to steward for a time.

My task is to stay focused on my call, to continue to teach on the power of faith and the importance of stepping out, and to stir that audacity up in others in whatever they are called to individually and in the Great Commission that we are all instructed to pursue.

———

EMBRACING APOSTLESHIP QUESTIONS TO CONSIDER:

- Considering the 'sent out', ground-breaking, and fire-starting nature of the apostolic function, who can you identify as apostolic in your life? Are there those who have begun something significant, aligned church culture or built health into a ministry that you have been a part of who you can identify apostolic grace in?
- Do any of the apostolic descriptions in this chapter resonate with you? Are you a leader or idea-generator that has an apostolic gifting?
- How can you do more to cultivate that gift for God's glory? Where are you using it to bring the Kingdom of Heaven to earth? How can you step up in that?

39

MOVING TO A COUNTRY YOU'VE NEVER BEEN TO

When you embrace an apostolic call, you attract apostolic people.

I want to tell you the story of Kris and Naomi because their story is one of an ordinary Christian couple that got their lives swept up in starting fires.

As Christians, they wanted to live in a way that made a difference. It seemed to them that the best place to have an impact was through their careers. They looked at the church in its current state and thought, 'That thing ain't gonna be changing the world anytime soon.'

Kris had landed an amazing job with an organisation in London helping millionaire philanthropists work out how to spend their money in the most meaningful and impacting ways. Naomi had gone on to have her own purposeful career as a social worker and was impacting poor people in inner city London. While deep in the rhythms of career and work, God woke Kris up one normal Monday morning and told him to walk away from this great job. He felt the conviction to share it with Naomi immediately. Her response? 'If God is telling you to do this, then you need to do it today.' He followed through on this leading, quitting his job and finding a new one out of London.

Kris and Naomi bought a home in the Cotswolds in central England, close to Kris' new job. They had never envisaged living there, but once again God's plans were different to their own. Naomi managed to get a job immediately and all the parts fell into place. 'This is where God has called us!' 'What a lovely part of the country to live in!' Everything seemed to make sense. And yet, they still couldn't find satisfaction.

Genuine peace appeared to be unattainable through pursuing their careers. They were renovating a beautiful cottage and making jam on the weekends. Life was good and successful but dull. There was this undercurrent of radicalism that was running through both of them. Their spirits were pining to live a life completely sold out for Jesus, but they were yet to find their own 'tribe'. God needed them to be disturbed once again. Part of this came through Naomi finding out that she was expecting a baby, and they would go from being a couple to being a family sooner than they had anticipated. But the other shaking up would happen through Kris' new job.

Instead of being the dream job that Kris thought it was, it was actually a pressurised environment that would cause Kris to be pushed to his limits. Kris is wired with a drive and intensity and the job preyed on the worst parts of this, pushing to get the most out of him and causing him to strive to achieve as much as possible. He had a relentless work rhythm, day after day, while at weekends trying to get their house renovated and ready for the baby.

It was a punishing season for them both, but it culminated in Kris having a nervous breakdown. He was medically signed off for two weeks of rest due to work-related stress. He spent two weeks on the sofa with overwhelming feelings of failure and depression. It would take him 6 months to recover any confidence and begin to get back to normal, but he never did go back to the job. God used these moments of desperation and hopelessness to strip him down so that He could rebuild him.

AN INVITATION TO CHANGE

An old friend got in touch, 'You need to come see this church I'm a part of.' Ever polite and obliging, they accepted the invitation and travelled almost 2 hours to come to church one Sunday. They were a bit shocked by the passion, the energy and life in the place. It wasn't like anything they had really experienced before.

Kris saw this authentic Christian brotherhood in the men. Guys that knew how to laugh together, loved each other but also worshipped their hearts out with one another, and they welcomed Kris in, even though they didn't know him. It was only on seeing these kinds of real relationships that Kris realised it was something that he didn't really have. The fire had begun to burn within Kris, 'We need to attend this church in Hereford'. They were living two hours away. But the radical seeds began to call out from within, 'Let's do whatever it takes.' And so their journey began into the heart of our church.

There was this holy ambition within our church that attracted them. We were talking about changing the world and living lives that were in line with that vision. They had looked for that purpose within their careers but not found it. But the call of the bride of Christ was beginning to amplify into their world. Through the process they had been on, they had been completely emptied out. Every time they visited our church, it was like fuel being poured over their lives, just waiting to be ignited.

They knew that if they got involved any more, it was going to be radical and consuming. But they couldn't deny the call any longer. Before long they had put their beautiful cottage on the housing market but also decided not to wait for it to sell. Instead they moved back to Hereford and stayed with family. They made their decision on a Saturday and moved on the Sunday. Sometimes you just need to move.

Two years later, Naomi was pregnant again with their second daughter, Abi. After a season of volunteering, taking on leadership roles and growing in culture, they were invited to that leadership meeting in late 2010 at the converted barn in Wales to hear our vision for church planting in 2011. As we shared the audacious vision of not only planting our first church into Cardiff the next year but also planting internationally into Kampala, they were amazed.

They didn't consider themselves as candidates to go for one moment. It wasn't because they were unwilling but because of all the rational reasons. They saw the leadership and gifting in the other couples in the room. They themselves had only been in this church for two years. They were not ready to take something like this on. But nonetheless they were excited and inspired by the vision and would get behind whoever was called to go.

In the months that followed, they went on to buy a house in Hereford and were busy once again doing renovation works. It was February 2011 and Abi had just been born, when Heather and I invited them over to have dinner with us. We had been praying as a leadership team and felt the Coppocks were the family that the Holy Spirit was calling.

I was holding baby Abi in my arms and it was not lost on me, the weight of this vision. Heather and I both found ourselves emotional as I prepared to ask them the big question. Would they be willing to lay down everything they had to go and start a church in Uganda? Well, they then took us by surprise. They responded immediately, 'Yes, God has been speaking to us about this, and we know it's right.'

Kris had been brushing his teeth one morning in the weeks before, just as any other day, when he had been interrupted by the Almighty, 'Where are you going to buy your toothpaste when you live in Kampala, Kris?' Naomi was ready too. On the way over, Kris had said, 'You know what they're going to ask us tonight, right? To go and lead the church in Uganda.' Naomi responded 'Yes. I know. And we're going to say yes.'

ANSWERING THE CALL

Kris and Naomi had never even been to the continent of Africa before. We told them the church didn't have any money to pay them. They would have to raise support to get themselves there and to sustain them month by month. They had never had an ambition to be pastors or missionaries, but all of a sudden their call had swept them up and out of their comfortable lives to take them on an extraordinary adventure.

But as they made the decision to say yes, a barrage of criticism, negativity and discouragement came their way. Kris had missionaries that had just come back from Uganda sit him down and do everything they could to talk him out of it. People sent articles about children in Uganda being abducted and then killed by witch doctors for child sacrifice. They said things like, 'You'll go with two children, but you'll only come back with one.'

People sometimes confuse obedience to God with naivety and foolishness. A seed is often most vulnerable when it first breaks through the soil and it is the same with vision. If you don't protect it, it can be trampled, crushed and even killed.

It is wise to go into a situation with knowledge and wisdom, but there is a difference between that and negativity or speaking out death. Naomi prayed for God to promise her that the girls would be safe. God responded, 'You are going to have to trust me.'

The difficulty to navigate for me as a leader is often how to not back away from these dangers and risks. If we think we are going to be able to bring redemption to the world, to beat back the powers of darkness, to see God's kingdom come to all the earth, without any cost to us we are living an unrealistic gospel. You only have to read the book of Acts to see that the early church did not have an easy life. They were persecuted, tortured and martyred.

As a 21st century church, we can want a sanitised version of ministry with a health and safety mindset to mission. I don't think the church would exist today if the brothers and sisters that had gone before us were so averse to risk that they chose the comfort of their circumstances. The truth is, I can't tell my people that I send that it is all going to be fine.

Church history shows that there is a cost. We have to raise up a church that is full of faith, brave enough to accept the risk and strong enough to be faithful even when harm does come their way. Kris decided that if God was calling us to somewhere that was deemed to be more risky, his family would be 'safer' in that place being in the will of God, than if they were in a place without dangers but out of the will of God.

Kris and Naomi put the plan together to move out to Uganda with a young team, mostly made up of teenagers that would have just completed our Academy training programme. Most of them had just recently finished their school education and moved out of homes and away from their families for the first time: willing but inexperienced. Kris and Naomi would move out in July to start the church in August, which is very different from how we would do things now, but we were at the beginning of our learning.

We had a trip arranged with myself, Kris and Josh to make plans for the big move and the church launch. We travelled through the night and landed in

Entebbe airport for Kris' first ever experience of Africa, the place he had already committed to and would be living in just a few months.

The red roads were teeming with people, lined with shops, sporting every kind of colour with their painted advertisements on the front, the smell of the air wafting into our vehicle. Kris looked out the window and absorbed the sights and sounds of his future home.

What had worked for us in Cardiff, (which we had launched by the time we took this trip) had been to find a prominent venue, promote it well, draw a crowd, and then build a church from those that had turned up. We managed to sort out accommodation for Kris, his family and the team in a group of flats. We even bought a motorbike for the team to use to get around Kampala. But our focus kept coming back to a venue.

There are so many churches already in Kampala, making it challenging to find a space that would be consistently available on Sundays that was not already being used by a church. We came across a huge theatre in the middle of the city. 'Theatre La Bonita' had 1000 seats, a capacity five times the size of our Hereford congregation. It would be a huge undertaking, and it was not cheap either.

To start in such a huge venue is not something we would recommend. But our mentality at the time was, 'Who is not going to come? We have something so special, it's going to take off!' We had this audacious faith that believed we would see something extraordinary happen as we took our church plant into the heart of Kampala.

We travelled back and Kris made the final preparations with his team. He and Naomi said all their goodbyes to life in Herefordshire. We did a final team night where we did some fun team games that included a race. Kris is a competitor, and so he put on some burning pace but ended up jumping over an obstacle and fracturing his heel. He was flying out in 3 days, moving with his young family and young team and doing it all on crutches!

They had just 3 weeks to get ready, which included moving into their flats, getting furniture made on the side of the road, learning where to buy groceries and sorting out transport, before we were sending a short-term team of 20 from our church in Hereford. The team was coming to help promote and get the word out to the city of Kampala that our church was beginning, and they were invited to be a part of it. Our mission team would take dance, drama and reams of flyers and completely immerse the university campus. We were ready to see a revival! We had over 150 people turn up to our opening event.

The church over the coming months dwindled from the opening 150 down to about 25 by Christmas. In fact, one team member told me that we dropped in numbers for 23 consecutive weeks! 25 people in a 1000 seat theatre is a horrible experience. You may have been clever enough to see this coming. Things had not panned out as our dreams had allowed us to imagine and our venue was not working. It was time to ditch Theatre La Bonita and try something new. We rented the local cinema out for a Sunday morning and the church really began to grow.

Over the coming 12 months, the church took strides forward and began building a life-changing, authentic community, integrating local people into the volunteer and worship teams, and most importantly seeing people find salvation in Jesus. The Coppocks, for the first time in their lives, were building God's kingdom every day and poured their hearts and souls into the church. They opened their home to all sorts of different people, made hundreds of brownies, sat in hour after hour of Kampala traffic and navigated living life in East Africa with perseverance.

Young adults were committing all of their lives to Jesus and were coming alive with vision. We had visited Uganda many times before and most of the young men we met were often morose and seemed numb. But the young men that we were discipling were full of joy. Life and hope was beginning to emanate from these Ugandan young adults, and it was a beautiful thing to see. This was the reason that we had started this fire and made this huge move. But just as we were seeing momentum building and real life change, a bowling ball was flying down our lane ready to knock everything over.

WHEN IT ALL GOES WRONG

There was an issue for the Coppocks that would not go away. They had problems with getting a visa that would allow them to stay in the country legally. The best way to deal with hold-ups in paperwork was to pay the expected bribe. That's what everybody does: accept the corruption and play the game. But Kris and Naomi had determined to live and work with integrity.

They refused to pay the bribe. This meant that their first visa took 50 visits to Uganda's immigration office to obtain, and these visits were usually at least half a day at a time, if not a full day. Now they were applying for their second visa as their first one was coming to an end. They even employed a lawyer to carry out the process on their behalf this time.

After the lawyer had been working on their file for months and with repeated visits to immigration, it had got to the point where they had run down the time on their current visa. The lawyer gave them a call that week and advised the only way forward was to pay a bribe. Kris and Naomi refused. They would not compromise on their belief. They called our leadership team and it was decided that they should head back to the UK.

God had shockingly closed the door to this wild chapter living in East Africa. This was such a difficult time. The Coppocks had not just built a church community but a family. A Ugandan couple, George and Desire and their children had joined the church just a year before and Kris and Naomi were now making them the pastors. Within just a few days, they had to pack their possessions, say their goodbyes and found themselves back in England, feeling disorientated from the whirlwind of life. Despite that, it was great to be home with both their daughters, and now Naomi was pregnant again. After the fearful words that had been spoken out over them about losing a child, they had gone to East Africa and gained one instead.

Kris and Naomi went about rebuilding their lives after moving back to the UK.. We restructured our leadership team at this point and I invited Kris to be part of the new team consisting of him, Dave Thomas, Josh and I. This would mean Kris was shaping the church, taking on significant responsibility and influence. Over the next years he would help launch our international church planting strategy, ministering to and supporting our overseas locations. Kris was key to helping us learn how we could plant church more effectively over the coming years. His and Naomi's experience and journey would be invaluable as we examined the lessons they had learned and set about improving our strategy.

After returning from Kampala, God took them on the journey of getting another home, despite all the financial challenges of being missionary pastors.

They sold the home they'd kept in Hereford while in Uganda and upgraded to somewhere bigger that once again needed a renovation but would fit their growing family. It had been an amazing provision for them to get this new house, a faith stretch. Their eldest daughters had begun education in a beautiful countryside school in England and the whole family was getting back into the swing of life in the UK.

SAYING YES AGAIN

The church in Kampala needed lots of support online through video calls and emails after a quick and dramatic leadership handover. Kris made several trips out to Kampala to go and see the new pastors and support them as they took on this daunting task they had been thrown into.

Kris was visiting in November 2015 and had coffee with one of the guys that had got plugged into the church the first time round that he had been there. As he began to share about some life decisions that he was trying to make, Kris' heart broke again for the people of the nation. He could see so clearly in this young man a fatherlessness and a lostness that rebirthed in Kris a deep compassion for Uganda, to see its people find the fullness of life in Jesus.

Later that evening, Kris heard God very clearly in his spirit, and it was one of those times where God spoke in a way that you couldn't miss. 'Move back.' In that singular moment, Kris knew that God was calling them as a family back to Uganda after almost 3 years of being in the UK.

But how could he go back and tell Naomi that after only just recovering financially from their last move, after having settled into their new house, after finally getting stabilised, that it was time to go back to Kampala? Well sure enough, God had already begun preparing Naomi's heart. After hearing the message at church one Sunday, Naomi had broken down into tears. When a friend went to support her and find out what was going on, she responded 'God is about to turn my world upside down again.'

Naomi didn't know the details, but her heart was prepared for another 'all-in', decision making moment. It would have been easy to think this test had already been passed, but here was God saying, 'Brace yourself, it's time to go again.' Kris came back and shared the news of what God had spoken to him. Naomi felt God wasn't forcing her to do this. He was asking her, and it was her choice to respond. But she knew the rejection of God's call would come at a price. So she quoted the Coppock family motto, 'We always say 'Yes' to Jesus.'

There was excitement, trepidation and so many questions that needed answers. Kris came to myself and the leadership team and told us what God had spoken. We didn't want to lose having him in the UK.

We trusted that Kris had heard from God, however, so we did all we could to help facilitate their move and support them as they set about transitioning back to East Africa. They were nervous to tell friends and family once again that they would be moving to East Africa for a second time. At this point, they were now a family of 6 as Oona and James had been added to their family. They were in for some criticism again. 'When are you going to grow up and take responsibility for your own life?' was one of the comments that came their way. Jesus warned us that people will misconstrue our motives. However, they were more prepared this time.

One of the different ways in which Jesus was calling them this time was to a deeper level of commitment. The Holy Spirit was whispering to Kris, 'I have more for you, and it's overseas. But you are going to have to give up everything to receive what I have for you.' So as they prepared to move in the coming months, there was nothing to go into storage this time. They sold their house. They sold all their possessions. It was an 'all in' move with no plan of coming back.

When Kris was flying high in his career in London, he valued possessions and success. His dream was to have a barn full of sports cars and his own racing track. But through this move especially, God was stripping away a love for the world. Through this process of letting go of everything, they would be able to seize what God had for them.

The first time around, they had taken their two daughters and they were so young that they were none the wiser to which country they were living in. It was not so easy this time, and they had to take their kids on the journey of their decision to move back to East Africa. They did it with excitement, explaining that it was a new adventure unfolding to follow Jesus.

Just a few months later, the whole family of 6 were boarding a plane once again, with a clearer idea of the challenge that lay ahead. They found a home to rent, got the older girls in school and once again pastored the church. It was like they never left.

The years that followed saw the church reaching the street children of Kampala, giving them support, care, education and even a home to those they could help. The church itself would grow from strength to strength, raising and releasing new leaders and seeing a fresh wave of momentum. The girls were thriving in school, and the Coppock family were far more comfortable in their missionary skin this time round. God had provided for every school bill and had given them a great home to live in an area of Kampala that they thought was unattainable. It was just when life was in its groove that once again God sent another change of direction.

WILL YOU GO AGAIN?

We had planted a church in Port Elizabeth, South Africa as a part of our 10|04 vision (planting 10 churches in 4 years) but had to wind it down after it lost momentum. But we really felt a strong call to the nation as a leadership team. We were praying into it, and began to get the city of Cape Town on our hearts. We also believed that Kris and Naomi should base themselves there.

This time around though, it was the most difficult to comprehend a move. Kris began asking, 'What are you doing to me God?!' He felt hollowed out and struggled with the thought of the daunting task that lay ahead of them if they said yes to this. The kids loved their school, they had great friends and community, and what would happen to the church if they were to hand it on? This was the baby they had poured their lives into and cared for. There was a lot of prayer and wrestling to make the decision. Life had already been so unsustainable and surprisingly expensive living as a missionary. How could they sign up to another chapter, in another country? They had already given everything up to get to this point. How can you give something up that you have already given up?

The heart of Kris and Naomi Coppock is willingness and obedience and so with a dose of caution, they took the plunge to trust God once more as they left their lives behind in Kampala, handing on the church to leaders they had raised up and began to get faith for Cape Town.

In Spring 2018 they headed back to the UK and Naomi was pregnant once again, (although there was no house to renovate this time). They raised up a team to go with them to plant this new church. Over 20 amazing, willing people were gathered to move to the other side of the world. A team from England, Wales, Poland, and the USA, along with some native South Africans burdened for their home nation, moved to Cape Town. It was like back to the future. Coppocks to Africa 3.0 but this time with more experience and wisdom as they got this new fire started.

New school. New Home. New city. New call.

The Church is built on people like the Coppocks, who go and go until we can start fires in all the world. They wouldn't have it any other way.

40

AN UNWELCOME SURPRISE

While the Coppocks were living out in Uganda for the first time, our world was about to be shaken.

My third son Jordan was born with a small hole in the front of his nose. It would get swollen regularly and would look like a sore spot. It's not very helpful for anyone but especially not when going through your teenage years in secondary school. It was a consistent nuisance for Jord. He had an operation when he was a child to try and deal with it, but it was unsuccessful and they didn't want to operate again until he was an adult and had stopped growing.

Jord had been church planting in Cardiff and Bristol and was working for our church, leading the way in creativity at just 21, when he went to have a test on his hearing after noticing his one side was more difficult to hear from. We thought Jord was just a poor listener and easily distracted as he was growing up. It turned out there was more to it. In the test, they confirmed to him that he was almost completely deaf in one ear.

The scan had also revealed that there was a growth on his brain. Heather and I were in Kampala, Uganda when we got the phone call through from Jord. This was not news you wanted to hear while you were halfway around the world. They had referred him to a specialist in Birmingham because what they had found was very unusual. Heather was particularly distressed, asking lots of questions, but Jordan didn't know any answers yet.

When we got back from our trip to Kampala, we went with him to the specialist in Birmingham to support him. They told us that the growth on the brain was called a dermoid: a cyst-like growth that was growing right under the forehead, on top of the brain. He told us that the 'spot' on Jord's nose was actually a cavity that linked to the dermoid, and gave direct access to the brain. This meant that at any point he could have contracted meningitis because his brain was open through the nose and had a direct connection to any potential infection. Then they told us about their suggested procedure; to cut a letterbox style incision on his forehead so that they could remove the dermoid.

Of course they had to tell us the potential side effects from the operation. He could lose the use of his limbs, and it could alter his personality as they would be operating on the front part of the brain. Heather fell on to the floor in shock and a nurse got called in to get her to lie out on the bed to recover.

They also told us there was a 50% chance of fatality.

What had always appeared to be an annoying spot was in fact a threat to the life of our son. With these percentages and side effects being spoken out, Heather roused herself, sat up, and said: 'Let me tell you something doctor. I am going to be praying for you'. I couldn't tell if she was trying to encourage her or threaten her, but she would be praying for sure.

The three of us drove back together. We were trying to put on a brave face, but we were devastated with the news, feeling so sad for Jord and the weight that he now had to carry: all these unknowns ahead with a major surgical procedure looming.

Jord was so kind, so good. He had done so much to build God's kingdom, and we just couldn't make sense of why this was happening. He was horrified, not only at the potential side effects, but that the best possible outcome would still leave him with a huge facial scar for the rest of his life. As a single man at the prime of life, none of these were pleasant thoughts.

In the weeks that followed, we went back to Birmingham to talk further about the procedure with the surgeon and two other specialists. Jord's particular case was so rare that they only had one other example of it recorded, in Canada. They wanted to do a recording of the operation to teach future students. They were proposing a ten hour operation but also had come up with an alternative method to go through his face, the cavity in his nose, and operate from the brain there rather than cutting through his forehead. This was a pioneering procedure that meant he would have to have his nose rebuilt. The date came through for the operation: it was to be on his 22nd birthday.

It was a horrible wait for the day to come around, and when it arrived we were all nervous. We had the church praying for Him, and we trusted and believed that God would bring him through this. This was where my friend Perry once again swooped in and made a huge impact. On the day of the operation, he got his church, Newspring, praying for Jordan and also posted a blog which was read by thousands more Christians from all over the world. We had 20,000 brothers and sisters lifting up our whole family in prayer.

It made a huge difference. We had hundreds of messages of prayers and scriptures being sent to us through social media. We could physically feel the power of the prayers and there was peace in our minds. It was such a tangible use of corporate prayer, using technology to mobilse the collective power of the church. We got the call that he was out of theatre and went to see him as he was being wheeled back to intensive care. We asked the surgeons how it went and they responded with a thumbs up.

———————

Over the coming days he began to recover, and this would be the time where we would see what the effects were. Jord had his whole nose rebuilt by a plastic surgeon and says, even now, that his 22nd birthday present was a nose job!

We met with the medical team, where the surgeon told us that he had to build a ceiling between Jord's nose and brain, and for the brain to be protected from infection that we would have to just hope that it would hold. If it collapsed they would have to rush him to theatre. He then told us that he didn't get all of the dermoid, they had done a scan and saw that 20% of the growth was still there.

Jord was obviously concerned, 'Will you have to operate again?' They said they would leave it. They told us one more thing, that the reason they had to operate so quickly was because the dermoid was growing in the brain, and could be creating a build up of pressure.

But when they had operated they had found another growth behind the dermoid. It was a layer of calcium 'like a shield' that had stopped the dermoid from creating pressure on the brain, hence why Jordan had never really had any pain, headaches or side effects. It was a God-given miracle, a 'helmet of salvation' that had protected him!

One of the things that the surgeon had told us was that as he was putting Jord under, he asked him one last question. 'What are you going to do after this?' Jord replied, 'I'm gonna change the world' and then lost consciousness. To have the courage and faith to make that kind of statement when he didn't know if he was going to be able to use his limbs, face permanent brain damage or even lose life itself, says everything you need to know about Jord.

He went on to make a full recovery, though he did completely lose his sense of smell, which seemed a small price to pay compared with the dreaded list of sinister side effects.

Within a few months, Jord had packed in his job he loved at the church, and it was time for another adventure. He got himself on to the Cambodia church plant team and moved out to South East Asia to plant our church there, just three months after his brain surgery.

As Part of Jan and Marleen's team, Jord had a significant evangelistic impact. He had a reputation for ending up in all kinds of different environments, whether it was a random house party or crashing someone's wedding. I think he even crashed a wake once, thinking it was a wedding, anything so that he could meet some new people and get the chance to connect them to Jesus and His church.

One day, Jordan was sitting in a restaurant with some of the other members of our church plant team when a group of young guys across the room caught his eye. He felt the Holy Spirit prompt him, 'You need to go and speak to them'. As Jord and his friends were about to leave, he couldn't ignore his conviction. He didn't have anything to say but walking up to the guys, he said the first thing that came to his mind, 'Hey… are you guys dancers?' They laughed and said no, but they did dance in the club.

They shared a laugh together and one of the guys shared his contact details with Jord, saying that he would invite him next time they were going to the club to dance. Jord began to build relationships with these guys, hung out with them, and invited them to church. None of them were interested, however Jord maintained a friendship with them. He got invited to a motorbike ride through the temple ruins with one of these guys, J-Den.

Straight away J-Den could see there was something different with Jord, as he heard about his life and his faith in Jesus. J-Den was not interested in this faith. He was dealing drugs, addicted to nightlife and had no desire to change. Jord's time ended in Cambodia and shortly after he left, he had a message through from one of the team. J-Den had been up all night, unable to sleep. He was hungover and decided to turn up at church the next morning. He heard a message about the prodigal son and had given his life to Jesus on the spot! That same day, he had gone straight to the tattoo parlour, asking for a new tattoo on his arm, 'Welcome Home' so that he would never forget what God did that day.

J-Den is now the pastor of our church in Siem Reap, currently our biggest location outside of our first ever campus in Hereford. He is married to Voleak and they have 3 beautiful kids; his life now completely transformed. It all started when Jord, being willing to listen to the Holy Spirit, crossed the room and started a random conversation that led him to J-Den.

J-Den's full story is extraordinary and you can watch it on Youtube: 'Freedom Church - The Butterfly Effect of God'.

41

PRAYER IGNITION

One of the themes of Jordan's story was the power of prayer. Through the reaching power of Twitter, other social media platforms, and blogs, we had seen how Christians could all be mobilised to pray together, seeing God move in such powerful ways. We had directly benefited from this, seeing our son lifted up in a potential life threatening situation.

What if we could mobilise the church to be praying more consistently? The church had been using the telephone for a prayer chain for many years, but could we make a 21st century upgrade?

I want to use the story of a paralysed man to talk about prayer, because I think that it makes for a great picture of what it feels like when we are praying into a specific situation and there is no way through. In the book of Mark we hear about the paralysed man who was carried to Jesus on a mat by his friends:

> They gathered in such large numbers that there was no room left, not even outside the door, and he preached the word to them. Some men came, bringing to him a paralyzed man, carried by four of them. Since they could not get him to Jesus because of the crowd, they made an opening in the roof above Jesus by digging through it and then lowered the mat the man was lying on. When Jesus saw their faith, he said to the paralyzed man, 'Son, your sins are forgiven.'

> Mark 2: 2-5 NIV

Sometimes it can feel like others are in the line ahead of us, the way to Jesus is blocked, and the door is shut. These four friends had a different mindset. They weren't going to wait nicely at the back, hoping that someone would let them through. They were going to find a way, even if it took tearing the roof open. What if we prayed like that instead of nicely waiting our turn?

If we don't treat something with value, it won't be a priority. It's amazing how many people say they don't have time to pray, but it's really because they don't value it as they should. Those same people are able to keep up with social media or their favourite sports team. They don't have to 'try to get into a good habit' because they value it.

I think one of the questions that we will ask ourselves in eternity is, 'Why didn't I pray more?' When we see from heaven's perspective the impact that our prayers had, we will be challenged that we could have done more. But here on Earth, seeing few of the immediate responses that we ask for, we don't value or prioritise it enough.

There is an urgency in these four friends that we need to have ourselves when it comes to prayer. Our prayer life needs rhythm and consistency, which can only come from making prayer a priority.

We also have to be relentless. We prayed and prayed that our son Jordan wouldn't have to have surgery at all. We prayed that God would take away the dermoid so that he wouldn't have to have this risky procedure. We did not get the answer we wanted, but we were undeterred. God delivered healing in the way that He desired.

In this story, the four friends were relentless. Imagine having carried your friend all the way to see Jesus, getting your hopes up, getting his hopes up, and then seeing the crowds. There's no way through. They can't access the doorway. They had a choice: be discouraged or be determined.

How many of us have been knocking on the door, over and over, when what we needed to do was to climb on to the roof to tear it open? These four friends were not invited to the party, but they gatecrashed it anyway; Jord would have got on well with them. As you will have seen as you read this book, our mantra in our years of ministry has been: if there is a closed door, find another way in.

Many Christians today have short attention spans. We look at the locked door, accept it and walk away. I believe that God is rebirthing tenacity across the world that will not be shaken off. A generation that refuses to give up: prayer warriors that hold on to their request like a dog with a bone, not letting go until God releases the blessing. When people pray like this, you see monumental shifts happen around the earth.

———

These kinds of prayers require the person to know the authority they have been given. The Greek word used for 'authority' in the New Testament means 'the legal right to demand or command'.

This is one of the often missed, understated features of who Jesus is in the Gospels. Luke 4:32 says, 'They were amazed at his teaching, because his words had authority.' He has given this same authority to us, as his followers, to utilise. It's like being in a battle with access to heavy fire-power but you pick up the paintball gun instead. We need to pray and speak with the authority to be who He has called us to be. Jesus didn't ask for healing, He commanded healing. We need to do the same.

> 'Truly I tell you, whatever you bind on earth will be bound in heaven, and whatever you loose on earth will be loosed in heaven.'
>
> Matthew 18:18 NIV

That's authority. When we speak things out, like peace or hope, they get released from the heavens. When we grasp the authority we have as sons and daughters of the King, then we can command things to be bound too, like despair or anxiety.

———

To answer the question about how to modernise our prayer coordination efforts, our team designed a prayer app, called 'Freedom Prayer', for our church to be able to pray consistently. We want to create a unity across our international church family, engaging in spiritual warfare together to see the things of God come to pass. As we pray as one, good will triumph over evil and breakthroughs will happen. We send out push notifications and put out a call for prayer in real-time as situations develop, and our whole church prays in unison. The app allows our church to pray corporately for themes and focuses across our whole movement and it also is designed for campuses to pray for their specific communities too. As well as global and campus prayer lists, there are ones that our people can write themselves for their own prayers and even share them with other people. The idea is we want to empower our people with what to pray for.

Our world needs prayer more than ever. The church needs to find a priority for prayer, to be relentless and know its authority. If the church can take personal responsibility to pray, we will see the earth set alight for Jesus.

PRAYER IGNITION QUESTIONS TO CONSIDER:

- In seasons of crisis, or in the small everyday challenges of life, is prayer your go-to solution or do you try to solve things in your own strength first?
- How can you prioritise the importance of prayer daily? What habits need to change for you to take things to God more quickly and more confidently?
- What are the issues, obstructions, requests and even people that you have stopped praying about because you felt that nothing was changing? What do you need to pick up again today and contend for once again?

42

SCATTERING SEEDS

Some of our church plants were really taking off. Once we had started planting churches we wanted to plant more and more. It was like we got the bug for mission and wanted to harness the momentum that we were seeing by continuing to plant with any resource we had in our hands. If we saw a bit of soil, we wanted to stick a seed in it to see what would happen.

Cardiff had been stunningly fruitful, and we had quickly taken it from a crowd to a church, with local people taking on volunteer roles and committing to the vision. Without this first experience being a positive one, I don't think we would have had the confidence to do what we did in the next 12 months.

In April 2011 we had planted Cardiff, and it was already showing signs of traction. We were preparing to send out our team to Kampala, doing team training nights. I felt that God had more for us in the UK. We had another leadership team day away and we reflected on what we had seen so far.

I told the team that I wanted us to plant again into the UK, in this year, in the city of Bristol in England. It is fair to say they were a bit stunned. Who would lead it? Who else could be sent without starting to impact upon Hereford? They came up with a solution which looked like Chris and Karin Cooke heading out to become the pastors. We made plans to launch our third campus in a year in October.

We found an amazing venue, the town hall right in the city centre, another prominent venue like those that had served us so well in our other locations. We hit the city once again with our teams of volunteers handing out flyers and putting up posters. We set up our venue in Bristol, fully equipped with the best production investment so far. It looked fantastic. On our opening night, we had 263 in attendance, it was the biggest launch we had experienced in our church planting journey up to this point.

We repeated our strategy by bringing teams of volunteers down from Herefordshire who would set up and serve after our service in the morning. We put on a killer night, with our passionate band, live dance and the use of media, it was a real buzz. But as we came out to the cafe after the church event, within about 20 minutes it was mostly our own church having refreshments. A marked difference from Cardiff when we had finished church and the underground basement cafe had been full of new people. We didn't think too much of it. There had been a great crowd of young people and international people, lots of potential.

We came back to our venue the following week to find it looking completely different. Outside the venue was a big green where many students and locals would congregate and have picnics in the warmer months of the year. It was now covered in tents. It was the 'Occupy All Streets' protest. They were staging a full time protest, as part of an international movement against capitalism, globalisation and financial powers.

The protest in Bristol was the biggest in the UK outside London. There were graffiti signs, rubbish everywhere and burning barrels, and it had attracted a lot of difficult and angry characters who had also set up camp. All of this was happening a week after our launch, right outside our new venue.

Once again, we could see that we were not fighting against flesh and blood, but that there was a different spiritual atmosphere coming to contend with us, right outside the doorway to our new church plant. It was an intimidating, rebellious and hostile atmosphere. That second week we only had a dozen people there, including some of the homeless that had been welcomed in by our team of church planters. There was a particular drunk who had managed to get hold of a rose and threw it at our new worship leader as she tried to navigate her set. What a start!

The protest continued and our church couldn't get off the ground. We tried to recapture some momentum with more flyers, more posters, and more outreach. We gave it our all to make it work. We even came up with a strategy where we bought 20,000 large envelopes and filled them with an invitation to our church.

Our team handed out 3000 and the result was two people coming through the doors. They didn't stay. Then we had the remaining 17,000 envelopes stored in our building in Hereford. We had some spare space in our office toilet where they were stored. You could be reminded every time you popped in there of the colossal failure the initiative was.

After five months, and seeing no difference, we took the church to a group setting and it slowly died out. Some of our young adults, including my son Jord, had moved there and set up a home together to help build a community in the church. They had found jobs and were there to build friendships and to see the city impacted for Jesus. It was incredibly difficult on all of them as the church wasn't bearing any fruit and looked like a dud compared to what was happening in Cardiff just 40 minutes across the Severn bridge, where the exact same strategy was working incredibly well.

One of our young team members had enough. He felt overwhelmed and exhausted so he called his parents, who moved him out of the team house. He left a note to say he had left the church. He had been with us since we had started at the Herdsman and was one of our young Barbarians. We never saw it coming.

We were now starting to see casualties of our church planting strategy. We were working the team hard and were so outwardly focused that it was easy to overlook their wellbeing. Again, another huge learning point as we would progress through the years.

In under a year, Freedom Bristol was finished, a blow to us as we sought to change the world. We had thought we were unstoppable, but we had learned that just because something had worked for us in one place, didn't mean that it would work somewhere else. One of the things that I learned is that every city has its own principality, its own spirit and battle to fight. We couldn't afford to make presumptions anymore. We wouldn't plant a campus model into the UK for another three years after this painful episode.

In the meantime, we had continued our connection with Elevation Church. When going to visit Newspring friends, we would make time to visit and learn from them too. One of the things that we grabbed hold of was Elevation Extension. It was a model that allowed anyone, after being vetted and approved, to take hold of their church resources and start a congregation where they were.

Instead of needing a campus building, a team, and financial resources, an empowered leader could take hold of a video message and start a mini-congregation in their home, community centre, office or army camp. We loved the idea and thought we could do the same, so Freedom Extensions was born in 2012. We had connections and friends all around the world who loved our church and the vision and wanted to begin an extension where they were.

We began an extension in Swansea, Wales in a student's bedroom. We had a group of 50 people meeting in Fiji in a community centre. We had a Ukrainian missionary who had been attending our church in Kampala who got hold of the vision, went back to his home city of Odessa, mobilised his friends, got our messages translated into Russian and started an extension there. We had a student from Singapore who had been attending our short-lived church in Bristol and was heading back home. She started an extension there too.

We had someone become a Christian through our extension into an army camp in Afghanistan, who is now one of our pastors in Rotterdam. All these pop-up churches were happening and we loved it. It felt like if there was anyone who wanted to join in the fight, we were there to put a sword in their hands.

But it was not long until we realised the amount of problems this had created. We had limited ability to lead and manage these extensions, one of which couldn't possibly be further away from us on the globe.

There were things happening that didn't represent our heart or vision. There were some that were struggling without proper support. There were others that simply couldn't get any momentum. We saw salvation and some impact, and some of the fragments from those extensions still bear fruit today, but none of the extensions that we started managed to last. We realised that to bear lasting fruit, we would need a different church planting strategy for the years ahead.

We had seen some success but lots of calamity too. We had seen failure; we had seen hurt. There was enough to discourage us. But the good that we did see was so good, that the bad wasn't even a rival to it. We were committed to this call and knew that God was drawing us to more.

As we began to prepare for our next stages, we spent lots of time learning and reflecting from our experiences of the past two years. We had a burning desire to plant more churches but planting as we go, and doing it as and when opportunity presented, had been chaotic and littered with failure. For this next chapter, we would have a thought out, structured plan and strategy of how we would go into all the world.

43

10 | 04

We went away at the beginning of 2014 with our newly formed Directional Leadership Team to plan the next phase of vision for the church. After days of prayer, discussion, debate and preparation, we had crystalised our vision: ten cities in four years. We would call it 10|04, a military term for 'message received' to echo the mandate from heaven that we would run with. We talked about what our church planting strategy needed to feature:

International Locations: We had this undeniable burden for the nations burning in us. The great commission was a call to go into all the world, and we felt our church planting strategy had to reflect that.

Local Locations: This didn't mean local to Hereford necessarily but local to where we already had a presence. It was one thing to shift a group of our church into another nation and leave them to it, but the support that our Cardiff plant had from the people close by in Hereford had been a huge help to getting it off the ground. We wanted to replicate that by planting churches that could have support from nearby Freedom locations when possible.

Timeline: A framework would give our teams and people something to gather around and plan for. Up to this point our planting had been fairly spontaneous and opportunistic. We wanted to have a clearer outline of where and when we would be planting. This would mean that if a plant was scheduled for two years time, it would give the planter time to get their life in order, think about ways they could fund themselves, and look into visas etc.

Limited Languages: We had already started translating into Dutch for our church in Belgium, Russian for our church in Odessa, and Khmer for our church in Cambodia. We had gone in way over our heads with the sheer work and weight of translating into so many different languages. We couldn't stretch ourselves any further with language at this point. Our next set of locations would be reaching countries with languages that we were already using.

Raise Strong Teams: We had made a lot of mistakes around who we would invite to be on teams in our first few years of church planting. We had a rigorous system for leading Sunday volunteering areas, (e.g. worship team / kids team) using applications and interviews, but somehow we had managed to not connect the dots that this should transfer over to people being on mission for us. We had a mentality that we needed to ask people to go, to 'shoulder tap' them.

We decided to announce to our churches the locations we would be going, and to give them the opportunity to apply and then be interviewed to be a part of the teams. We turned the tables from us asking people to go, to them getting a conviction from God that they were called, putting the emphasis on them to convince us of their conviction and calling.

That proved to be a game changer in terms of people's ownership. It shifted a mentality from planting the church because the leadership asked you, to knowing that God has called you to go, and needing to submit and process that vision with leaders. When the inevitable tough times would come, it would be that conviction that would keep people going. This is what they had applied for, prayed for, and fought for.

Team Size: We were looking for seven volunteers for each location to move and relocate to be a part of each plant, so a total of 70 people for all ten plants

Significant Investment: We wanted to back the church plants by investing cash into them.

Ten cities, four years - from 2014 - 2017.

We had our first city in mind, but the others we would choose alongside the pastors once we found them.

2014: (1) Worcester (UK)

2015: (3) India, South Africa + a local location in a country we were already in

2016: (3) Kenya, The Netherlands + a local location in a country we were already in

2017: (2) Scotland + a local location in a country we were already in

If you were counting, you'll notice that only makes nine. As we prayed I had felt that there was one that we were to reserve. It was unclear why or how that would look. God showed me an island though, far away somewhere, that was calling out upon the name of God. In 2017, God revealed that island to be Cyprus, which was to be the final 10|04 plant.

This was an audacious, wild vision. We didn't have the leaders for it, and we didn't have 70 people to sow. We didn't have the money, and we still had very limited experience. But what we did have was a lot of heart and faith. We felt resolute as a leadership team that our God was able to do this through us. With the plan in place, it was time to take it to the church to see who would answer the call to come start fires with us.

44

THE CAVE

As our church family became more and more spread out around the world, it became increasingly important to take time each year to regroup and to speak in vision and purpose. It wasn't meant to be a conference where we would just fly in visiting speakers but a sense of bringing the tribes together as one Freedom Nation. We looked for a name, and came up with some really 'Christian' ones.

Then Chris Cooke shared this scripture with me:

> 'So David left Gath and escaped to the cave of Adullam. Soon his brothers and all his other relatives joined him there. Then others began coming—men who were in trouble or in debt or who were just discontented—until David was the captain of about 400 men.'
>
> 1 Samuel 22:1-2 NIV

That sounded like a bit of a description of our church: the debtors and the troublemakers coming together in unity. The Cave didn't sound like it was a church event at all, and after all these years it still intrigues people across the world when they hear about it.

We had gathered our locations for the first Cave in Hereford in 2012 and it had been a great success. Our people had been out on the streets, volunteering, driving to new cities, and going on expensive mission trips to set up churches across the world. Having an opportunity to have an internal party, celebrating all that God had done so far, sharing vision for what was to come next and imparting a new teaching and spirit for the season ahead made the Cave electric. We are very aware of new people on Sunday events, trying to cater our services for them. On the contrary, this wasn't for the guests, this was just our church family.

It's always rowdy. With the untamed worship, inspired creativity and a people brimming with expectancy. Even when you walk in you can feel the bubbling of the eruption that is about to come, a prophetic sense of God about to pour out His spirit on His people. It is our favourite time of year. I can't tell you how many lives we have seen transformed at the Cave as we have met with God, heaven touching earth.

When it came to sharing the 10|04 vision with the church, we knew that the Cave was the place to do it. We prepared our presentations, messages, and creativity to bring the vision to life for our people. Our leadership team unveiled the vision of 10|04 in the morning sessions of the Saturday, sharing that our little church was going to reach into ten new cities in the next four years.

We unveiled the nations that we knew we were going to; South Africa, The Netherlands, India, Kenya and Scotland. As we put up the flag of the nation for each one, there were shouts, there was jumping of joy, there were tears. It was wild! The place was a picture of emotion, overwhelmed with what we were taking on but enveloped by the vision and heart of our God. There was an enthusiasm and belief in the place that was infectious: we could do this.

That night, I spoke at the final session to our troops, our church family that had gathered from across our locations to grab this vision.

As I mentioned at the start of the book, we had calculated that we would need 70 people. We were hoping that maybe 40 would respond to go on this uncharted adventure, to answer the call to mission. Bearing in mind that we had already sent dozens over the past years, 40 would have been a huge number.

I was determined not to make this an easy call for people. I didn't want people to be manipulated or just respond out of emotion, to sell them the 'adventure' of this call. The Holy Spirit confirmed this in my spirit. I went the other way and made it as hard for people as possible, warning them of the difficulty. Jesus didn't offer the disciples a wage, or a nice benefits package or even their own safety. It was to be the same for us. I spoke on the Hebrews 11 scripture that starts with the heroes of the faith but ends with torture, imprisonment and being sawn in two!

As I finished the message, I had ensured I had painted such a realistic picture of death-to-self and sacrifice that I thought 40 was more likely to be 20 now. But before I had even asked anyone to respond, there were people coming out from their seats in front of the stage, kneeling down, faces full of tears. One of the worship band put down his mic, got off the stage and knelt with the others.

The call and weight of God was so heavy in the room, it was tangible. God had given me a picture of His call, landing deeply on His church. As I gave the opportunity to respond, the call hit the people like a wave. Couples came out holding hands, others responding who totally surprised us as we had no idea that this was in their hearts. Maybe they didn't either until this moment. Young adults and youth came as well. We had 14-year-olds responding, who had worked out that they would be able to finish school and get on one of these church plants by the time the vision was coming to an end.

It was humbling to see. It was like the same weight of calling that I had in the salvation army at 10-years-old had multiplied onto a whole body of people. It was the same weight and conviction of emotion that I had been exposed to as a boy, and now God has used me to mobilise a small army for this same purpose.

We had hoped for 40, but we had 130 respond, more than three times the amount we had anticipated, and over half of the room in attendance!

Every one of those responses has a story that led to that moment. We can't tell them all, but here are the stories of one couple who got swept up in the 10|04 vision.

TWENTY TWO AND READY TO CHANGE THE WORLD

Amy was a Welsh girl, born and raised in Cardiff, and not from any kind of Christian background. She was from a broken family: her parents had divorced when she was still a child. The trauma of this spring boarded her into a life of drink, drugs and smoking from 10 years old. The makeup of her life was violence, arguments, peer pressure and being exposed to things no child should be.

She was a very angry young person with virtually no relationship with her mum and surrounded by unhealthy friendships. Amy did have family members that went to church though. Freedom Cardiff had begun in March 2011, and a few weeks later, Amy's cousin had come through the doors. She loved it, made it her home and invited Amy along in May. Amy was 18 and doing her A Levels at the time and felt she was failing them after neglecting her education.

She was desperately searching for more, believing for something greater than her reality. When Amy's cousin invited her along to our church, Amy said yes, despite the fact that she was incredibly shy and scared to come for the first time. She had never been to any sort of church before. But as she came that first night, she was blown away. She had no idea that a church like this existed. She was moved by the life, the worship music but most of all the people.

She couldn't believe how relevant it was, that church and this Jesus could really connect to real life. Amy went down to the cafe area after the service and people came up to her, talking to her like they knew her and having a genuine interest in her life, something she said she had never truly experienced before.

These people really seemed to care. As she spoke to these zealous Herefordians who travelled each week to Cardiff to plant the church, she saw joy in them. It was infectious and attractive and she was drawn to it. When she went home, she couldn't stop thinking about Freedom Church, the people she met, and about Jesus whom they had shared with her.

Three months later, having carefully considered the call to give her life to Jesus, she responded in a message to become a Christian and found the grace, life, forgiveness and hope that only Jesus can give. A month later she signed up to do our Academy in Hereford where she met James.

James was from a very different background, having grown up on a farm in the countryside of Herefordshire in a Christian home. He grew up going to church and had a good foundation of Christianity. But at age 15 he drifted away from church, as his home church went through conflict and fall out, which caused James to be disillusioned with what it was about. Simultaneously, things of the world had become more and more attractive. He had an influential group of friends and got into a non-christian relationship. He embraced the party lifestyle, lots of drinking and lots of fun (so he thought). The church seemed to become increasingly dull and the pull of this new lifestyle became stronger.

As the fallout had happened in James' home church, he ended up coming to Freedom Church in Hereford. He was attracted to the music, the relevance and the young people. Having been to great youth conferences in bigger cities before, he couldn't believe something like this was happening in quiet little Hereford. But even though he liked what he saw, and started coming along to the church regularly, he wasn't ready to repent, to change his life, to give up his sin and his relationship.

We would hold Thursday morning prayer, and one morning, Chris Cooke texted James afterwards to say: 'James, I am in intercession, and praying for you this morning. I don't know what is about to happen, but God is wanting to prepare you to be ready.' James was at a music festival but got news later that day that one of his close friends had tragically died in a car crash. James was shaken.

Just after that, James' girlfriend had become pregnant but decided to have an abortion. James had been to the clinic to be with her for the procedure. As he left the clinic, travelling home on the train, he was still high from the night before but was now hitting a low. He felt like his parents hated him, felt the weight of shame and guilt because of the abortion, and felt that he had ruined his life all at the young age of 18. He was depressed and believed the lie that he had no-one to turn to. A wave of loneliness washed over him. He was grieving, not just for his friend that had died, but for his own life that was a ruin.

While he was sitting on that train still sick to the stomach and downcast, his soul reached out and he began to pray, 'Jesus, if you are who you say you are, if you can forgive, like you say you can forgive, if you can change life, like you say you can change a life - then I'm all in. Take this broken life, it's yours.' This was his salvation moment. It's amazing how you can spend your life in church but never actually have submitted your life to the father or entered into a relationship with Jesus. James turned his life around, ended his relationship and made some brave life choices to put God first by throwing himself into pursuing the kingdom.

As James and Amy met each other on our Academy, they were finding out about their identity in Jesus and learning about the bride of Christ. They had a foundation being built, a new understanding being forged, and they were each being made new. Amy was still painfully shy, incredibly insecure, and didn't like to speak out loud, especially around people she didn't know.

Prayer times were her worst nightmare. Every week in group prayer time, Amy was always silent. We would encourage her, but she wasn't ready to make that step. There was an inner fight and tenacity within Amy though, and on the last day in the last session of the whole year, she prayed out loud for the first time. What a triumph!

By growing her personal relationship with God, through friendships and the teaching on Academy, she was growing in confidence. She also had a passion growing inside of her for the church. Jesus had so dramatically changed her life that she was completely committed and would never miss any church event we were doing. In April 2012, we asked Amy to go and join our team in Kampala to help build the church there. Some of the people we had originally sent out the year before were returning and we needed to replenish their team support. Amy didn't need time to think and pray, or to think about how she would afford it, or the implications for her family. She said yes there and then.

She headed out that summer to become the kids pastor in our church in Kampala, and her heart got set on fire for the nations and for mission. It wasn't long before Amy fell in love with building church and realised that this is what she wanted to do for the rest of her life. She got involved in a street children's project, helping bring care and education to boys who had no parents or who had run away from home and were now surviving on scraps in the squalor-filled centre of Kampala. After serving for a year, it was time to head back to Cardiff, to get a job and earn some money. But she had been changed by Kampala forever. Before long, it was clear to Amy that she wasn't called to live in the UK for this time; she had itchy feet and a heart being pulled towards mission again.

At the end of James' Academy year, we had approached him and asked him if he would move to South East Asia to go and be a part of our team heading out to Cambodia to plant church in Siem Reap. In just a few months, he was living in the Far East, standing in the heat of Asia, dripping with sweat, handing out thousands of flyers to people that he couldn't even speak the local language to, all for the sake of the Gospel that had turned his life around.

He was a new man. He had gone from helping friends deal drugs in Herefordshire to finding himself on the other side of the world building relationships with Cambodian drug dealers to introduce them to their Saviour. He learnt about building team, about pastoring people from a different religion, culture and background, and about what it takes to build church from scratch. He had taken the things he had learned in the Academy and transferred them into building church on a daily basis.

Even though James and Amy had become friends on the Academy, they weren't in a relationship until the following year. When James was halfway through his stint in Cambodia, he came back for a friend's wedding and he and Amy got together. They then were in a long distance relationship for 8 months - what no new couple wants.

Amy made a huge impact through being a kids pastor in Kampala, and so we approached her and asked if she would be willing to become the kids pastor for our church in Brugge where they needed some additional support. James had been involved in lots of aspects of ministry in Cambodia, and we wanted him to grow through another opportunity, so we asked him to be our youth pastor in Brugge.

They were about to head to Belgium together, finally being in the same place. But first they attended the Cave 2014. As we announced the 10|04 locations, they saw the flag of India come up on the screen. I shared that this nation had been put on our hearts. As they saw it, they were both immediately lit up with vision for India, wanting to be a part of this church plant. They looked at each other with smiles and amazement.

As the call landed on their lives in the evening of the Cave 2014 and as I spoke about the value of the pearl, giving up everything for the it and this kingdom life, James and Amy's conviction grew and grew. When the response came at the end, James says it was like something hit him as this life call came so tangibly upon him. God was saying to him 'You're going to go.' The two of them came out together kneeling down at the front of our church with over a hundred others, holding hands, and answering the call as a couple, even though they weren't even engaged yet. This young couple wanted to give it all for the kingdom.

Within a month they had both moved out to Brugge but were already thinking about India. Going out to a restaurant together, they talked about the prospect of being on the team. That quickly progressed to, 'What if we were to become the campus pastors?' Did they have the audacity that God could use them for that?

———

Back in the UK, without knowing all this was going on, we had been passionately praying for them as a leadership team, and believed they were called to be our pastors for India. We didn't feel it right to approach them however, as they were not even engaged. We needed to start getting plans in place for India, and selecting the pastors was the first port of call. So we prayed that God would bring the India pastors to us. A few of us were at an outdoor wedding that weekend, with some open fires and a grass dance floor.

While at the wedding we had a message through from James. 'Just in case you haven't yet found your pastors for India, we would like to put ourselves forward! ;)' The winky face reflected their doubt that we would actually accept them! I shared the news with Josh, and we celebrated the answer to our prayers.

God had called out the leaders for India just as we had prayed, and we danced madly round the fire in gratitude and amazement. We texted back to say they'd have to go and get themselves married of course, but we would love to have a conversation with them about it. We interviewed them and felt a peace that they were who God had called for Freedom India.

In the year that followed, they would go on investing into Belgium, continuing to grow and to learn, and then return to the UK to get married. James flew out with Kris to go spy out the land and pray into which city we would be planting into. They settled on the city of Chennai in South East India, a city of over 7 million people. We then opened applications to our whole church for people to come and follow James and Amy and move their lives over to India. They had 16 people join the team, far above the 5 that we had anticipated.

They got married in August, went on honeymoon in September, and then moved out to Chennai on the 3rd, October 2015. Both aged just 22, having been married a month, they flew into Chennai to plant church, a city that Amy had never been to before. She felt overwhelmed by the smell, the heat, and the sheer volume of people everywhere.

They had a delayed flight, so it had taken them 36 hours to get there, leaving them exhausted as they entered this chaos. The felt lost in this mega-city, wondering how on earth they were going to be able to do this. Amy had never seen Hinduism before, and seeing the big statues of Ganesh, she could feel a tangible sense of heaviness in the nation. It was an atmosphere that neither of them had really experienced before.

They checked into a very rough guesthouse. They could smell the sewer from outside, stinking out the room. There were dirty handprints on the wall, the sheets were stained, and the honeymoon was well and truly over. But they carried a relentless vision and optimism within them that began to look for things to love in the city and for the potential of the church.

The team was going to need somewhere to live. It was very difficult to try to negotiate accommodation for a group of foreigners, and even to get an Indian SIM card it required an unbelievable amount of paperwork. A day before the team started to arrive, they still didn't have a house, and pressure was mounting as they desperately looked for a solution.

As time was running out, they found an 18-bed house on Airbnb and booked that out for the foreseeable future. It was an answered prayer, right at the last minute. They moved in and scrubbed the place. It was so filthy, cockroaches seemed to be inhabiting most of the rooms. The newlywed couple were living with 16 others, including a family with two teenage boys, and an experienced Christian couple more than twice their age! They were the leaders having to balance team dynamics with people living on top of each other in a new place, not an easy job for anyone. Not many pastors start out by living communally with their whole congregation.

They had been looking for a venue, but no one wanted to take them. It is illegal for Christians to convert others to their faith in India, and there can be a lot of suspicion and accusation towards international people bringing in a foreign religion. Previous church plants we had launched had included putting up posters and handing out flyers. In India, however, this was going to be impossible, as it could lead the team to being booted out of the country.

Almost all of the team had only one way to get into India: utilising tourism visas. So they had to invite people to our new church plant through relationship building only. No workplace evangelism, no office faith talk. Every time they went to a cafe or a bar, they would look to strike up conversation. When they would jump into a rickshaw, the small Indian version of a taxi, they would pay an interest in the driver's life, see if he could speak any English and do their best to forge a relationship.

As they couldn't secure a venue, they started in their home. Their first Sunday finally arrived, all that they had been building into and preparing for over the last year and half, and they had two in attendance other than the team. One was the guard on duty outside of their house who didn't speak English. But they didn't care about that. They danced and celebrated for these first souls that had come through the doors. Freedom Chennai had begun!

Three weeks later, Chennai was hit with the largest floods in four decades. The streets were full of flood waters and floating sewage, and the region was completely devastated by this disaster. The city had ground to a halt with electricity cables breaking off into the floods that were killing people everyday by charging the water with current. It was very difficult to get bottled water and there was no power across the city, including at the team house. This was meant to be the prime time of building church, getting people there this Sunday off the back of the relationships they had been making over recent weeks.

The team house was the only house on the whole street that had not been flooded. Church wasn't going to happen at the house that week as people were stranded. The team looked at what they did have: a stove and a big bag of rice. So they cooked it all up and gave it out to the people of their street. If they couldn't do church, then they would take church out to the people. They had queues of people wading through the water to come and get some rice. They fed 200 people that day. Not bad for a church that was three weeks old. After the flood subsided, they continued to meet in the house, and over the coming weeks saw handfuls of people coming in through the doors.

In February 2016, they finally found a venue that would accept them as a church. It was a hotel in the middle of one of the biggest Hindu districts in the whole city. To get to the hotel you had to drive past one of the most prominent Hindu temples in Chennai. This is where God opened a door, right on the Hindu doorstep. The space the hotel gave us was two levels underground. We were out of sight, but the noise of our worship echoed up the stairways, sending out a sound of hope and lifting up the name above every name even from the depths of the ground. We weren't allowed to advertise the church outside of the building, so to find our church, you had to come with someone or know exactly where to go and then follow the music.

As soon as we opened up in the hotel, the church really ignited into life. In our opening event, they had a better attendance than they had ever had at the house. They attracted and welcomed all sorts. Atheists, Hindus, disillusioned and broken Christians. There was such a buzz and momentum that happened over the coming weeks that James and Amy contacted us to say they wanted to launch an Academy evening course in June.

We would never have thought this possible, but they saw this as a key way of increasing discipleship and raising up leaders within the campus. They took on 6 people in that first year group.

Over the coming years, the church would go from strength to strength and they would impact many lives along the way. When they were still meeting at the house, they had a 15-year-old, Dinesh, join the church who was from a staunch Hindu background. He came through a friend and never left. He gave his life to Jesus and got transformed. When he turned 18, he signed up to our Academy training programme.

Dinesh is now passionately sold out for Christ, and if you get him talking about what Jesus has done, he becomes a sobbing mess. Recently, Dinesh was walking and praying along a street with a friend when he saw a man drunk in his vehicle. Dinesh approached him to offer help as the man seemed distressed.

He realised that it was his best friend's dad, who had been missing for a week. After having an argument with his wife, he had just not returned home. In a city of 7 million people, Dinesh just happened to walk right past him. After praying with him, and supporting him, the father returned home. He and his whole family came to church that week, and Dinesh's best friend gave his life to Jesus.

In the weeks that followed, Dinesh was meeting with his friend, reading the Bible with him, teaching him about this new found faith and who Jesus is, taking someone who made a decision and turning them into a disciple. This young Indian has broken free from Hinduism and now has the Holy Spirit living within him, prophesying boldly to others. Dinesh knows what he wants to do with his life. He desperately wants to be used for mission and church planting and is willing to go anywhere in the world for the Saviour that took his broken life and redeemed it and gave him a hope and future.

Shifali was a young woman who had grown up as a devout Hindu and would worship regularly at the temple that was on the same street as our church. She noticed that inside the temple there is a special place set apart for Jesus. The guru of that temple had always said there was something important about Jesus. Through seeing this, Shifali got a revelation that Jesus was the only one and true God. It is amazing that even through the falseness of other religions, the Holy Spirit is still working in places that we haven't even set our feet.

After going on a journey of discovery, Shifali gave her life to Jesus and later ended up coming to one of our Christmas events, knowing that she needed to be around other Christians. She found home, a place of relevance and life that could help her know how to become a disciple of Jesus. Shifali is a pilot, and got posted in Delhi 1400 miles away. But such was the authentic community and life that she found in our church, that she travels to Chennai every Sunday, flying 3 hours there and 3 hours back, so that she can be in church. Has anyone got a good excuse for missing church again? This is what happens when you find an oasis in the desert, when you have found the pearl worth everything you have. You'll do whatever it takes to get it.

A young woman called Shilpa met one of our team in a bar. She was a Brahmin, which meant that her family was from the highest tier of the caste system in Hinduism. These were the most serious and intense in their faith and often the hardest to reach. She struck up a friendship with our church planter, Emily, and came along to church. After about a month, she gave her life to Jesus. She couldn't come to groups and she could not sign up to the Academy course as a lot of her peers were doing because of the control and limitations upon her through her devout Hindu family. So Amy met her one-on-one every Saturday morning for a year and took her through the Academy course teaching personally in order to disciple her.

Her life began to transform. She got baptised and fell more and more in love with Jesus. Shilpa made the decision to tell her family about her faith and it went down incredibly badly. They rejected her, became aggressive, and felt betrayed by Shilpa's decision. They wanted to send her North to undergo a ceremony where she would have to renounce her Christian faith and be baptised in cow urine.

Shilpa fought against this, and so her family reached out to a radical Hindu organisation. They obtained the phone number of our team members and began to track them. It was becoming more and more dangerous for Shilpa, as she was beaten and persecuted by her own family. She eventually had to move away from them to the North of the country so she could pursue her faith freely and has plugged into a new church there.

India was number 10 in Open Doors top watch list for persecution against Christians. With aggressive radical Hinduism causing the country to be labelled at the 'extreme persecution' level. It is one rank behind Iran. Some-times James would be reaching people in a restaurant and then have a convic-tion from the Holy Spirit that he should withdraw, not exposing his faith in front of this particular stranger. Some Sundays a certain guest might be sat at the back of the room with their arms folded, frowning, and James was left wondering if they were a member of the radical Hindu organisation who had come to watch him.

We have had to conceal James and Amy's real names in this book, as we cannot afford to expose their work in India. Just a year ago, a pastor was hanged by Hindu radicals within the same district. When Freedom Chennai have baptisms, they do it in secret up on rooftops, and they don't post it online as social media is closely watched by the extreme organizations.

By early 2019, Freedom Chennai was filling up their space in the hotel. After looking at hundreds of properties online and visiting dozens of those proper-ties, it was again proving very challenging to find a new venue. In Chennai, they require 10 months rent as a deposit, and most venues didn't want to have anything to do with Christians. James got his Indian Barbarians together and they committed to praying and fasting until they had a building.

Three months later, they moved into their own building, coming out from the underground onto one of the most prominent streets in the whole city! They found out from the agent, it had become available the same week as they had begun the Barbarians prayer. The people of the church raised up all the money they needed for the deposit and the works to the building.

Only 12 months before, they had been struggling to afford the rent at the hotel. It was a miraculous provision. The next year they planted out into another Indian city, Bangalore, having raised up their own pastors and team. This mission is multiplying. Marriages are being restored, individuals are finding purpose, and Hindus converting to Christianity.

A Cardiff girl from a broken family, who couldn't speak to a stranger or pray out loud and a young man who was in the pit of despair after a life of drink, drugs and living for his own agenda had been raised up to start fires. Only God could have seen this couple and known that they would be changing lives in the South of India.

4 6

LIONS AND BEARS PREPARE YOU FOR GIANTS

As 10|04 began, we were still based at Coningsby St. in Hereford. We were teaching Academy sessions there and running our support teams for the global Freedom movement from our converted warehouse. It was like a fridge in the winter and an oven in the summer.

As we didn't own the building, we had done a limited renovation to it. If you pulled back the theatre curtains in the auditorium you could still see the breeze block walls. That breeze block wall was the only barrier between us and the surrounding houses. It was like a skin. There was no insulation, and there were holes in between the roof and the wall. We were also leaking sound, which made us extremely unpopular with our neighbours. We had strict limitations on the times that we could use amplified sound, but as the years had gone by, the people in surrounding homes had become increasingly irritated. They would march in to our events, shout abuse at our volunteers and take numerous complaints to the local council to try and stop us from meeting.

All this was going alongside our never having been fully granted planning permission. We had been given 12 months in 2008 and had continued to string that out in conversations with the council about the future. They had all kinds of sound tests done and recommended we have work done to insulate the place for hundreds of thousands of pounds. That was more money than we had spent converting it in the first place.

This put us in a very sensitive position. The complaints were investigated by the local council, and they would conclude that we needed to have structural work done, but we would respond to say we didn't have the money for that. This was on repeat. We felt vulnerable: they could take away our permission to be there at any point. We needed to find a new base to operate from and to support the work that God was doing through our church.

We had a trip arranged to go visit Newspring in February 2013, partly because we wanted to go and report back to them about what God had done since they had invested in us in 2011. We wanted to be accountable and show them how God had moved in incredible ways through our church. We had a day with Pastor Perry and their whole leadership team.

We took them through a presentation, during which they asked lots of questions. They had been aware of a lot of our struggles with our building and our ongoing challenges. They asked us what we were going to do.

If you present a problem, then you have to be ready with a solution. I believe that Jesus wants us to have specific things that we are asking for; we have to ask to be able to receive. But the asking comes before the receiving, so we have to pray and understand what desires God has placed in our hearts.

Before David fought Goliath, he fought a lion and a bear as a shepherd. All those years ago, we had battled with our lion to see Brook Hall miraculously come into our hands against all the odds. Over a decade later we had fought our bear in the shape of the Coningsby Street warehouse, where we had been warned by council officials to not go through with our renovations. We had seen the situation transformed and the council make way for us after originally threatening to push us out.

We wore the teeth of the bear and lion around our necks, remembering the victories and the breakthroughs on the other side of big asks. God had used all of these years to prepare us to make our biggest request yet. So we decided to run towards our giant and make the biggest ask of our lives.

I showed the Newspring team the plans of a group of buildings in the south of Hereford City.

It was a Lord's manor house that had been owned by the Polish Catholic Church in the 1800s. They had added buildings to the site over the coming hundred years including a chapel and dormitories. It also had a separate building, a classroom that had been used for raising up monks and missionaries to be sent across the world. It seemed very appropriate.

Josh and I had been to visit the site before we had visited the USA. It was in a dire state. The Polish Catholic monks had stopped using it as a mission training centre and used it instead as a retirement home for the monks that were coming to the end of their lives after completing their service.

After they had passed away, their governing body had leased the buildings to another organisation who had been on an utterly bizarre decorating spree. It was one of the ugliest and most dated interiors I had ever seen.

There was mould, damp, leaking roofs, and broken heating systems. There was renovation needed in every single room in every single building. There were 98 rooms in total. As we were shown around the rooms, it was like a rabbit warren or a maze.

Having renovated buildings for years, I could see the staggering potential of what we could do if we got our hands on the place. We could take hold of it and redeem it, using it as a staging ground to send out missionaries into all the world. It was up for sale for £1.1 million.

We shared it with the Newspring team, and told them this is what we were dreaming about and praying into. They were interested by its rich history and potential. They asked a lot of questions about our current staff team, which was, and still is, mostly made up of volunteers who were supporting this work happening across our international church. A paid day here or a half a day there was keeping everything going.

They were shocked by the limited man power and volunteers that were powering and resourcing this missional movement. They spent the majority of the afternoon helping us restructure and giving us input and counsel from their experience to take our church to the next stage of growth. It was so valuable as we had never had this kind of input before. These guys were not just consultants, they were friends that loved us and wanted to do the best to help us steward what God had put in our hands.

Later that week, Newspring was holding a roundtable leadership event that we had been invited to. During the break, they asked to speak to us. They pulled over myself, Heather, Josh and Rose to tell us that they had some news. They told us with smiles on their faces that they were going to be helping take our staffing to the next level. They were going to give us the financial equivalent of five full time paid staff members and would do so for the next three years.

Not even I was taking a full time wage from the church; every one of us was working part time and having to create other incomes. This was a complete game changer! It was overwhelming. We never would have expected Newspring to help us in this way, such was their generosity and their hearts for us.

But they weren't done. They told us, with tears in their eyes, that they were also going to give us the money to buy the Polish Catholic buildings. Heather fell to her knees, Josh started hugging the Newspring guys, Rose stood in shock and I went straight up to Shane Duffey, one of the leaders, to see if I had just heard right... were they really going to buy this million pound building?

We had never dreamed that this would be the response. Perhaps they would have a heart to help in some way, to contribute something but to purchase the entire building? As well as what they had already pledged with the staffing? It was completely stunning, a rich and lavish generosity that bowled us over. It was a dream coming true. They would even contribute some money to begin the renovation work. They told us that we were the most fruitful investment they had ever made, and they wanted to help establish us in a place of strength as we purchased this site.

It was only a dream at the time, but that building, now known as 'The Forge' would go on to house offices for all our staff and volunteers, film studios, classrooms and accommodation wings for our Academy students, as well as having a Chapel that was renovated to become a stunning worship space that many of our church family have got married in.

We went back home, full of awe at how God had moved on our behalf, and wide-eyed that we got to be a part of another miracle once again. All this had begun with a bunch of our Academy students worshipping their hearts out on a Sunday night to songs they didn't know, not knowing that they were going to facilitate the future of the Academy for decades to come through their passion and zeal in those moments.

The Academy has been a consistent theme as I write about our church journey over the last few years. When it started in 2009, I don't think anyone could have imagined how monumentally important this program would become in achieving all that God was asking our church to do.

The willingness we have seen in people is astounding, but early in our church-planting journey, we recognised that we would need more than willingness. We would require leaders to be trained, equipped and prepared for the task ahead of them, whether they were moving to East Africa or running a ministry area in their hometown.

In 2010, Rose received a prophetic word that there would be people travelling from all over the world to receive this training. We are a church that says the word 'global' regularly now, but at the time, with only one church location in quiet Herefordshire, this prophetic word seemed hard to imagine.

To date, we have seen over 200 students take part in the course in our Hereford location. People from all over the world, Australia, across Africa, Poland and Belgium, Latvia and Singapore, Canada and the United States and beyond, have made the journey to Hereford to prepare themselves for what is next. The Academy has grown from a training program that people travelled to one morning a week, to a residential course in a beautiful facility where students receive classroom teaching from leaders who have built church across the world, personal tutorship from mentors who guide them, internship opportunities, and get to serve and learn in a thriving local church.

Soon realising that this should not only be available to the under 30s, we also extended our courses to include Academy+, a one-year course that happens one night a week, so that parents, people in full-time work, and emerging leaders of all ages could get involved in the training.

Currently, Rose and the team are working on developing a second residential Academy site in the USA, with dreams of more to come around the world in the future. Almost all of our locations have now run their own Academy+ courses in their campuses in order to train up the leaders that are passionate to grow.

So many of the students have gone on to have huge impact around the world. I've already mentioned people like my son Jord, and James and Amy, but there are so many more. Leaders have gone on from the Academy to build church within our locations and other churches. They have gone on to become pastors in Hereford, Cardiff, Birmingham, Worcester, Rotterdam, Mombasa, Kigali, Kampala, Cape Town and Chennai. There has been such great fruit from taking the time to raise the next generation of leaders, and we know there is far more to come.

47

HURTLING ALONG

Through 10|04, we began to plant churches at a phenomenal pace for our still relatively small church. God would sustain us with his grace and wisdom as we stepped up our energy and mission.

'You have a lot of flow'

This statement was made to me in 2018 by the senior leader of a large apostolic movement of churches in Brazil. He had been looking around the headquarters building of our church, The Forge, in Hereford, and I was explaining to him what we are doing and in which countries. He went on to explain that when a new 'stream' of churches is initiated, it is like a stream of water in the natural world. It flows busily and noisily. It is full of oxygen and life, it's fun, and it's interesting. It is also vulnerable, as in a drought time, it may dry up. He said that humanity is always keen to reduce risk and to build in sustainability, and hence we build lakes. We dam up some or all of the outflow of the stream in order to create a lake, which protects us against 'dry-times'. Except that, of course, without an outflow, the lake can become stagnant. It is more predictable and less noisy or chaotic, but it has less life. If the lake continues to build its capacity, at some point it will grow to be above its source. Once that happens there is no longer an inlet or outlet. Just a stagnant, dead lake.

I'm not interested in lakes.

I'm far more concerned with where we can see the water flow.

See, I am doing a new thing!

Now it springs up; do you not perceive it?

I am making a way in the wilderness

and streams in the wasteland.

Isaiah 43:19 NIV

The 10|4 vision was about going to new cities and new countries. Teams of bold, radical, faith-filled young people and young families looking to 'Live Full, Die Empty', and have fun doing so. They were aiming to write a better story, stories they could tell their grandchildren. And boy, do we have some of those!

It was just three years since we had planted our Cardiff church when the 10|4 vision began, but with that apostolic culture and grace that I explained earlier, we found that our new churches were becoming sending centres too. Over the four years that the vision ran, Cardiff sent out 54 people on church plants or to our Academy. I could still remember when even having 54 people come to church seemed like a distant dream.

Our first church plant of 10|4 was into Worcester, a city just 45 minutes east from Hereford. It was there that we first met Jordan. A friend of his had joined our Cardiff church and when Jordan started University in Worcester his friend told him to check out Freedom. He was living life with one foot in the Kingdom and one foot out; including being quite absorbed with his Sunday-league football team and his non-Christian girlfriend, Saffron. Saff later told me that they were walking back from football one Sunday, and Jordan's mother rang him. She asked how church was that day and he said that I had preached up a storm, (even though he hadn't been!) As Saff witnessed this, she was furious and told him he was not to lie to his mother like that ever again!

Jordan started to commit to attending regularly and will now say that this was where he found faith for himself, rather than riding on that of his parents. Eventually, Saff asked him when he was going to invite her. He did and she went the next week. At first she was a bit of a 'rabbit in the headlights', as she had a very traditional view of what church would look and sound like, and we did not match that at all. Initially, it was the community that impressed her and helped her to settle into church life. She was invited to dinners and social events, and people talked about their faith and asked about her life. Over time, she could not deny it any longer. Jesus was real, and she wanted that faith and life too. Saffron made that decision and committed her life to God, and not much later, committed her life to Jordan too as they married.

As soon as Jordan finished his degree course, they were ready to go, and the two of them joined our plant-team for Mombasa, Kenya. They were a brilliant part of the team and made such a difference. A year or so later, though, they felt the call to 'go again', and joined our plant team to Glasgow, Scotland. It was becoming clear that this was a special couple. After a while, they returned to Hereford for some further training, and one beautiful baby boy later, Heather and I asked them whether they would take on pastoring the Worcester campus that they had originally joined and Saffron had been saved in. They said yes. It is such a joy to see local leaders raised up, sent out, gain experience, and return to the very place they were ignited in to help bring that fire to others.

Another city around 30 miles from both Hereford and from Worcester is Cheltenham. We launched a church there that has built a really strong community. One person that came in is Molly. She had grown-up in a non-Christian household, had served in the British Army, and had been due to get married. There was a lot of relationship mess in her life, though, and she called the wedding off. Quite quickly, she got into another relationship with a guy that was a Christian.

Molly listened to a worship song that he had, and it affected her quite deeply. She had a dream where God spoke to her to go to church. She found Freedom Church through another army friend that she had and started to attend Freedom Cheltenham on her own. She says that the day she walked into Church, she found home. She quickly realised that she believed in God and in all that Jesus had done for her. Within a few weeks, she said the salvation prayer and has urgently followed Jesus ever since.

For a while, she felt that she had 'made it' but decided to attend our Academy and found herself going to whole new levels in God. She had physical healing for damaged knees, and perhaps even more importantly, she has learnt who He is as her father, what it means to be His daughter, and how to let the Lord deal with her insecurity. She is now beginning to ponder what church planting might mean for her, and to look to further horizons than she has ever done before.

48

GO ONE MORE TIME

We have a number of stories of where one of our people going just one more time, has made all the difference to someone's life and eternity. Don't expect everything to fall into your lap on your first outreach, and don't be discouraged if it seems to take multiple efforts to get the result you were looking for.

When we launched our Chennai campus, the team were evangelising with passion, whenever and wherever they could. But at times, this seemed to produce limited results. One day, one of the team, Ffion Cooke, was taking a taxi called a tuk-tuk. As she was about to get out, she gave the driver an invite card to Freedom Church and spoke to him about it. He said that he would come, something a church planter has heard many times but not always seen come to pass.

What Ffion didn't know was that this man, Arul, was a Christian who had been on a 100 day partial fast. He had a very sick, young, adult daughter, and was seeking God for direction about which church he and his family should be a part of. On his 100th and final fast day, had God brought him an answer? That Sunday he travelled the two hours from where they lived and came to church. Over the next few months he and all his family became absolutely core parts of the church. This happened despite the fact that his wife's English was quite limited, and that his daughter was so unwell. In fact, she had tuberculosis, and so the team prayed for her, got her access to free treatment, and soon saw her completely healed.

The church realised that Arul had sold his own tuk-tuk to pay previous medical bills and was now paying most of his earnings to hire one each day, just to earn a living. After a few quick conversations, our church joined together to buy him a brand new tuk-tuk, meaning that those hire costs have disappeared and he can provide well for his family. I love the church!

PAYING A PRICE

It was amazing to hear that for some time Arul and his family were traveling for two hours each way to just come to church. In some of the settings we have started church in, people have paid an even higher price for faith.

We sent a team to plant church in Limassol, Cyprus. Cyprus is an island in the Mediterranean Sea, and you can hear the shelling and bombing in Syria from there. It is also close to Turkey, Israel, Jordan, Lebanon and Egypt, and behind those lie Iran and Iraq. Given all those names, it is not surprising to find out that our church there has a high proportion of asylum seekers and refugees. There are few things more humbling than hearing the stories of those people and how they have suffered for their faith. A number of them have lost everything for their belief in Jesus. One of those was an Islamic extremist, who was a part of the community that went on to found the Islamic State terror group. Our firestarting had got us into some places and meeting people that we could never have imagined in quiet Herefordshire.

As well as providing a home for many of these people, our team have befriended many others from these communities, even while they continue to ascribe to Islam. As a result, many have come to faith in Jesus. One of our team there, a quiet unassuming Welsh guy called Aled, said that he has baptised a number of Kurdish Iranians, and every single one of them has had physical signs of torture on their bodies.

I hear people in the West sometimes talk about how 'persecuted' or 'oppressed' we are as Christians, and there is no mistaking the fact that things are getting darker and harder. But our brothers and sisters in countries where there is significant persecution set an example for us in love for Christ and perseverance for His kingdom.

UNEXPECTED EVENTS

Sometimes God uses truly bizarre events to bring people to Himself and to His family. We planted into Cape Town, South Africa in 2018. Our original pastors there, Kris and Naomi Coppock, brought their wonderful family back to the UK after 10 years of church planting in Africa, and handed it on to a young couple, Josh and Meg Cooke. Josh was out one day and drove to a local shop. He thought that he had locked his car, but the remote key lock hadn't worked, and whilst he was in the shop a thief opened the car and stole a bag that had Josh's laptop and a journal/notebook in it. He had quickly hailed a taxi and driven off. Someone had seen what had happened and tried to stop the taxi but to no avail.

As always, such an event is hugely frustrating, as well as being expensive. Two weeks later, Josh had an extraordinary phone call. It transpired that the taxi driver had not gone far when he figured out what had happened, grabbed the bag back off the thief and threw him out of the car. He had driven back to the scene of the crime, but Josh had already driven off. The taxi driver left the bag with two young women in an office beside where Josh had parked his car when it happened in case he came back. In the intervening two weeks, the young women had been reading all of Josh's notes and been inspired by what he had been writing about building a multi-ethnic church. Eventually, buried deep within the notes, they found a phone number and rang it. It was Josh, and they told him that not only did they have his laptop and notebook, but they were interested in joining the church! Josh was not only astonished and relieved but became even more grateful when the very next Sunday the two young women came to church, loved every minute, signed up for mid-week groups and are now thoroughly integrated into the church family there. The Holy Spirit is lighting fires even when we think it's an attack from the enemy.

SECURITY

One feature that loomed large for me when we started to talk about our 10|04 vision was security. I am grateful when people step up to add their gifting, passion, time and resources to the mission. I am humbled when they move cities, or sell everything and move countries. But when they put themselves into vulnerable and threatening situations, it weighs heavy on me. I have to trust God's protection and remember that the New Testament is littered with examples of where the believers went where they would be in danger.

It is my experience that as leaders and parents, we consistently work hard to keep our children and our people far from danger; but that biblical testimony indicates that God often inspires His people to travel into dangerous territory. G.K Chesterton said that, 'Jesus promised the disciples three things: that they would be completely fearless, absurdly happy and in constant trouble.' I see that so often with our church planters.

We have faced a variety of security challenges for our guys. In India, the young women in our plant team felt a certain sense of sexual threat, and recognising this, the guys in the team chaperoned them everywhere. In South Africa, the guys have faced the threat of personal robbery. In fact, a number of members of the plant team were held at gunpoint and robbed when they were volunteering at a childcare facility. You can't imagine how I felt when I heard about this episode. We also planted in Mombasa, Kenya, which is down the road from Somalia and Al-Shabaab, the jihadist terror group. They have bombed and attacked people in Kenya on a number of occasions. More than once our pastors were tipped off to possible concerns there and shepherded the team to safe settings.

In recent times, we have actually launched churches in closed nations, where the threat levels are higher again. We are not reckless in what we do, or in who we release on such ventures, but we are bold. We pray for God's protection over all our people, but we also know from biblical examples that things won't always go well. This is hard for me, but I have a conviction from God that 'we do not belong to those who shrink back and are destroyed, but to those who have faith and are saved.' Hebrews 10:39.

IN HINDSIGHT

Looking back, 10|04 was an incredibly audacious vision for our church. We knew it was bold, but I don't think we realised just how wild it was. To send so many people, to so many cities and countries, with so few resources, in such a short space of time was incredibly stretching. We must have been mad! But God has been so good and so faithful. He has provided and protected. And whilst not every plant has taken hold in quite the way we would have wished, others have surpassed our expectations and are now planting new churches themselves. It is that exponential growth that I feel God has been pointing me towards for years.

49

SEEING BEYOND THE MIST

After starting fires around the world with 10|04, we had tried to curb our church planting addiction for a few years, giving some time for the new churches to really start burning. Between 2017 and 2020 we began a couple of new churches but slowed the pace in comparison to the previous six years. It also allowed us to strengthen the rest of our church. We had expended so much energy on outward focus over the last years, that we needed to spend some time internally focusing, to get stronger for what was next.

In January 2020, it was time for our Leadership team to think about vision for our next season as a church. Josh flew back to the UK from Raleigh, North Carolina, where he and Rose had moved to plant a church just a few months prior. Kris had also flown in from South Africa. Dave and I met them in the airport and we travelled to the Isle of Skye in the Scottish Highlands.

We drove from Inverness, through the stunning snow covered mountains, excited to see each other again and filled with anticipation about what God was going to do in our week ahead. After driving for hours through the spectacular Scottish landscape, we had arrived at the other side of the country. We drove over the bridge from the mainland on to the misty Isle, which seemed shrouded in mystery. The wind was howling, the rain beating down. The sun would miraculously show up for 10 minutes at a time before being enveloped by the clouds again. It was a picture of our time together: beautiful but difficult to see the whole scene. We arrived at our cottage rental right on the north coast, and over the coming days would pray, discuss, and eat some knock-out food, taking it in turns to cook for one another.

We had been praying and fasting in the lead up to our time away. The whole church was covering us in prayer whilst up on the Isle of Skye. Now it was time for us to begin to share with each other what God had been speaking to us as we had been preparing on our different continents.

We had a huge focus on church planting through the 2010's and it had been all-consuming. We had questions through that past decade. What would be next? We had planted 10 churches in 4 years. Should we just increase the amount of churches for our next target? Could we do it all again? Would that be the right thing to do? Some of our church plants had succeeded, others had not taken root. Some people had thrived church planting, while others had, heartbreakingly, left the church.

We had talked over previous years about our hearts to church plant more, but it became clear that we had a heart for 'anyone, anywhere'. It wasn't just for one people group or one country. It was for people all over the world. If we committed our leaders, teams and resources to one area, it would mean not being able to go to another.

One of the big revelations that God gave us in 2014 was that we should be planting church digitally as well as physically. We set a whole team on it, doing research and investing resources. We did what almost every church similar to us was doing. An online service, streaming our church gathering online on Sunday mornings. Services that were designed for the person in the room, rather than created with those online in mind. For a certain time, we were even doing online small groups too. The team did a great job, but it never lived up to what we had imagined digital church was going to be online. There was so much more, but it was kind of like the misty island of Skye. It was so opaque. Planting digital church had become a frustrating and confusing side project.

When we met in January 2020 though, it was clear that God was putting it front and centre for our agenda in the 2020's. It was like the mist cleared revealing a sudden clarity of the picture.

We had always treated digital ministry as just one of the offshoots of our church vision. A separate department. What God was showing us through our time in Skye was that we needed to make everything digital. This meant making all of our ministries digital instead of making digital its own ministry. Digital was going to be the big thing for us in the 2020s. Our kids ministry, youth ministry, our training programmes, our church planting strategies.

One of our great burdens has always been evangelism. How do we reach people in a world where it has become more and more difficult to actually get people into a physical building? What God revealed to us was that He wanted us to dream much, much bigger about reaching our world digitally. It would blow away our simple church-online streaming services. We were being called to create digital evangelistic content that would reach far beyond the confines of our resources, our leaders or visa limitations. How can you reach into the Muslim world? How can you reach into places where you cannot move church planters because of government restrictions? How can you plant a church where it is illegal to gather as Christians? Physical gathering and practical movement would still be an essential part of our work; however, we are accelerating towards the finish as Jesus is set to return. The Church needs innovative ways to spread the gospel like wildfire, beyond what we have seen to this point. We believe that this is the very reason that God has allowed us to come up with the internet and smartphones. It's all for the culmination of the finish. It's all for the bride of Christ to be able to spread this Good News around the world so that more may come to Him.

We would still continue to plant physical churches, but we made plans to refocus our time, resources and energy into digital ministry for the next decade.

FIRESTARTER

This is where God downloaded the vision 'Firestarter' to make church planting available to anyone anywhere. What if we could record specific resources that would equip people with a heart to reach the people in their lives with the Gospel and empower them to build a Godly loving Christian community? Anyone can play a message on Youtube with their friends round, but this would be about something so much more. It would be worship, communion, and authentic relationships. From our decade of church planting, we knew that the relationships to support the people who had a desire to be firestarters would be key.

All those years ago, Heather and I had ignited something that would touch the nations, all from the familiarity of a tiny living room in the town of Leominster, beginning with a few friends. Over 30 years later, things were coming back to full circle. Our vision would go back into living rooms and offices and community centres. Like-minded people would gather all over the world, being equipped to step out in faith and reach their world.

It would not be pretty, and it would be a little messy in places. Some firestarters would catch alight and some wouldn't. Whatever happened, we just knew that we had to ignite more hope in this world.

Through the last 10 years, we had sown-out ordinary people into the nations and our extraordinary God had done some beautiful things through them. But now, instead of only sowing people, we would be putting out the call to people all over the world that they could be a part of this. If they would just believe, make themselves available, God could use them. This would mean we could take the Gospel into countries we had never been before and expand into places it was previously impossible.

Firestarter would be a community of people planting churches worldwide. They would gather people and build churches in their homes or any other venue they could make work.

We would offer three things to equip and support these new churches as they got started: Culture + Community + Content.

Culture that fuels church planting

We know who God has called us to be, and when we live this way, He changes lives. Our strong, defined DNA fuels reaching people, changing lives and releasing leaders to multiply the impact.

A global leadership community

The Firestarter community will ignite and sustain Firestarters by connecting them to friendship, inspiration and support. We become stronger leaders and make a greater impact when we care for and encourage one another.

All the content someone needs to plant

Teaching, worship, creativity and more. Our digital library provides training to grow our peoples' leadership and strengthen their approach to building church. We're also providing content that will turn up the heat when they gather.

The last decade of church planting had been staggering, but perhaps through Firestarter the next decade could be even more special as we set the world aflame.

But God didn't stop there. There was more he wanted to speak to us about.

50

SALTWINDS

I saw this tweet recently: 'I saw a guy at Starbucks today. He had no smartphone, tablet, or laptop. He just sat there drinking his coffee... Like a psychopath.' It made me laugh. We don't just sit anymore in the Western world. The average person can't even have a few moments just with their thoughts, they are always consuming content. I walked into a public restroom recently and saw a guy scrolling through his feed while using a urinal, could he not wait 20 seconds?! Think back a hundred years ago about how much more silence there would have been, how much more thinking. From the moment we wake, to the moment that we put our head on the pillow, there is a device in our hands. Our screen time is becoming so significant that even the big tech companies are trying to help wean us off it by creating apps to help us monitor our usage.

Humanity has an insatiable appetite for content. With all the shows, films and content available though, we still end up trawling through Netflix for ages because we 'can't find anything to watch'. How is that possible with so many thousands of hours of footage at our fingertips? We are looking for something that isn't there.

We had a word spoken into our church in 2010 through Clem Ferris that said this:

'The Lord is going to begin to move that outreach heart of yours over the airwaves. You won't be able to go through natural doors, you won't be able to knock on doors on Saturday mornings and hand out tracts, that's not going to work, but they'll go to their internet, and they'll turn on Facebook and they'll turn on their favourite search engine, and their favourite shopping page, and there will be this little lion that comes up in the corner.

Church as we've known church, that it's a gathering of people on a Sunday to come and feel better, and make it through the next week - it's not going to be about that. It's going to be about reaching out and the whole system is going to shift, and the activity Monday through Saturday is going to so overshadow what happens on Sunday. There will be a constant flow of traffic. This whole room is going to change....it's going to become an incredible production studio

I see broadcasting coming out of this building for the whole city, for the region. The Lord says get ready to broadcast the gospel. There will be Christian broadcasting, there will be controversial broadcasting. There will be battle over the airwaves and there will have to be intercession going out. There's something about warfare and intercession that you're going to have to do, because you're going to do battle with the prince of the power of the air. He thinks he owns the airwaves, but God owns them. The Gospel is going to run on that invisible internet track and God says 'I'm going to increase spiritually the bandwidth of this house. It's going to run on a whole new bandwidth with new speed and new penetration into darkness

God says I want to break into some new arenas of people, new people groups, I want to break out of old systems and into new regions with the Gospel. It's going to come because you're going to use current technology and current ways.

Get Creative!'

God has been preparing this in us for quite a while. This word was before we had ever planted out from Herefordshire. We just couldn't see how to put the jigsaw puzzle together. We had tried a number of ideas and outreaches over the last 10 years but never felt that we had landed on the format or concepts that these prophetic words were speaking into.

On the Isle of Skye, God spoke to us about sowing seeds all over the earth. Our church planting strategy to this point had been to take a potted plant and put it into a new environment and hope that it takes to the soil. Now we were going to take seed, and scatter it everywhere, not knowing where it may land. Some would fall onto pathways, some strangled by the weed, but there would be some that would return a hundred fold. We just have to scatter the seed. It wouldn't be able to fit into our nice oversight models of pastoral groups; we would have to trust the Holy Spirit that if we were faithful to scatter the seed, He would be faithful to grow it.

There are huge amounts of the Christian population in the world who are becoming sick of what the world has to offer on its shows. 50 years ago, TV was relatively wholesome and innocent. Now we watch dark content, showing graphic violence, adultery, sexual scenes, homosexuality, and atrocious language, and then go to church the next morning. It is coming to a breaking point where it feels like too much of a compromise to engage with our world's TV broadcasting in the same way as we may have once. We see a huge opportunity for us to give people a new option to feed their hearts with content that inspires them and doesn't cause them to walk away feeling dirty after.

There are so many people that are not Christians that are waiting for us to tell some different stories.

> 'Jesus spoke all these things to the crowd in parables; he did not say anything to them without using a parable.' Matt 13:34 NIV

Jesus was a storyteller and almost never spoke without using stories! Yet we as Christians have become almost exclusively focused on services rather than stories. We need teaching to build up the body, but if we want to reach out, we need stories. People are desperate for good stories. The world is more likely to listen to a story than it is to watch a preacher talk to camera for 40 minutes, yet that's the way, for the most part, the church is trying to reach them.

What if the modern missionary carried a camera? Wrote scripts? Was able to design motion graphics? Artists and creatives have so often found limitations within the church and gone on to try and fulfill themselves within the entertainment industry instead. We are losing our best artisans to the world because we don't know what to do with them other than putting them on a sound desk or getting them to make a video for our worship experience. Imagine if we harnessed their energies and creativity to change this world.

What if they were able to be resourced to be fully utilised by the body of Christ? What if they were able to produce content that will equip the church, bringing a wave of fresh relevance, dynamism, humour, debate, drama, documentary, reality and more?

We are going to produce premium Christian content, in a Netflix-style app to wage a culture war and to take out the good news of the Gospel in a creative and engaging way for this generation.

We don't have the money, we don't have the expertise, and we don't have the contacts. But those things never stopped us before. We will trust God for what we lack.

We plan to raise millions of pounds and partner with other like-minded Christians across the world to bring life changing content to nations and languages all over the earth. Maybe, even now, you are reading this and the Holy Spirit is stirring you to be a part of this vision. Get in touch with us.

After an afternoon walk on the Isle of Skye, trying to put our brains back together after God had monumentally blown them away, Kris observed the name of the house in which we were staying, 'Saltwinds'. He told us that it was a prophetic name, that the vision that God had given us was going to take the 'salt' and blow it all over the earth. Salt is so small, yet it packs such flavour, changing the taste of a whole dish. Our clips would be like salt; to some small, even insignificant, yet carrying the power to bring a mouthful of flavour.

Saltwinds was born with a mission to connect anyone, anywhere to a life changing relationship with Jesus.

God was expanding our vision once again, from having a heart for 10 cities, to global impact.

Kris then shared this word that God had spoken to him on the plane on the way over, confirming that God was wanting us to see the world, not just cities:

South America. The awakening. There is a groaning in the spirit. A yearning in the spirit. A tossing and turning of things unborn, moving deep within the continent as a prelude to arrival. But the mother is not well. Fever in the body, a temple under attack. Old roots of religiosity have arisen out of the ground and try to pull her into their under-the-surface, damp, dank grave.

But the Holy Spirit says 'Go!', be my medicine. Treat the fever. Raise an army of healthy blood cells. Send them out into the body, that she might arise, this daughter, this princess, and deliver an heir that is the church for the next generation.

Within the Americas, there is a northern and southern army that needs to awake. The mission movement of the next century. 2020 to 2030 is seed sowing for the 2050, 2060, 2070 harvest.

The North American army will gather and move from the east & west coasts of America, to reach across the globe into continents, meeting in the middle. The South American army is destined for Europe, retracing trade routes of the first ships that sailed... driven by a blizzard from the south.

There will be war and peace, famine and plenty. All these elements are the visible signs of a spiritual undercurrent driving the church around the world and towards the 'finish line'.

Europe will experience unparalleled economic growth in the days ahead. You may expect Asian economies to arise, but some of these nations will turn inward not outward. Again, all part of God's plan for redemption this century.

China will become like a mixing bowl with a huge spiritual whisk thrust into it, propelling pieces around and around. Corruption will trigger a vortex movement... as it spins, the Gospel will spread through the batch, and after an 'oven season' of relative isolation, it will emerge, baked to greater spiritual health.

Russia will break apart into multiple pieces, governed by warriors. Isolationist, wealthy... people of strength will rise up to spread the Gospel. Kingdom highways will cross the fractured nation, carrying hope and redemption from place to place.

Africa. Cleanse the bride, purify. She will once again arise.

Transportation is going to get quicker and easier. There will be a radical new breakthrough. Tipping towards what seems impossible. People will look back on how we move around now and say, 'Can you believe we used to do it like that, what a pain. How slow. How inefficient.'

The greatest driver of technological innovation in this century will be the Holy Spirit.

God is going to become so visible under the microscope. As a precursor to the final times, where some people will harden their hearts to God in the face of undeniable evidence that he is real, God is going to reveal himself step by step and stage by stage in the coming decades.

Each decade of this century will provide greater evidence of the 'One True God' reality. Like stepping up a flight of steps to arrive at the top, face to face with Him. His 'being real' will become clearer and clearer to humanity. 'The only explanation: There is a God.' will head-line in the coming years.

This is the century that will break up the news media giants. New platforms will aggregate news from other sources - from on the ground experts, to on-scene novices. There will be a new way of grading or assessing 'trust-ability'. The trust index or score will help people identify what's true and what's false (a Holy Spirit innovation, by the way).

Banking and finance will be controlled by businesses and billionaires in the days ahead. The influence of governments will erode. Digital currencies will be the currencies of choice, not Dollars, not Euros, not Yen. The furious thrashing to maintain financial control will yield little fruit for governments because those receiving the money will embrace the alternative technologies. Life will just be much easier that way.

And with all this happening, what of the Church? It will thrive! It will do well. There will be challenges, there will be shutdowns, there will be rejection and attacks. But it will do well for all of this.

Again, step by step, moving forward with confidence, consistent in a way the world around it is not. Many moderate people will come to faith in the years ahead. Watch the moderates, reach the moderates. They are looking and watching you. They will look around at a world spinning out of control, hear the witness of the church and will think 'this has got to be the way to go'.

Extract from 'State of the Nations' prophetic word

January 2020

We headed to our different homes after our week in the Isle of Skye. full of excitement about implementing the vision that God had given us.

Little did we know that just weeks later the whole world would change. Coronavirus had already begun to be reported in China, but we had no idea that it would spread all over the world, shutting down schools, communities, economies and church buildings: an unfathomable tragedy, cutting short so many lives.

Everything that God had been speaking to us just weeks before on the isle of Skye was now powerfully coming to life. Churches were being forced to become digital overnight, reaching people they had never reached before, who would never have set foot in a church building. It was a confirmation of everything we had begun to dream with the Firestarters and Saltwinds vision.

51

THE STORY CONTINUES

As we conclude this story of what God has done so far through us as a couple, and through our church as a whole I am moved by the faithfulness of God. I am not someone who looks behind but someone that is constantly forging ahead with fresh vision and dreams for the future. Through this process, it has made me reflect and look back upon things that I don't often dwell on. It has filled my soul with gratitude for all the things that God has done!

As you have read this book, I have no doubt that you will be left with the realities that we are not the perfect leaders or the perfect church. Far from it. We have been honest about our shortcomings and mistakes. Undoubtedly though, we have seen God do some truly amazing things through the years. Miracles, provision, breakthrough - time and time again. I believe that is because God can use anyone. Anyone that wholeheartedly believes in Him and his power. That person can make a difference. I can't tell you how excited it makes me to think of you having read this book and now having this knowledge - that it is not your experience, qualification or status that determines whether God will use you. It is about faith. Believe in Him that is within you.

There were moments where it seemed that our story was destined to be limited. But we refused to give up or to remain in obscurity, we hungered to see the world changed, to make the name of Jesus famous. We didn't stop praying. We have not allowed our limitations or weaknesses to ever define us but instead invited Jesus to be our strength when we knew we could not do it ourselves. Whatever you see about yourself that you don't deem to be enough, take confidence that if God can use me, he can certainly use you!

As well as faith, a journey following the Lion of Judah also requires courage, and the truth is that not enough Christians summon the courage that is required to live with audacious faith. I pray that this book makes you a little braver, a little bolder to believe God for impossible things. Our world needs it! Likewise, it needs us as firestarters, those that burn with the fire of God to shine hope and faith in this dark world.

> *Neither do people light a lamp and put it under a bowl. Instead they put it on its stand, and it gives light to everyone in the house.*
>
> Matt 5:15 NIV

We know that the story of what God wants to do through us is far from over; there are many more chapters that God wants to write. Just as we did, right from the start, we will practice gratitude for the small things and keep pursuing the pearl with all that we are. As our story continues, we pray that your story would be ignited too. Choose faith over comfort and just wait and see what God does in you as you commit to be a firestarter in your world.

NEXT STEPS

So what to do now? This story can serve as an inspiration to you, a testimony to what God can do if you believe in Him and are willing to be used by Him.

Perhaps you are part of a church community already and you can take the faith and fire from this book and apply it to the way you serve and take your place in the local church.

However, if you are not actively engaged in a church right now, you could start a fire of your own and help write the next chapter of this story.

Look around at the community around you, the friendships that you have, the people that you know. Do you have faith and vision for what Jesus could do in you and through you to reach these people? The fire you start could become a great blaze that brings the hope of the Gospel through building relevant church. This is not about exceptional people who know everything or have all the answers, it is about those willing to love others and live wholeheartedly for the Kingdom. You could become one of our firestarters and build relevant church to reach the people where you are.

We have set up **www.firestarter.church** to equip anyone, anywhere to start a fire, to plant a church. If you want to be a part of this movement you can apply to be a firestarter.

Whatever you do go on to do, burn for him brightly so that the world may know Jesus.

ACKNOWLEDGMENTS

From reading this book you would have seen that none of this would have been possible without Heather. Apart from being superwoman and the most phenomenal mother to our boys she has been my greatest encourager, my soul mate, the unfailing rock in trouble and the tonic of laughter that I have needed through every chapter. She is the greatest evangelist I know and her passion for the gospel has become the motivation of our church to reach anyone, anywhere.

To Josh who literally made this book happen with his dogged determination, his selfless conviction and vision to chronicle the journey which he has played a massive part of since being 16. Thank you for being my supporter, my inspirer, my confidant and friend, no man could wish for a greater armour bearer, you are a gift to us and a gift to the church.

Thank you to Rose who has owned every step of our strange journey no matter how hard since she was 16yrs old, for the time she has taken to work through and shape this story. Thank you for being so loyal and faithful, for your heart to train and raise leaders all over the world which has become the engine that fires the mission, you were born for this.

My leadership team of Dave and Kris who have stood by us in every challenge and every crazy vision never faltering, I know you have given your lives for the cause and I am forever honoured to be in your company and to have you as captains, you have epitomised what Heart and Soul really means. Also, honour and gratitude to your mighty wives Saz and Naomi, whose steadfast commitment to the Bride is an example to many. You all have given me the prayers and encouragement to bring this book to life, your support is second to none.

Chris and Karin Cooke for the many years of standing with us through every change no matter what, God sent you to be the greatest friends anyone could ask for, you have fought for our children and been God's voice of faith in so many situations. We have laughed late into the night, eaten the best food and you've run with the vision. The significance of your lives is astounding and eternal.

To my precious family - Josh and Rose, Luke, Jordan, Charlotte and Isaac, Sol and Winter and my grandkids - Judah, Nathan, Cleo, Jesse and Rohan who have brought unspeakable blessing into our lives, the legacy of which is yet to be seen. The greatest cost as a family is being separated around the world but the greatest blessing is to see you all follow your dreams, your call and to see you love His church.

To my 5 boys who were there throughout for the good, the bad and the ugly. Who discovered what it was to pursue the Lion, who loved me even in my mistakes as a father, for the price you each paid growing up, the things you endured, I could not be more proud to be your dad, to see the Godly men you have become.

My parents for their decision to raise me in a home of faith and always making God's House a priority. Their decisions launched me into my calling and for that I'm forever grateful.

Anna Roberts whose suggestions and edits took the book to its finishing point making the whole narrative flow so much better. Chris and Rose too for their editing and improvements.

Richard Welch for his final tweaks, adjustments and ideas. Richard worked so hard to prepare the book for publishing.

Finally, I want to honour the many volunteers who may not feature in this book but are part of the vast army that refused to settle for normal, and chose to pick up their cross and give their all for the love of the Bride. This story is theirs.

ABOUT THE AUTHOR

Gary Snowzell lives in Herefordshire, England with his wife Heather. He is the father of five sons and the Senior Pastor of Freedom Church, a global church-planting movement. With over 30 years in ministry, Gary writes with a passion for people, the church and the gospel through the highs and lows of life and leadership.

Printed in Great Britain
by Amazon

75230200R00183